About This Book

Here, in one volume that you can keep by y... ... ...
information you need to create your own Web pages in Microsoft Word—everything from
how to write them and link them together to how to set up your own Web server and use
it to manage forms and create special programs to process them.

In addition, this book provides hints, suggestions, and examples of how to structure your
overall presentation—not just the words within each Web page. You also will learn the
HTML language as you go so you'll be able to identify tags in the final stage. This book
doesn't just teach you how to create a Web presentation—it teaches you how to create a good
Web presentation.

Who Should Read This Book

Is this book for you? It is if

☐ You've seen what's out on the Web and you want to contribute your own content.

☐ You're representing a company that wants to create an Internet "presence" and
you're not sure where to start.

☐ You're an information developer, such as a technical writer, and you want to learn
how the Web can help you present your information online.

☐ You're doing research or polling and you're interested in creating a system that
enables people to "register" comments or vote for particular suggestions or items.

How This Book Is Structured

This book is intended to be read over the course of a week (and it's a real week—seven days—
not a business week). Each day you'll read two chapters that describe concepts related to the
design of Web presentations. With this book in hand, you should be able to start with a
simple web presentation and move on to putting a more creative presentation up on the
Web—and all this in a week, maybe even less.

Conventions

Note: A Note box presents interesting pieces of information related to the
surrounding discussion.

Tip: A Tip box offers advice or teaches an easier way to do something.

Warning: A Warning box advises you about potential problems and helps you
steer clear of disaster.

DO read the DO/DON'T boxes. They clarify procedures and tasks for you.

Teach Yourself
Web Publishing
with Microsoft® Word
in a Week

Herb Tyson

201 West 103rd Street
Indianapolis, Indiana 46290

President, Sams Publishing	*Richard K. Swadley*
Publisher, Sams.net Publishing	*George Bond*
Acquisitions Manager	*Greg Wiegand*
Development Manager	*Dean Miller*
Managing Editor	*Cindy Morrow*
Marketing Manager	*John Pierce*

Acquisitions Editor
Mark Taber

Development Editor
Angelique Brittingham

Software Development Specialist
Kim Spilker

Production Editor
Kristi Hart

Copy Editors
Nancy Albright, Tonya Simpson

Technical Reviewer
Kevin Horst

Editorial Coordinator
Bill Whitmer

Technical Edit Coordinator
Lynette Quinn

Formatter
Frank Sinclair

Editorial Assistant
Carol Ackerman

Cover Designer
Dan Armstrong

Book Designer
Alyssa Yesh

Production Team Supervisor
Brad Chinn

Page Layout
Charlotte Clapp, Terrie Deemer, Steph Mineart, Susan Van Ness, Michelle Worthington

Proofreading
Michael Brumitt, Michael Dietsch, George Hanlin, Kevin Laseau, Paula Lowell, Donna Martin, Brian Kent-Proffitt, SA Springer

Indexer
Cheryl Dietsch

Dedication

This book is dedicated to the people I love: Karen, Katie, Tom, Sharon, my mother and father, and the rest of my family. As I'm writing this, my father is in critical condition in a hospital recovering (hopefully) from a 39-day (so far) ordeal resulting from triple-bypass surgery complications. Writing this book has been an especially difficult struggle because my heart and mind are 200 miles away. Now that the book is done, I can join my heart and mind to see if I can be of any help or comfort. Dad, I love you, and I hope you will be able to read this. You taught me the most important lesson I've learned from anyone: *Never stop trying.*

Overview

Contents

Acknowledgments

I would like to acknowledge the fact that I don't have a fast connection to the Internet. So, if you build fancy Web pages with lots of graphics, demonstrating what you learn from this book, then I—and others like me—probably won't see them. Just keep us in mind when you see that empty *Alternative text* space staring back at you. What's that? Not that kind of acknowledgment? Oh, well.

I would like to acknowledge the persistence of Mark Taber, acquisitions editor at Sams.net, who, when confronted with my enthusiastic response to an invitation to write this book, said, "I'm not going to let you weasel out of it *that* easily." I also would like to acknowlege the support of my family who always manages to inspire me when I need it most by saying things such as, "Who are you, and what are you doing in our house?" And most of all, I'd like to thank the little people who made this all possible...Sleepy, Dopey, Doc, Grumpy, Dancer, Prancer, Donner, Blitzen.... Well, you get the idea.

About the Author

Herb Tyson is an internationally respected consultant, developer, and writer. He is a consultant to OS/2's I.V. League, for which he has prepared, evaluated, and reviewed technical materials. Oddly enough, he also has been awarded the status of MVP (most valuable professional) by Microsoft Word's technical support team for his contributions on CompuServe's MSWORD forum. He is the author of a number of books for computer users, including *Navigating the Internet with OS/2 Warp, Word for Windows 6 Super Book, Your OS/2 Warp Consultant, XyWrite Revealed, Word for Windows Revealed,* and *101 Essential Word for Windows Tips.* He also was a contributing author to *Using OS/2 Warp, OS/2 Warp Unleashed,* and a number of other books. His articles appear regularly in *OS/2 Professional* (his adjectives and verbs, however, appear elsewhere). As a Team OS/2 member, he also is an active participant and moderator on forums on FidoNet and the Washington, D.C., Capital PC User's Group BBS (the MIX). Tyson received a bachelor's degree from Georgetown University and an interdisciplinary doctorate from Michigan State University.

Introduction

Are you ready? I hope so. I also hope you've already spent a fair amount of time browsing the World Wide Web, or the *Web*, as I'll call it throughout most of this book. If you haven't been on the Web, you might be reading this book because the boss put it on your desk with the simple instruction: *Web it!* Do you know what your boss meant by that? It *might* mean that your boss has been reading too many computer magazines. Or, it might meant that your boss somehow has become E. B. White. No? I didn't think so. However, seven days from now, you will know enough so you can go back and ask what he meant.

In the meantime, here's the book—*Teach Yourself Web Publishing with Microsoft Word in a Week*. It's a seven-day plan for learning how to use Microsoft Word to create HTML documents suitable for publication—on the Web. Do the words *publication* and *publishing* sound odd in this context? Well, perhaps they do. What exactly does it mean to *publish*? According to the *Random House Unabridged Electronic Dictionary*, publish means "to issue (printed or otherwise reproduced textual or graphic material, computer software, etc.) for sale or distribution to the public."

If you're at all familiar with the Web, you know that it contains millions of pages of information available to the *public* over the Internet. Guess what? That means that simply by putting something onto the Web, you're publishing it. But, wait! Don't close the book yet. There's a little more to it than that. Just as publishing a book means more than slapping a cover on some printed pages and sticking it into a bookstore or library; publishing a Web page means more than sticking a text file onto a Web server. It means knowing what to put on those pages, where to put it, and how to put it there.

A Web *what*?

A Web server. A Web server is your publishing media. However, this is just the introduction, so don't worry about that yet. This book teaches you what that means. By tomorrow, you won't even bat an eye when folks toss around words such as *client* and *server*.

What This Book Is

This book is a complete guide to using Microsoft's Internet Assistant for Word to create Web publications. However, it's more. It's a compendium of working examples and samples that you can use to quickly get your ideas onto the Web. It's an idea book that shows you what you can do on the Web, how to do it, and why you might want to do it this way or that. It's a source book that shows you where to go to publicize your Web pages. It's a how-to book that teaches you how to accomplish specific effects on the Web. It's an advice book that tells you what to aim for and what to avoid.

Who Should Read This Book?

When you see **bold** or *italic* Words on the Web, do you wonder how they got that way? If so, you should read this book. This book tells you how they got that way. It also tells you how *not* to get them that way. There's a right way and a wrong way, and the success of your Web publications depends on your knowing the difference.

When you see cute pictures that seemingly take forever to appear on your Web browser, do you wonder how they got there? If so, you should read this book. This book tells you. It also tells you when to put them there and how to make sure that text shows up instead of the picture if readers don't have their graphics turned on. It also shows you some neat ways to make sure that your Web pages bring others considerably more pleasure than pain while they're browsing the Web.

When you see those neat fill-in-the-blank forms with check-boxes, option buttons, and pull-down lists, do you want to know how to do that? If so, you should read this book. This book shows you how to create those forms using Word's own built-in features. It also shows you which form elements to use, how to create them, and how to use them.

If you wonder how you can create polished and professional-looking Web pages without leaving the comfortable and familiar surroundings of Word, you should read this book. If you need to know how to convert exiting Word documents into Web documents, you should read this book. If you're ready to show the World Wide Web what you can do, you should read this book.

How This Book Is Organized

This book is set up as a seven-day teach-yourself course. It works best if—when I say something like "Now, let's…" or "First, you…" or "If you do this…"—you actually do those things. It's called *learning by doing*. You'll learn much more quickly if you actually try the things suggested. If a picture is worth a thousand words, then an action is worth a million words. Go for it! Here's the seven-day plan.

Day 1: Understanding the World Wide Web and Hypertext

On the first day, you'll learn about the World Wide Web—what it is, where it comes from, how it gets to you, and why it's so *hot*. You'll also learn about the myriad things you can put on the Web, the primary goals most Web publishers have, and how to incorporate the Web into your game plan.

Day 2: Quick Start—Creating Simple Web Documents

On the second day, you'll quickly get started with the Internet Assistant. You'll learn where to get the latest version—for free, assuming you don't already have it—how to install it, and how it works. You'll begin by creating simple Web pages using tools you already know how to use—Word styles.

Day 3: Presenting Information and Ideas with HTML

On the third day, you'll get an intensive course on how to format just about anything for presentation on the Web. You'll learn about lists, character styles, and tables. You'll also learn about hyperlinks—the key to making it all work.

Day 4: Multimedia on the Web Pages

On the fourth day, you'll find out how to give your Web presentations pizzazz. You'll learn how and when to include inline images directly in your Web pages, as well as how to give users options they can see, watch, and listen to with external graphics, video, and audio. You'll also discover two great free tools—Microsoft Imager and WordView—that make creating and viewing Web presentations easier.

Day 5: Creating Web Documents that Work for You

On the fifth day of Christmas, my true love sent to me…. Oops! I got carried away. On the fifth day, you won't find five golden rings, but you will find loads of ideas and advice on how to create specific kinds of Web presentations. You'll learn—step by step—how to create online resumes, catalogs, and support pages.

Day 6: Going Public

On the sixth day, you'll learn how to put it online. You'll learn where to go and what you need to install your Word-created HTML presentations onto a Web server (there's that word again). Heck, by the sixth day, you won't even quiver when you hear the word *server*. You'll learn what you need to put onto the server, how to prepare it before putting it there, and where to put it. You'll also get a crash course on being your own Web publicist. You'll learn about the major places on the Web where you can advertise your home page to attract some attention.

Day 7: Advanced Webbery

On the seventh day, you can rest. Did anybody mention that these seven days don't all have to be consecutive? So, for heaven's sake, take a day off. Then come back and learn all about forms and image maps. On the seventh day, you'll learn how to design forms so you can get data from folks who stop by your Web page. You'll also learn about some additional tools for Web publishing that don't require Word 6 and the Internet Assistant. I'll give you a guided tour of some of the most popular alternatives and tell you where to find them.

What You Need

Web publishing never has been this easy. All you need is this book, Microsoft Word for Windows (version 6.0a or later), and access to the Web. Starting points are hard. Because this book is called *Teach Yourself Web Publishing with Microsoft Word in a Week*, I'm going to have to assume three things. First, you are familiar with the World Wide Web and have a connection to the Internet and access to a graphical Web browser. Second, you have Microsoft Word 6 and you know how to use it. If you don't know how to use it, then rush out and buy a copy of the *Word for Windows 6 Super Book*. Or, visit `http://www.mcp.com` and order a copy online. Sorry, I got carried away. And, the third assumption is that you don't mind books with excessively long titles. Look on the bright side. They *might* have decided to go with the title I suggested, which was *Teach Yourself Web Publishing with Microsoft Word in a Week or Your Next Pizza Is Free!* Unfortunately, they didn't, so you won't find any free-pizza coupons. However, if you have a pizza parlour, perhaps you could set up an online pizza ordering form, as shown in here. Seven days from now, you'll know how to create this form. *Bon voyage!*

Conventions Used in This Book

Geneva, Shriners…. Nope, we don't use those conventions in this book. Instead, we use special typefaces and other effects so you can tell what's what. Each time you see a new term, it is shown in *italics* so you'll have to tilt your head to read it. It's a proven scientific fact that this simple act wakes the reader up. Because I'm not a scientist, however, I don't have to prove it. Text that you type, as when I say, type the following:

```
why am I typing this?
```

is presented in a `monospace` type to mimic the way text looks on the DOS command line. Because you probably won't be typing much of the stuff in this book on the DOS command line, one wonders about this convention, but that's another matter. I also display *URLs* (uniform resource locators) and Internet addresses in monospace. If you don't know what URLs are yet, you will shortly.

Whenever I say to type something with a variable in it (that is, text that varies depending on what you're doing), the variable is shown in *monospaced italic*. For example, type:

`mailto:your-email-address`

You would type `mailto:` just as it's shown, and replace *your-email-address* with, well, your e-mail address. Here's an example: `mailto:smith@jones.com`. If there really is someone at `smith@jones.com`, let me apologize in advance for all the mail you're going to get. Your Web server, at `http://www.jones.com`, also is going to get quite a workout. Did you notice, by the way, that we've already started using those conventions?

Whenever I tell you about menu commands, I'll refer to the menu parts, separating them with a vertical bar (|). For example, under the File menu, there is an Open option. I would say, "From the menu, choose File | Open." This means for you to choose the File menu, and then choose the Open option from that menu.

Filenames are shown as they usually appear in context. If you generally would encounter a filename in uppercase, that's the way I show it in this book. For example, `WINWORD.EXE` usually is encountered just that way. If you generally would encounter it in lowercase—as you might on a UNIX server—then that's the way I'll show it. For example, most home pages are named `index.html`. Because filenames sometimes can be mistaken for regular words in text, particularly when they are lowercase and without a file extension, all filenames are presented in monospace type.

For your convenience, figures and tables are numbered randomly throughout the book. Randomly? Just testing to see if you're really reading this. Most people don't, you know. Figures and tables are numbered consecutively by chapter. For example, the first figure in Chapter 1 is numbered 1.1, the second is numbered 1.2, the third is…. Well, you get the idea.

DAY 1

Understanding the World Wide Web and Hypertext

1

The World Wide Web

You have a week to learn how to turn out Internet-ready Web documents. Let's get started. Today, this chapter and Chapter 2, "The Basic Plan," teach you the following:

- [ ] What the World Wide Web is and why it's generating so much excitement
- [ ] What Web browsers are and how they work
- [ ] What HTML is and why you should care
- [ ] What Web servers are and how to find them
- [ ] What URLs and home pages are

What Is the World Wide Web?

The *World Wide Web* (henceforth *the Web*, sometimes called *W3*) is a way to present resources and information over the Internet. For the official definition, let's go right to the source—the birthplace of the Web at CERN (European Laboratory for Particle Physics)—at `http://www.w3.org/hypertext/WWW/TheProject`. According to CERN, "The WorldWideWeb [*sic*] (W3) is the universe of network-accessible information, an embodiment of human knowledge."

That makes the Web a computerized information system. To cut to the chase, however, the Web is a versatile hypertext *GUI (graphical user interface)* for accessing resources on the Internet. The Web has the following attributes:

- [ ] Graphical
- [ ] Multimedia
- [ ] Hyperlinked
- [ ] Dispersed
- [ ] Dynamic
- [ ] Versatile
- [ ] Multiplatform

Graphical

Graphical has come to mean nontext. Often, it means text that is presented as graphics. In this context, however, it means that navigation of the Web is based on visual guides, including icons, pictures, and text. There's even an *image map* (a picture that produces different results depending on where you click on it), as shown in Figure 1.1.

To paraphrase the Oldsmobile commercial, this is *not* your father's Internet. The image of Internet Past, now quickly fading into history, is one of ancient academics and scientists pounding away at the command line, invoking UNIX-based incantations to summon mystical powers from aging mainframes. Not anymore. In many ways, the Web is the very

antithesis of the Internet that existed a few short years ago. Navigation on the Web is designed to be as simple as possible. The hallmark of a GUI is the capability of pointing and clicking on what you want. The Web is designed with that in mind. If you see something interesting, you click on it.

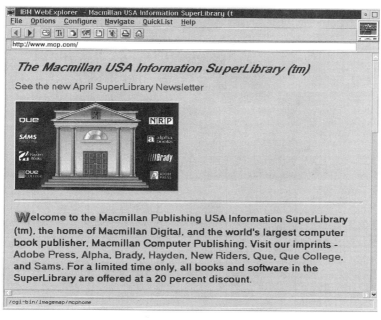

Figure 1.1. *Image maps are an intuitive way to present choices.*

Multimedia

The graphical aspect doesn't stop at mere pictures. It includes both audio and video presentations as well. You might think of the Web as a gigantic online multimedia encyclopedia. Visit the White House home page http://www.whitehouse.gov, for example, and you find that you can hear Socks (the presidential cat) meow or Bill play the saxophone (see Figure 1.2). Visit http://www.met.fu-berlin.de/DataSources/MetIndex.html and you discover video clips of weather for the past 24 hours or so (see Figure 1.3).

If you're fairly new to computers and own a multimedia encyclopedia, you might not be very impressed by all this. Not too long ago, however, the notion of seeing video clips on a personal computer wasn't within the realm of possibility. If you wanted to hear a sound file, you first had to *FTP (file transfer protocol)* the file, then load it into your audio player. Now, thanks to the magic of the Web, it's all integrated. Just click on a picture or an icon, and within seconds (often), you are listening to the sound of whales (http://www.physics.helsinki.fi/whale/greetings.snd).

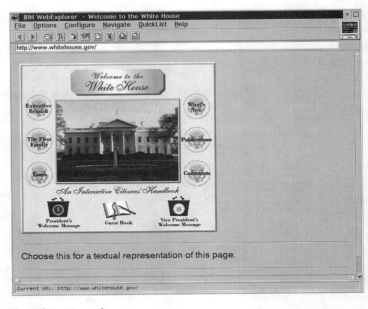

Figure 1.2. *The White House home page.*

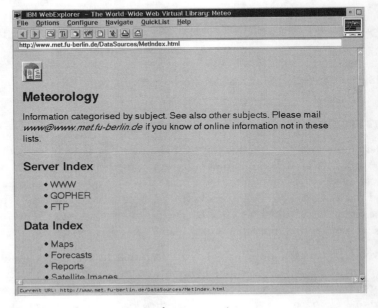

Figure 1.3. *The Meteorology page is not about meteors!*

Hyperlinked

The Web is a collection of hyperlinks. *Hyperlinks* are text, icons, and pictures that lead to other text, icons, and pictures as well as to video clips, files, sounds, and a variety of games and services. The temptation is to call the Web a *hypertext* system. The term hypertext is too limiting. It makes you think only of text. There is also *hypermedia*. However, that focuses too much attention on the output form (text, pictures, sound), and might also be just as limiting as hypertext. After all, we have other senses as well, as yet untapped by computers. Perhaps they too fall under *media* in the word hypermedia. However, I like to think that smell, taste, and touch interfaces for computers are just around the corner.

Imagine, if you will, a virtual city or a virtual shopping mall, in which you can follow your eyes, your ears, your fingers, and your nose to things that interest you. Trust me—it's not too far away. If you think people have pushed the limits of good taste with pictures, sounds, words, and movies, just wait to see what they can do once you add in smell and taste!

"Hyperlinked" describes the key feature of the Web: linkages. The Web is a vast collection of *HTML (hypertext markup language)* documents, all ultimately linked together over the Internet. The Web page shown in Figure 1.4 contains links to more than a dozen different Web sites. Each of the icons, as well as each highlighted text item, is a link or pointer to additional information.

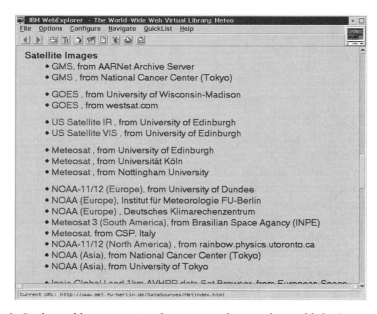

Figure 1.4. *Links enable you to point the user anywhere in the world that's connected to the Internet.*

Thinking of the Web as hyperlinked also focuses attention on Web publishing, which is the main topic of this book. Ultimately, Web publishing is the presentation of hyperlinks in a way that provides quick and easy access to information. "Easy" is pretty simple once you have the basic tools. "Quick," however, often presents more of a challenge—largely because speed is determined by how the user connects to the Internet.

Dispersed

The Web is everywhere. It's not contained in one central location. There is no single computer you can point to and say "That's the Web." Unlike some services, such as CompuServe, GEnie, or America Online, the Web isn't all located on one computer. Instead, it's contained on thousands of computers all over the world. Potentially, the Web extends to every computer directly on the Internet. From a user standpoint, this means that it has practically an infinite capacity for information.

Dynamic

The Web is dynamic. In this book, you'll see numerous Web addresses (known as *URLs*, or *uniform resource locators*). There is no guarantee that they will all still exist by the time you read this. They're constantly changing as their owners improve, upgrade, downgrade, and move on. If Web residents discover a more economical service for their Web documents, the underlying addresses could change. To the extent that they obtain and propagate alternative names or *aliases* for their Web presence, they can ensure some continuity when the underlying addresses change. However, if Web page designers use the underlying addresses rather than the aliases for linking to other Web pages, the dynamic aspect of the Web renders such links useless. Does the phrase "Moved—Left no forwarding address" strike a familiar note?

Not only are the physical locations on the Web constantly changing, but so are the contents of Web pages. The World Wide Yellow Pages (`http://www.yellow.com`) bills itself as "The yellowpages for the next 100 years" (see Figure 1.5). With a slogan like that, it's a pretty sure bet that the underlying address isn't going to change. The contents, however, do change. Daily. Have you ever searched the yellow pages in a hotel room while traveling? You find a restaurant that looks perfect, and you set off to enjoy the "best Greek pizza in Boston." When you get to that address, however, you discover that it's now a punk hair salon. You check back and find the yellow pages directory is three years old. Even if the yellow pages were current, however, businesses come and go—often before the next edition of the yellow pages gets printed. There's no guarantee that a business that was current when the directory was published is still there even a few weeks after the directory is published.

A dynamic online directory, however, has the potential for always being current. Like the electronic directories that telephone information operators use, when a customer's listing changes, the directory changes—by definition, because the directory and the customer listings are the same.

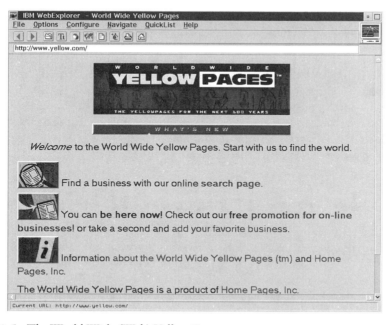

Figure 1.5. *The World Wide (Web) Yellow Pages.*

Versatile

The Web provides access not just to Web (HTML) documents, but to other kinds of Internet resources as well, including newsgroups, Gopher sites, FTP sites, and various terminal-base services, such as WAIS (wide area information servers) and Netfind (a terminal-based service for locating individuals on the Internet). One of the basic ideas underlying the Web is to simplify what you must do to access resources on the Internet. By making just about everything available from a single piece of software, the Web designers have done just that. Rather than having to learn different interfaces for Gopher, FTP, and newsgroups, you can learn just one. The Web doesn't yet encompass everything—it still doesn't appear to work for e-mail and for posting to newsgroups. However, it's a good start.

Multiplatform

One of the continuing problems businesses face in the computer world is the fact that there are so many different computer platforms. How do you make your products available for every platform for which you have potential customers? There's Macintosh, OS/2, DOS, UNIX, and Windows—and those are just some of the more popular desktop computer platforms. What about minicomputers and mainframes? Even within the desktop computer

platforms, there are additional varieties to worry about. UNIX comes in at least a dozen different flavors. Heck, even with Windows, there's Windows NT, Windows 95, and Windows for DOS.

The beauty of the Web is that it works across a wide variety of different platforms. First, Web browsers (a computer program for accessing the World Wide Web) have been developed or are under development for virtually all the popular platforms. Second, even if a Web browser is not yet available for a specific platform, users can still connect to a UNIX host and run a browser (such as Lynx) on the host computer. Thus, one way or another, the resources on the Web are available to virtually everyone on the Internet.

Who Is in Charge of the Web?

Nobody, really, is in charge of the Web. The Web—like many aspects of the Internet—is a nearly perfect form of anarchy. The Web exists by virtue of the exchange, propagation, and proliferation of URLs. You become part of the Web by setting up a Web server and giving your Web address to others. To the extent that you get other Web sites to include your URL in their own Web pages, you establish a presence. Once your Web address is public knowledge, virtually anyone can contact your Web page merely by specifying your URL. Nobody can turn you off or prevent others from accessing your site. There is no governing body saying who can and who cannot, or what can and what cannot, be on the Web.

Ultimately, the Web is as open and as limited as speech. If you put something on the Web that deprives others of their rights, they can take legal action—suing you for damages, libel, or what have you. However, there is no master Web governing body that can pull the plug. The Web—like light and sound traveling through the air—is open to all comers, and accessible to all who want to partake.

A better question is: *Who sets the standards?* The Web is largely the result of work performed by CERN in Switzerland on a project called the World Wide Web Initiative (sometimes called the Web Project or the Project). Since the Web Project first bore public fruit in 1990, the HTTP protocol and HTML (the basis for all Web documents) have taken their direction from the developers at CERN. For additional information on the history and future of the Web, you can visit CERN at `http://www.w3org/hypertext/WWW/TheProject.html` (see Figure 1.6).

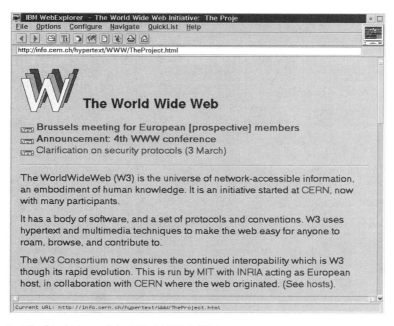

Figure 1.6. *The birthplace of the World Wide Web.*

Web Browsers

To drive along the highways of the world, you need some kind of vehicle, whether it be a bicycle, a car, a truck, a bus, or what have you. To travel along the Web, you need a Web browser. A Web browser is a special communications program that reads and interprets HTML documents. At the simplest level, you usually can use a text-based Web browser that's installed on your Internet provider's computer. If you have a SLIP or PPP connection to the Internet, you can use a graphical Web browser installed on your own computer.

Note: *SLIP (serial line internet protocol)* and *PPP (point-to-point protocol)* are popular methods for connecting desktop computers to the Internet in such a way that the computer actually is a host on the Internet. An Internet *host* is a computer that is connected directly to the Internet. If you have only a UNIX shell account (command-line access to the Internet only), chances are good that

your computer is not itself directly connected to the Internet. You are limited to running only those programs that are installed on your provider's computer, or those to which you have telnet access while logged onto your provider's system.

When you connect using SLIP or PPP, however, full access to the Internet is provided for programs installed on your computer. These programs, often known as *clients* (for example, SLIP clients), include FTP, gopher, telnet, news readers, e-mail programs, and—of course—Web browsers. Your SLIP clients are able to send and receive signals directly over the Internet. This enables you to use the new generation programs, such as Netscape, the WebExplorer, and Mosaic, for Web walking.

Most Internet providers have a nongraphical (text-only, that is, no pictures or sounds) browser similar to Lynx, shown in Figure 1.7. To browse the web using Lynx, you use the cursor keys or Tab key to highlight an option, then press Enter. Depending on your software, you might also be able to click your mouse pointer.

Figure 1.7. *Lynx is a text-only Web browser.*

At the other end of the spectrum, there are full multimedia, graphical browsers, such as the WebExplorer that comes with OS/2 Warp, Netscape, and Mosaic. The WebExplorer—used to show many of the Web pages in today's lesson—integrates text and graphics, and uses

OS/2's multimedia extensions for displaying higher-quality graphics, sounds, and video. Netscape (for Windows) and Mosaic (for Windows, Macintosh, and X Windows, the graphical user interface for UNIX systems) provide similar capabilities.

With the Internet Assistant, Microsoft Word also joins the list of browsers, technically. Don't delete Mosaic, Netscape, or the WebExplorer from your hard disk quite yet, however. Although the Internet Assistant provides Word with browsing capabilities, the performance as a browser isn't quite stellar—at least not at the time this book is being written. Rather, the strength of the Internet Assistant for Word is more of a *WYSIWYW (what you see is what you web)* HTML editor than a browser. Nonetheless, as shown in Figure 1.8, Word is now a member of the Web browsers club.

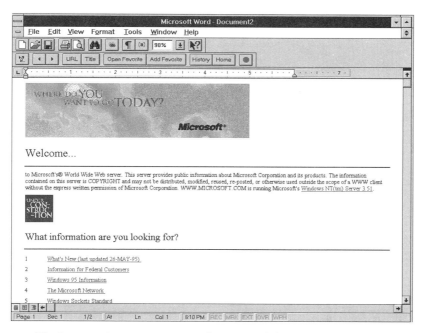

Figure 1.8. *The Internet Assistant turns Word into a Web browser.*

Why Do You Need a Web Browser?

Web pages are written in HTML. If you could gain access—apart from using a Web browser—to the directories where Web pages reside, and could display a Web page using an ordinary editor or file browser (such as Buerg's LIST or Windows NOTEPAD), it would look something like that shown in Figure 1.9. Not a pretty picture.

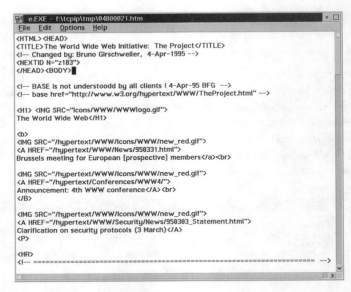

Figure 1.9. *Raw HTML—where are the pictures?*

Using a Web browser, the same page takes on the appearance shown in Figure 1.6. Much nicer, right?

Besides giving a nicer picture, Web browsers also are communications programs. Thus, when you see a pretty picture, an icon, or some highlighted text and click on it, a Web browser uses its communications capabilities to travel (electronically, of course) to the location associated with the picture, icon, or highlighted text.

Hypertext Markup Language (HTML)

As mentioned previously, HTML is the language of the Web. HTML is a way of formatting documents so that they display as Web pages. Unlike the formatting of many word processors, HTML does not depend on high-level binary codes embedded in file headers. HTML is all just plain ASCII. In fact, to get right down to it, if you know all the HTML format codes, you don't really need Word, the Internet Assistant, or any other HTML editor. All you need is a plain text editor.

HTML coding is accomplished by including HTML tags in your text before and after text you want formatted. There are tags for on and tags for off. If you're familiar with WordPerfect, you might find HTML to be rather similar in concept and in application. Instead of reveal codes, however, you use plain angle brackets (< and >). For example, to make

the title of this section "Hypertext Markup Language" into an HTML level 1 heading, you precede and follow it with HTML heading codes:

```
<H1>HTML</H1>
```

The code `<H1>` means "begin Heading 1 formatting," and `</H1>` means "end Heading 1 formatting." As simple as that is, it gets even simpler. When you use the Internet Assistant for Word, you don't have to type the `<H1>` and `</H1>` codes. Instead, you apply Word styles. When you apply the Heading 1 style, for example, Word automatically supplies the necessary HTML codes when you save the document as an HTML document.

You learn a good deal more about HTML—what styles to use and when to use them— beginning on Day 3. For now, all you need to know is that getting your documents into HTML format isn't going to be difficult.

Web Servers

To make your Web pages available to others, you need a Web server, which is a computer program that responds to requests from Web clients (browsers). Web servers reside on Internet hosts (a computer connected to the Internet). The job of the server is to make files available when requested by Web browsers. For example, the text version of the Microsoft Web home page is shown in Figure 1.10 (`http://www.microsoft.com/default.htm#textmenu`). Note that each of the highlighted text strings (links) corresponds either to the name of a file or to another Internet address. When you click on a link that corresponds to a file, the Web server uploads that file to you. If you click on a link that corresponds to a different Internet address, control passes back to the Internet as another server is summoned.

When browsing the Web, it's not uncommon to visit dozens of Web servers in a single session. Because of the way HTML documents are linked together, however, you're scarcely aware of that fact. Only when your browser encounters an obstacle—such as an address that doesn't work or a Web server that doesn't respond—do you realize that you're really playing electronic hopscotch across the globe.

Mind you, all that you encounter while using a Web browser isn't necessarily the Web, strictly speaking. One of the goals of the Web project is to make a variety of Internet resources available using the Web interface. If you click on a file, chances are pretty good that it will be transferred to you using FTP rather than using HTTP. You'll also encounter gopher servers, news servers, and telnet servers while webbing along. After a while, you can recognize the changes in landscape as they appear. Novices browsing the Web, however, sometimes don't notice when they've veered off onto a non-Web server.

Even so, the integration of text, sound, and graphics into seamless online documents is the domain of the Web, so, although you might want or need to integrate your Web creations with the assistance of FTP and gopher servers (after all, why reinvent the wheel?), you use HTML to weave it all together.

So far, all the data flow seems strikingly one-way. The Web isn't limited to one-way data flows, however. Using forms and other interactive Web pages, Web servers can be used to accept data as well. Many organizations use interactive Web pages for accepting orders and getting product feedback, as well as for conducting online surveys.

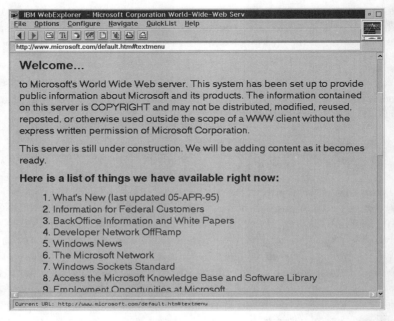

Figure 1.10. *The text version of Microsoft's home page.*

Uniform Resource Locators

Recall that URLs are addresses that you feed Web browsers for browsing the Web. (Although a few descriptions indicate that URL is pronounced "earl," most people just say the letters: "U-R-L" (like FBI, CIA, and KGB).

URLs are a consistent method for specifying Internet resources in a way that all Web browsers understand. For example, in `http://www.microsoft.com`, the URL for Microsoft's home page on the web, the `http` tells the Web browser what protocol to use. This enables the Web

browser to know how to retrieve the information at the link, as well as what to do with it. The remainder of the URL, www.microsoft.com, is the Internet address.

Some URLs are more complicated than that. This is the general form:

protocol://*address*[:*port*][/*directory*][/*filename*]

The *protocol* is the method that the Web browser uses to retrieve the information at the URL. Accepted protocols include http, ftp, gopher, file, news, mailto, and telnet.

The *address* is the name of the location on the Internet, such as www.microsoft.com, ftp.microsoft.com, comp.os.ms-windows.apps.word-proc, or gopher.psi.com.

The *port* is seldom used. However, some servers have special-purpose access channels that are needed for accessing different drives or computers on their network.

The *directory* is the location on the server disk where a specific file is located. For example, at this writing, the beta version of the Internet Assistant is at ftp://www.microsoft.com/deskapps/word/winword-public/ia/wordia.exe. The *directory* portion of the URL is /deskapps/word/winword-public/ia/, and wordia.exe is the *filename*. Note that on the Internet, because most host systems use the UNIX operating system, the slash (/) character is used rather than the backslash (\). Note also the absence of a disk specification. One limitation of directory specifications on the Internet is that no provision is made for specifying disk drives (yet). Some hosts get around that by using different *port* specifications. For the most part, however, that should not concern you at this time.

What do you do with URLs? You check them out, of course. A regular feature in the *Washington Post*, for example, is a cyberspace column that contains interesting items on the Internet. Usually, the author mentions the URL. One such URL, for example, provides a way to get in touch with Santa Claus. The URL is http://north.pole.org/santa/talk_to_santa.html. If you installed the Internet Assistant, you can check it out using Word. From the menu, choose File, Open URL, type the URL, and away you go.

URLs are the currency of the Web. In any HTML document on the Web, you find links to other documents, files, and Internet addresses. Each of those links is specified as a URL. Using a Web browser such as Netscape, Mosaic, or the WebExplorer, the URL is specified at the bottom of the window as you move the mouse over links (see Figure 1.11). This provides not only a good way to know where you're going before you jump on board, but also a way to see just how vital URLs are to the Web concept.

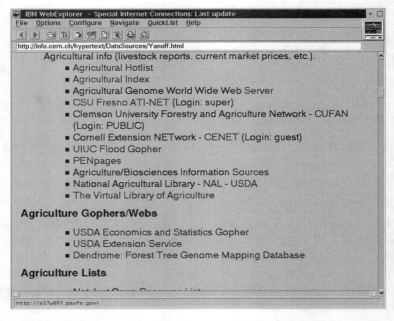

Figure 1.11. *Most Web browsers display the source of the highlighted links.*

Home Pages

The phrase *home page* gets used a lot in talking about the World Wide Web. Like many other computer-related terms, however, it now has several meanings. On the one hand, home page has come to mean any Web user's starting point. Most of the Web browsers have some kind of built-in starting point referred to as the home page.

For example, Mosaic's starting point is the NCSA (National Center for Supercomputing Applications) at `http://www.ncsa.uiuc.edu/SDG/Software/Mosaic/NCSAMosaicHome.html`. The starting point for Netscape is Mosaic (ironically enough) at `http://mosaic.mcom.com/home/welcome.html`. If you use OS/2 Warp's WebExplorer, the starting point is the IBM Internet Connection home page at `http://www.ibm.net/`. Each of these is a distinct address or document accessible via the Internet.

If you set the Internet Assistant up as a Web browser, however, its starting point is not on the Internet. Its default starting point is a local (on your own computer) HTML document called `DEFAULT.DOC`. `DEFAULT.DOC` comes as part of the Internet Assistant package and is used to introduce you to the Internet and to HTML. If you prefer, you can replace it with your own creation.

It should also introduce you to the idea that the default home page you use need not be way out there in cyberspace. Instead, it can be located on your own hard disk. As you navigate the Web and develop a feel for where things are and what you like, you can collect the URL references and create your own home page. Most Web browsers, in fact, have a feature—sometimes called quick list, Web map, or favorite places—that enables you to collect URLs for quick return later on. There's nothing stopping you from using that list as a starting point for your forays onto the Web (unless, of course, you're using Word as your browser, for which the only choice is DEFAULT.DOC). If you like the default starting point that is associated with your Web browser, you can use it. The following are other popular choices for user home pages:

World Wide Web Virtual Library
`http://info.cern.ch/hypertext/DataSources/bySubject/Overview.html`

Yahoo
`http://akebono.stanford.edu/yahoo/`

Table-of-Contents, Inc.
`http://www.mag-browse.com/`

The Awesome List
`http://www.clark.net/pub/journalism/awesome.html`

The Best of the Web
`http://wings.buffalo.edu/contest/`

Starting Points for Internet Exploration
`http://www.ncsa.uiuc.edu/SDG/Software/Mosaic/StartingPoints/`
`NetworkStartingPoints.html`

So far, I've talked about home pages exclusively from the user perspective. The term home page also means the principal point of presence for many businesses and institutions on the Web. Although someone might ask, "What do you use for your home page?", another might proclaim, "I have my own home page." They sound similar, but they're really quite different. For the most part, the HTML document that you use as your jumping-off point for exploring the Web is conceptually the opposite of what people mean when they say they have their own home pages—particularly businesses and other organizations. A business or other dedicated home page is designed more for exploration of that business and its capabilities, rather than for exploration of the net. You might think of the home page for a business as being its corporate résumé.

Look at Investor's Galleria, for example, `http://www.webcom.com/~galleria`, shown in Figure 1.12. This home page is Galleria's storefront to the Internet. This is Galleria's opportunity to tell the world who and what they are, and to encourage the browser to stop and look. Does this home page draw you in? Does it tell you what the Investor's Galleria does? Does it give you something interesting or informative to do?

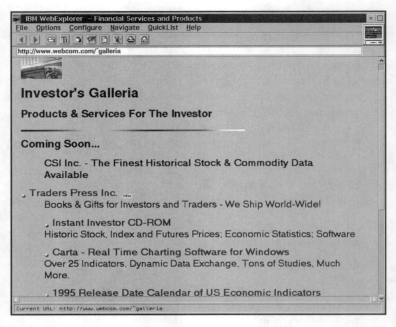

Figure 1.12. *Some Web pages are a bit dry.*

Now take a look at Blue Mountain Arts' 5-D Stereograms Home Page, http://www.ais.net/netmall/bma, shown in Figure 1.13. How about this one? Does this one draw you in? Does it pique your curiosity? How might you change Galleria's home page to make it more homey?

Pay close attention in this section of the book. Designing and building your own home page—your storefront or résumé to the world—is important. In order to do a good job, you become a media critic of sorts. You have to be able to look at home pages such as the ones just cited and see what's right or wrong with them. You want to see what ideas you can borrow and what ideas you want to shun. For starters, you would do well to fire up your Web browser and aim it at the WWYP at http://www.yellow.com. Using WWYP as a starting point, you have thousands of home pages at your fingertips. Here you find zillions of ideas of what to do and what not to do. Stay tuned. In this book, you will learn what to look for!

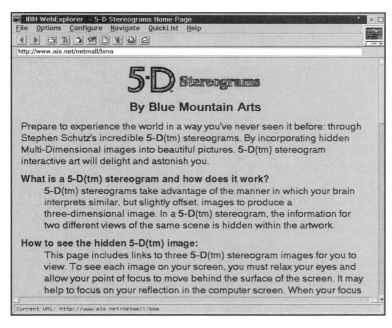

Figure 1.13. *Other Web pages instantly grab your attention.*

Summary

Today, you learned what the World Wide Web is and explored a few samples of what it has to offer. You also learned some basic terminology, such as URL (uniform resource locator), home page, and HTML (hypertext markup language). You've taken the first step toward Web publishing by looking critically and analytically at the home pages you encounter.

Q&A

Q How large is the audience or market for the Web?

A Audience and market are good terms. They describe the Web's potential quite nicely. Unfortunately, it's really hard to say how many people have access to the Web. Some of the more credible numbers I've seen estimate the current online world population at anywhere from fifty million to about two hundred million.

Q I hear that there's a Web site that enables you to type a few words of a song's lyrics and it can tell you the name of the song—as well as the lyrics, original artist, and so on. How can I find that Web site?

A Unfortunately, there really isn't a great way at present. However, two pretty good starting points are the World Wide Yellow Pages and the World Wide Web Virtual Library. The WWYP (`www.yellow.com`) enables you to search or browse by topic heading, name, and geographical location. As the name implies, the WWYP is geared toward businesses and institutions offering services. The World Wide Web Virtual Library (`http://www.w3org/hypertext/DataSources/bySubject/Overview.html`) has topic listings that might ultimately lead you to your destination. Other sometimes-useful ways to track down Web sites are the WebCrawler (`http://webcrawler.cs.washington.edu/WebCrawler/Home.html`) and Lycos (`http://fuzine.mt.cs.cmu.edu/mlm/lycos-home.html`). See Appendix A for additional resources.

I spent about 30 minutes searching so I could provide an answer to this question and ultimately stumbled onto a gopher that searches a large lyric database. Unfortunately, it's now so busy that I couldn't actually get a search to work (see the next question). Perhaps you'll have better luck. Try the Book of Metal gopher server at `gopher://spinaltap.micro.umn.edu/11/fun/Music`. Unless it's changed, the third item on the list is Lyrics Search.

Q Isn't there a danger that the Internet is going to get so busy and crowded that it will cease to be useful?

A Perhaps. At the moment, there are numerous traffic jams on the information superhighway. One thing that will make some of these go away is wider roadway (bandwidth). Right now, many of the millions who are connected to the Internet are using modems and telephone lines. Most such connections are limited to 28,800 bps or slower. The technological rumor mill suggests that much faster communications are on the way. So, rather than occupying a link for 30 minutes to get a 3MB file, you'll suddenly be able to get it in seconds. Of course, with wider roads comes more demand. Instead of wanting 3MB of pictures, you'll be wanting a 300MB movie.

Ultimately, the answer is technology. As demands increase, so will the response of technology. Those of us who are on the superhighway while it's still being paved will, on occasion, face the inevitable steamroller as it crushes our bits and bytes. I guess that's the price we pay for progress.

Q I'm a cynic. What's going to stop the Web from becoming just like television—that is, an overcommercialized ghetto that robs viewers of their creativity and motivation?

A You. Unlike television, the Web is interactive. Moreover, most of the viewing audience has the opportunity to become a part of the Web. If you don't like what you see, tell the parties responsible. Better still, create something new. Create a home page that draws others in and makes it interesting, exciting, and fun to discover new things. Frankly, I'm a cynic, too. I stopped watching television about six years ago because—even with 120 cable channels—I couldn't find anything worth watching. Oddly enough, though, when I visit Europe, I find myself watching television again. Why? Because it's different. Because it's not the same old commercial-formula television I'm used to.

On the Web, you get world service. You have potentially hundreds of millions of channels to choose from. Each one has the potential for being designed, produced, and sponsored by folks like us. There's nothing stopping cynics from making the Web into exactly what we want. If we leave the Web to others, it might become yet another commercial wasteland, filled with mind-numbing quicksand that invites our children not to think for themselves. If we seize the initiative, it can be an oasis. It can be an electronic canvas onto which the coming generations' Monets, daVincis, and Einsteins can work their magic. Television could have been that way if each viewer had been given transmitting as well as receiving capabilities. With the Web, you have it. Viewers and producers are one and the same. If you have genius to share with the world, the Web provides the forum. Go, and be heard!

2

The Basic Plan

Most successful endeavors begin with a goal and a plan. Presumably, you have some kind of goal in mind before you start to establish a Web presence. In coming up with a plan or approach to use the Web, you need to ask yourself the following questions:

- ☐ Will the plan accomplish the goal?
- ☐ Is the approach something that you can maintain easily and without too much expense?
- ☐ How can you measure whether your approach is working?

Today's lesson is designed to show you what's possible and what kinds of approaches typically are used to accomplish specific purposes. Today, you look at a variety of different goals and approaches and lay out some guidelines for deciding how to proceed.

In this discussion, it's hard to find an appropriate noun to use to characterize exactly what you use the Internet Assistant to create. You'll hear the terms home page, Web page, Web site, and a variety of others. I like to think of your entire Web presence as a presentation. In fact, you can even use Web tools to publish multimedia presentations—for selling ideas, proposals, and products. If you put together a snazzy presentation for use over the Web, you can just as well put the needed files onto a laptop or notebook computer and use it as the basis for a road show. In fact, when the files are already on your computer, you don't have to be nearly as restrained as you do when you have to worry about how long it takes to download files over the Internet.

Decide on a Main Purpose

It might sound simplistic, but you should have some definite ideas about what you want your Web presence to accomplish. In the hurry to establish a presence, a lot of companies and individuals rush headlong simply to get *something* onto the Web. Sometimes that's a mistake. Hundreds of items are being added to the Web each day. Some of them, unfortunately, aren't very well thought out. After all, you don't want your foray onto the Web to do more harm than good, do you?

Some common goals include:

- ☐ Advertising
- ☐ Providing information
- ☐ Public relations and building corporate image
- ☐ Collecting contact information (that is, addresses and names for mailing lists)
- ☐ Providing product and technical support

□ Collecting survey information

□ Education

Let's look at each of these to see which apply to you. Don't be surprised if you have multiple goals. Many Web users do.

Advertising

Perhaps the number one reason most businesses establish a presence on the Web is advertising. With hundreds of businesses establishing Web pages every week, nobody wants to be left behind. Surprisingly, however, advertising is very difficult to accomplish over the Web. Unlike billboards, commercials, printed ads in newspapers, magazines, and the telephone yellow pages, public exposure for Web advertisements is not easy to come by. So far at least, online versions of magazines and newspapers are highly text-oriented and content-oriented—largely due to the fact that many who are connected to the Web have relatively slow data connection rates that make graphics-laden Web pages difficult to tolerate.

Another reason public exposure for advertising is difficult is a lack of anything equivalent to public thoroughfares. When you travel around the Web, you often are making hyperleaps from link to link, seeing only those links that you explicitly want to see. Most advertisements are advantageously placed. You place them in high-traffic areas where interested parties are likely to see them. For example, you place ads for movies on posters in movie theaters. You place ads for restaurants in vacation and leisure magazines. You place ads for computers in computer magazines. The basic idea is to take advantage of opportunities, knowing that people in your market will be in the neighborhood.

On the Internet, that's difficult. Because data transmission rates are slow, there is a premium on packing as much useful and relevant information as possible into as little bandwidth as possible. When a Web surfer drops by an automobile Web page to see what kind of performance the new BMW delivers, he or she doesn't want to waste valuable online connect time by having to wade through ad copy for Satan's Used Cars.

Thus, if your purpose in establishing a Web presence is to advertise, you're going to have to be especially creative. Except for minimal listings in something like the World Wide Yellow Pages, you're not going to be able to litter the landscape with posters advertising your business. Instead, you might consider creating a useful service that itself draws people in, creating your own neighborhood in which you just *happen* to have information about your products and services.

Consider the CBS home page (http://www.cbs.com), for example, as shown in Figure 2.1. The CBS home page shows you a 3- by 3-inch image map, highlighting CBS's strongest points. Note, however, that the image map doesn't always remain the same. The one shown here is what was current when today's lesson was being written—by the time you read this, of course, it will have changed. Among other things, the NCAA basketball tournament—a big draw for CBS—was underway. Thus, the CBS home page features a "Road to the Final Four" (the last four teams left in the NCAA playoffs), an NCAA trivia quiz, and a sweepstakes in which viewers can win a trip to next year's Final Four.

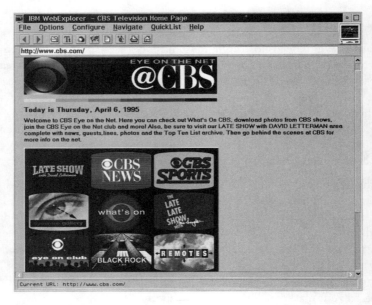

Figure 2.1. *The CBS home page.*

One of the big draws is the Late Show with David Letterman home page. If you travel down the Letterman path, you find the Top Ten list from the previous night's show, as well as an archive of all of the Top Ten lists since Dave moved to CBS from NBC. The Top Ten list is even searchable, in case you're looking for Top Ten lists having to do with a certain topic.

Because CBS can't put flashy commercials in locations where you'll stumble over them, they do the next best thing. They've made their Web home page an interesting place to visit. They've filled it with a number of interesting things to do. They also hint broadly about future plans to give you a reason to return. All the while, they're advertising. They're telling you what's on CBS, making it seem more interesting than it would seem otherwise.

Providing Information

Another major goal of many Web home pages is to provide access to information. Although commercial utilization of the Web is growing daily, the roots of the Internet go back to education, science, and national defense. Unlike advertising, where you have to devise clever ways to attract and maintain attention, information providers don't generally need to be quite so clever. After all, their mission is to make information available. It's not as if they're trying to sell anything (well, at least not overtly, although virtually every organization in the world usually is trying to find ways to increase or justify their funding).

Some Web sites succeed quite well in providing information. Others are less successful. As you cruise the Web, you'll notice lots of variation. The key difference between information providers that are successful and those that are time wasters is meat—something useful to sink your teeth into. Many information providers don't really provide any useful information, or at least don't provide the kind of information you think you're going to get. Take the National Archives, for example. Anyone who's ever visited the National Archives to do genealogical research drools at the prospect of having access to an online version of its collection. When I did research on my family tree about fifteen years ago, I discovered that many of the documents in the Archives from the 1600s and 1700s are available only on microfilm and microfiche, and often are handwritten. Finding a family name means hours of tedious searching, fiddling with ancient microfilm readers, and copying by hand any discoveries you make (the printing capabilities were not working when I was there).

Now imagine, if you will, having all that information transcribed into text files, with online search capabilities. That's the picture I had in my mind when I saw the National Archives (`http://www.nara.gov/`), shown in Figure 2.2. However, the reality doesn't come anywhere close to what I had imagined. When I saw an item entitled `The 1790-1890 Federal Population Censuses`, I got very excited. When I displayed the document, however, it turned out to be just a catalog of the microfilm holding. I spent a good three hours exploring every nook and cranny I came across, but never actually found any online data—only information about data. The Metrorail subway still appears to be the only way to access the National Archives data collection—at least for now.

On the other hand, there are some excellent examples of online data—weather, for example. The home page of the National Climatic Data Center (`http://www.ncdc.noaa.gov/`) includes several topics (see Figure 2.3).

These items take you directly to pages that offer many megabytes of weather data for direct download. I was tempted, but 9.5MB of data for 8,000 weather stations seemed like more data than I was ready to handle at the moment.

Similarly, you can get weather maps, both satellite- and radar-based—often just minutes old—for any part of the planet.

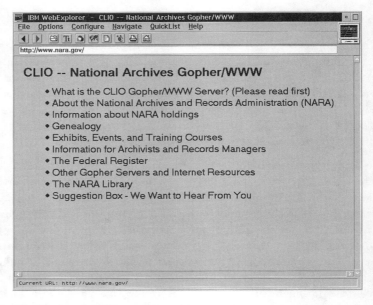

Figure 2.2. *The National Archives.*

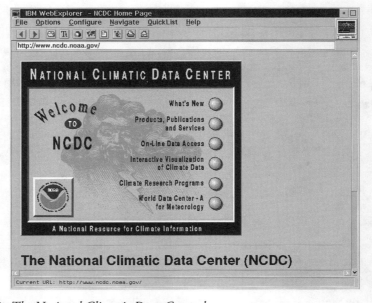

Figure 2.3. *The National Climatic Data Center home page.*

To summarize, if you're going to use your Web presence to provide information, you need to decide what kinds of information people want and then make it easy to obtain. One of the first computer games was something called Adventure. It was a text game, wherein you type commands, hoping that the game rewards you by opening new doors and paths. Usually, you wound up in a "twisty maze filled with winding passages" (a description from the Adventure game). Very often, however, trying to find information on Web sites seems like a game of Adventure, filled with many false clues and blind alleys. You can avoid frustrating your audience by saying up front what you have and don't have, so the user doesn't have to zigzag all over the Webscape (Web landscape) looking for things that might not exist. The key to doing it correctly is organization, using clear and accurate headings with concise and informative descriptions.

Public Relations and Building Corporate Image

Another goal for many Web sites is to provide the public with a strong positive impression of your organization and activities. This is sometimes known as PR (public relations). Actually, almost anything you put onto the Web falls into this category, whether you want it to or not. So, even if PR isn't your primary purpose, it will be a primary effect, and thus should be a consideration in your planning.

The first thing to remember in establishing good PR via the Web is not to aggravate or frustrate visitors. Having a pretty home page with nice graphics might seem like a good idea at first blush. However, recall from Day 1 the discussion of Lynx and the fact that some users connect to the Internet at fairly slow data rates. The best education for someone designing a Web presence might be to tour the Web while connected at 9,600, using a graphical browser such as the IBM WebExplorer in graphics mode. When graphics and text are in the Web pages you encounter, the WebExplorer displays the progress. If—after a minute—the progress indicator shows that you've downloaded only 25 percent of the main graphic contained in the home page, there's a good chance that the reader isn't going to hang around for another three minutes to get the other 75 percent.

For the sake of PR, plan your home page to have minimal graphics so that the home page can be displayed on a not-so-high-speed connection within 10 seconds or so. If you keep users waiting longer than that, you're inviting them not to hang around. Once there, you should offer users a choice of full graphics or a text-only route. People with higher speed connections or more patience can choose the graphical route. People with lower speed connections or text-only browsers can go the text route.

Note: Out of curiosity, I wanted to see what kind of PR image Coca Cola likes to project via the Web, so I typed `http://cocacola.com` as the URL. To my surprise, I connected not with the Coca Cola company, but with a Web server called MindSpring. One of the top items on their list was something called Core Values and Beliefs. Intrigued, I clicked on it to reveal the Web page shown in Figure 2.4. What a neat idea. So many organizations you encounter don't seem to have any kind of corporate conscience at all. Yet, here is one that puts its core values and beliefs right there on their home page. I'm still wondering why the `cocacola.com` address got me MindSpring's. It appears that Coca Cola uses them as a Web server, and I just wasn't able to find the right link. However, discovering MindSpring was refreshing.

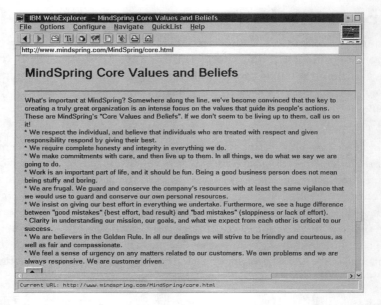

Figure 2.4. *Core values at MindSpring's Web site.*

Collecting Contact Information

Another useful mission for Web sites is collecting information (which is covered in Day 13). Using the HTML forms feature (as described in Chapter 13, "Web Forms and Image Maps"), you can provide a method for visitors to your Web site to leave contact information.

At its simplest, you can gather the e-mail addresses of visitors, or you can provide an entry form for them to leave their addresses and telephone numbers.

Many organizations simply provide e-mail and regular mailing addresses and invite you to send mail to those addresses. One of the advantages of the Web, however, is the capability of soliciting information then and there. In the Netsurfer's home page, for example, you find the form page shown in Figure 2.5 (`http://www.netsurf.com/nce-mail.html`). If you force your visitors to defer responding, they might not respond at all. If you offer them a convenient method to respond right now, you get a much better response rate.

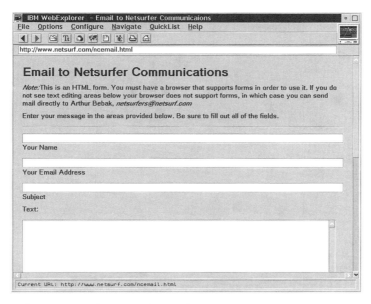

Figure 2.5. *A form page at the Netsurfer's Web site.*

Another example of how you can use this feature to provide interesting things for Web visitors can be found at the Macmillan Computer Publishing (MCP) Web site. One current attention-getter is the Mac Madness Computer Tipoff contest, shown in part in Figure 2.6 (`http://www.mcp.com/hayden/madness`). Borrowing from the NCAA "March Madness" (which has something to do with basketball), this is a contest in which Mac users offer their favorite tips to be used in a Tip of the Day feature. Winners can win books and have their names celebrated at the MCP web site (`www.mcp.com`). Of course, there's no guarantee that the Madness URL will still be in place by the time you see this book. MCP also has a monthly Top Ten contest you can enter to win a T-shirt (I even won one for my entries to the Top Ten ways that surfing the Web is more fun than watching the O.J. Simpson trial).

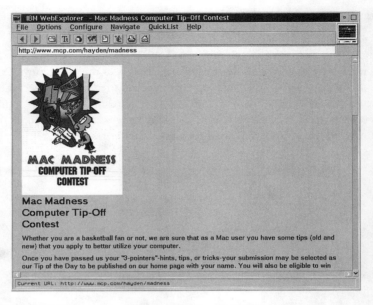

Figure 2.6. *Mac Madness at Macmillan Computer Publishing.*

Once you get your Web site set up, by the way, you will want to use the forms page for the World Wide Yellow Pages to start publicizing your Web presence. Set your URL to `http://www.yellow.com/cgi-bin/online` and submit a listing using the form shown in Figure 2.7. At the moment, it's free!

Providing Product and Technical Support

Another popular use for Web sites is providing online product and technical support. In addition to providing a direct feedback channel, you can also use your Web resources to make information about recalls and updates available. Many computer hardware and software companies provide direct support over the Web as well, often providing access to files for updated programs and drivers.

For an example of a company that provides product support via the Web, see the Abstract Technologies, Inc. home page (`http://www.abstract.co.nz/abstract-y.html`), as shown in Figure 2.8. Here, they've neatly divided their page by product, support, and information headings.

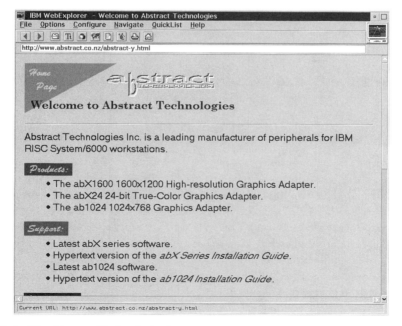

Figure 2.7. *The World Wide Yellow Pages.*

Figure 2.8. *The Abstract Technologies home page.*

If you choose the option to download the latest abX series software, you then see the page shown in Figure 2.9. Here, there are direct links to files contained on an FTP server. The fact that they've neatly hidden the details of the FTP directory from you is a nice touch. Rather than having to navigate directories and figuring out which filename you want, you just click on the highlighted text description.

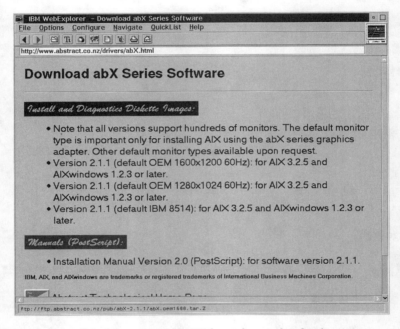

Figure 2.9. *Downloading software over the Web can be painless for the user.*

Education

Another goal you might have for placing your Web site into service is to educate. Indeed, some of the best advertising is educational. However, some educational efforts are for education in their own right—especially those set up by universities. Consider, for example, a Web site called The English Server, whose home page is shown in Figure 2.10 (`http://english-server.hss.cmu.edu`). This server acts as a supereducation site for a number of topics ranging from arts and architecture to technoculture. There's even an entry for Recipes that contains "helpful hints for preparing dead animals for consumption" (`http://english-server.hss.cmu.edu/Recipes.html`). I guess that's the kind of spin you get when you put a vegetarian in charge of a recipe server!

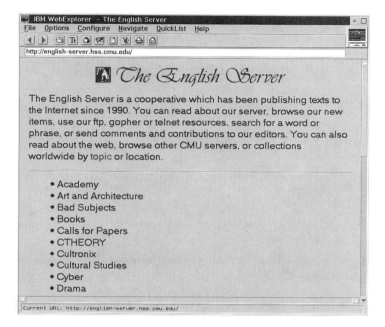

Figure 2.10. *The English Server.*

Or, perhaps you'd care to set up a poetry server, such as the one shown in Figure 2.11 (`http://english-server.hss.cmu.edu/Poetry.html`). Among other things, you'll find Carl Sandburg's complete *Chicago Poems*. The same education server also has a page called Reference, shown in Figure 2.12 (`http://english-server.hss.cmu.edu/Reference.html`). If you are looking up an area code, information from the U.S. Census, a dictionary, e-mail directories, or a variety of other topics, this might be a good starting point.

This type of education Web site is simple and succinct. You aren't compelled to wait for dozens of irrelevant graphics or wade through twisty mazes or passages to find the information you want. If you want to use your Web site to educate, keep these basic principles in mind. Once you have someone's attention, don't throw it away by challenging his or her patience or playing hide-and-seek with information.

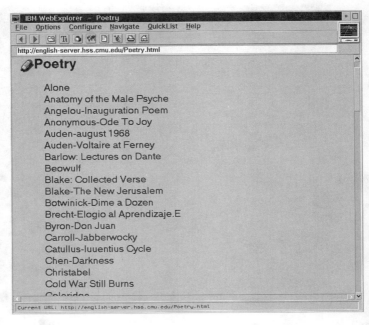

Figure 2.11. *A poetry server.*

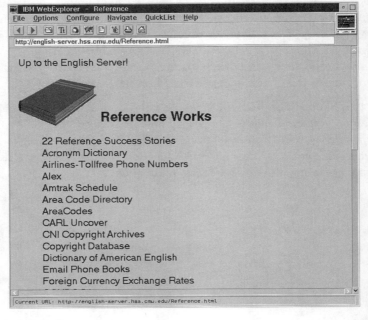

Figure 2.12. *The Reference page.*

What Can You Include
in a Web Page?

Technically, the World Wide Web is an extremely versatile medium. Almost any comput-erized resource can be placed onto the Web, with most limits being those imposed by practicality and bandwidth. The following can be included in a Web page:

- ☐ Text
- ☐ Local text links to other parts of the Web document and to other HTML docu-ments
- ☐ Inline and external graphics
- ☐ Sounds
- ☐ Videos
- ☐ Forms
- ☐ Links to other HTML documents
- ☐ Links to other Web sites
- ☐ Links to FTP, gopher, and Telnet

Let's take a quick look at each of these, especially why and how you might want to use them—and circumstances in which you might *not* want to use them.

Text

Text is, of course, the most obvious thing you can include in a Web page. It's essential to conveying information in a literate society. However, too much text can present problems as well. Keep in mind that visitors to your Web site might be trying to ascertain quickly whether what they want is there. It's not uncommon to cruise onto a very wordy Web site and conclude that what you want *isn't* there, when in fact it *is*.

Use text wisely and succinctly. Make use of headings as links so that the reader can quickly zero in on a topic of interest. One way to do this is to organize your Web presentation in an outline. On your home page, include just enough descriptive text under each major heading so that the user knows what to find.

Another use of text is to provide a text-only alternative to your graphical Web presentation. Not everyone has a T1 or ISDN line (fast Internet connections) connecting them to the Internet. Many users connect to the Internet using 28.8Kpbs modems and slower. A 100KB inline graphic of a corporate logo might instantly snap into focus on your system. On a 14.4Kpbs modem visitor's system, however, the same file takes about a minute to download. Some people don't have the patience for logos that take a minute or longer before they show up on a computer screen.

An even more compelling reason for providing text alternatives, however, is the fact that many users use Lynx rather than a graphical Web browser (see Chapter 1 "The World Wide Web "). A picture might very well be worth a thousand words. If you're using Lynx, however, the pictures are worthless.

Local Text Links

Another useful thing you can do in long Web pages is to use links to other parts of the same Web document as a kind of table of contents. This type of presentation has several advantages over using a number of different HTML documents to accomplish the same thing. First, the user has only a single download. Once the document has arrived, browsing it using local links (links contained in the same document) is very fast.

Second, some documents—especially online manuals and directories—are most useful to users if they can save them to their local disks for later reference. If the Web presentation is broken into a number of separate files, however, saving the entire document to disk can be very tedious. Moreover, on a Web server, files typically are named `something`.HTML; on local systems, they typically might be named `something`.HTM. The internal references are all to HTML using the original filename, many of which exceed the file-naming capabilities of a typical DOS FAT file system. So, in order to have such a document continue to be useful as an HTML presentation by users, they have to rename all the links. If you really want to perform a service for your users, make such presentations a single document.

There is the other side, of course. If the presentation is a 300KB text file, it's going to take the average user several minutes to download it. That's not a very pleasant option, either. One thing you can do for such documents, however, is to provide the user a choice of browsing online or downloading the entire document.

Inline and External Graphics

A Web page can contain two types of graphics: inline or external. Inline graphics often are used for items such as logos and image maps, using either GIF or JPEG format (files with the extensions `.GIF` or `.JPG`) (see Figure 2.13). Inline graphics show up in the Web document when using a graphical Web browser. Very often, the quality of the browser's graphical display is not nearly as good as that of the higher-end graphics programs. In addition, in order to save time for users who want to browse quickly, Web page designers deliberately don't include high-resolution graphics as part of a Web page.

If you have fine artwork that requires high-resolution graphics, such as pictures from an art gallery, a detailed schematic, or a detailed map, it's much better to include a reference to a file—for example PCX, TIF, BMP, GIF, or JPEG. That way, users can download the file (as a conscious choice) and use their favorite dedicated graphics program to view it, rather than the more compromised view you often get from a Web browser (see Figure 2.14).

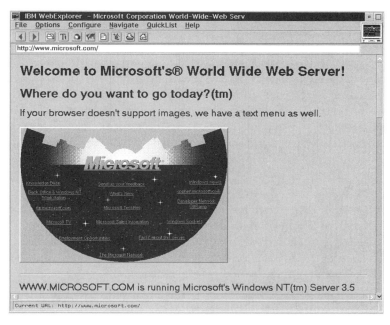

Figure 2.13. *Graphics can be used as image maps.*

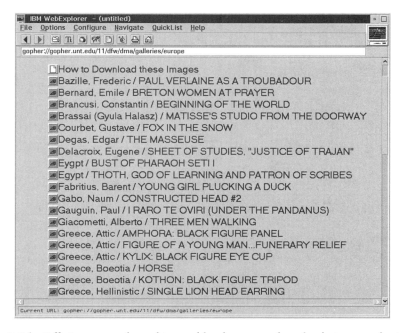

Figure 2.14. *Offering external graphics enables the user to download pictures selectively.*

41

Sounds

Unlike graphics, sounds cannot be made to be automatic parts of a Web page. One common use for sound files is to provide some kind of welcome message from the CEO of a company. Just as in multimedia encyclopedias, other uses include bits of historic speeches (Martin Luther King's "I have a dream" speech and John F. Kennedy's "Ask not what your country can do for you..." speech), popular musical themes, and so on. As bandwidth (data transmission speeds) on the Internet increases, the use of sound will increase, including items such as trademark themes and commercial jingles.

Videos

Another emerging element to include in Web pages is a file containing digital video. Using a Mac, OS/2, or Windows, most users now have the capability to display (or play) digital motion video on their personal computers. Bandwidth being what it is, at present, digital video is not often relied upon for most Web presentations. Instead, such items are ancillary, as in the case of multiframe weather satellite images.

Forms

One of the most useful things you can include in your Web presentations are data forms for collecting information and feedback from users. Several examples of forms were shown earlier. The form shown in Figure 2.15 is used to collect customer feedback. Due to security considerations, however, transmission of credit card numbers is not very popular over the Internet at present. There is—right now—no clear way to guard against interception of credit card numbers transmitted over the Internet. However, many companies are willing to accept orders for COD, as well as invoiced, making the Internet at least somewhat useful as an ordering medium.

Links to Other HTML Documents

As implied earlier, any HTML document can also contain links to other HTML documents. This can be useful when documents are specialized or are maintained by different individuals. Those other HTML documents can be local or anywhere else on the Internet.

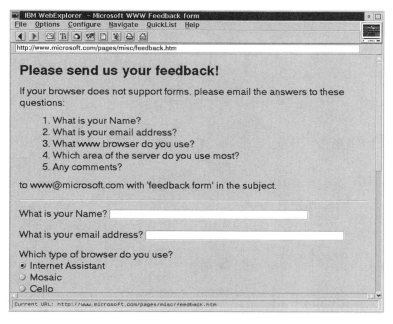

Figure 2.15. *Forms are a great way to get instant customer feedback.*

Links to Other Web Sites

Popular items to include in many Web presentations are links to other Web sites that are of likely interest to visitors. For example, as shown in Figure 2.16, some Web sites are set up exclusively as points of redirection. Larry McGoldrick's Bookmarks (`http://cpcug.org/netmarks.html`) is a collection of hyperlinks to interesting and useful Web sites collected by Larry—a member of the Washington, D.C., area's Capital PC Users Group. The World Wide Web Virtual Library and Yahoo are also Web sites whose main function is to direct you elsewhere.

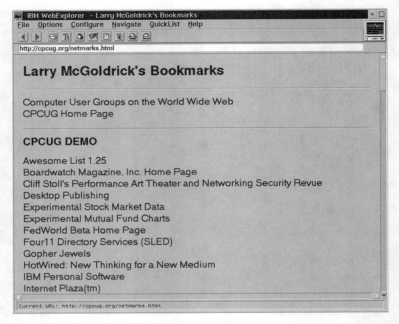

Figure 2.16. *Larry McGoldrick's Bookmarks provide a number of useful starting points.*

Links to FTP, Gopher, and Telnet

The Internet is a collection of many capabilities, and the Web, although big and growing, has not yet replaced all other capabilities. In particular, there still are a number of functions that currently are best handled by FTP, gopher, and Telnet sites. Most Web browsers are capable of performing FTP and browsing gopher sites. You can include links to FTP and gopher sites in your Web pages. In fact, in the case of files, it often is best if you can include a link directly to a specific file, with a description of the file, rather than forcing the user to navigate through directories often containing hundreds or thousands of files. Presenting files in this way performs a real service to the user, providing both convenience and insurance that the right file gets downloaded (assuming the FTP site is up and running, of course).

Most Web browsers are not capable of performing Telnet functions (at least not yet). Instead, most of the popular ones enable users to designate a Telnet client to invoke when their browsers encounter a telnet URL. Thus, it's generally safe to include Telnet references in your Web pages. Telnet references are frequently used for searches, such as Netfind.

Start Simply and Build

Usually, simplicity is best. Complicated Web presentations not only confuse the user, but the author as well. As you cruise the Web, you very likely will encounter Web pages that are still under construction. Although many users find that Web pages that are under construction are a bit frustrating (like blind alleys), they're actually a good sign. They're a sign that the user hasn't just slapped something together and then abandoned it. Rather, they're likely proceeding deliberately and slowly, gradually building their Web presentation into something that does the job. It's also not unusual to see solicitations such as "Tell us what you want to see here." Unfortunately, that kind of solicitation is *not* always such a good sign. It's an indication that the Web site author really doesn't know what they want to do with his or her Web site, and has placed establishing a presence above establishing a well-thought-out presence. Moreover, if site authors don't know what they're doing on the Web, how the heck can they expect their readers to know?

If you don't have a long agenda to accomplish with your Web site, that's okay. You can set up something that accomplishes a simple purpose at first. You don't have to do it all at once. Then, as your needs grow, or as you discover additional needs that could be addressed by expanding or enhancing your Web presentation, go for it.

At the very least, your Web presentation should contain the following:

- ☐ Who you are (usually at the bottom of the Web page)
- ☐ The purposes of the Web site
- ☐ A brief description of how your site is organized (where to find what)
- ☐ The substance of your presentation
- ☐ How to contact you or otherwise provide feedback

Outline, and It Practically Writes Itself

One of the best planning tools ever devised is the outline. Nearly every computer book on the market starts with one, and almost every successful business became successful because somebody paused to put the ideas on paper. Successful and effective Web pages begin with outlines as well. For starters, you need at least the following:

A. Goals or problems
    1. What do I hope to gain by having a Web presence?
    2. What problems will having a Web presence solve?

    3. Do I want the Web presence to disseminate information, collect information, advertise, warn, or educate?

  B. Methods and materials

    1. What do I want to include in my presentation: text, graphics (inline or external), sound, links?

    2. Where can graphics or other files be found?

    3. Do I make files available locally (at my site), or set up links to other locations?

    4. Should I beta-test my Web presentation (try it out on others in my organization before going public)?

  C. Measuring success

    1. Collecting feedback—providing a method in the Web page for people to respond to how well you're achieving your purpose

    2. Asking customers where and how they heard about me (if the Web directs people to write, call, or visit)

If you are in an organization and plan to delegate the task of putting together a Web presentation, you should ask that person to prepare an outline. Before you go online with anything, you also should assemble all the components and see how it all plays. Test it out for a week or two, testing all the external links at various times of the day and night. Keep in mind that there's a reason why the World Wide Web is called the *World* Wide Web. Sometimes, links you think are available are tied to various schedules. Did you know, for example, that some university sites close down during Christmas and spring break? Did you know, for example, that some businesses pull the plug on their Internet links at 5 p.m. every day? International links are especially susceptible to interruption. Either have contingency links in place, or include notices to indicate the times that users might expect to encounter problems.

Summary

Today, you explored ideas about what goes into a Web presentation. You learned that Web sites can exist for a variety of reasons, and that the approaches should be determined by the purpose. You discovered that a Web presentation can contain many different elements, and that choosing the elements carefully can make the difference between having a good Web site and one that people avoid. You also learned that it helps to outline your plan of attack. Before you set up your Web site, you should have a definite plan in mind—and on paper.

Q&A

Q Hey, I just want a little fun place to tell the world who I am. Do I really need to do all this stuff?

A Yes, but not necessarily in such a formal way. Do you work for other people? Even if your Web page is just for fun, there's a good chance that your employer, customers, clients, or family could stumble onto it, either accidentally or out of curiosity. If they do, you owe it to yourself, your livelihood, and your relationships to make sure that you don't embarrass yourself.

Q When linking to other resources on the Web, how can you guarantee that they'll always be there?

A You can't guarantee that links will always work. If something is vital to your Web presentation, the only way you can guarantee that it will be there is to have it available locally on your Web server.

Q What if I goof? Are Web presentations carved into stone, or can you change them?

A Web presentations can be changed. Depending on your Web server, some are easier to change than others. For most, changing is simply a matter of FTP-ing replacement files onto your server and setting the appropriate access privileges.

DAY
2

Quick Start—
Creating Simple
Web Documents

3

The Internet Assistant for Word

So far, you've seen a lot about what can go into or onto a Web page, and you've seen a lot of Web pages in action. You're probably wondering when and if you're ever going to start learning about the Internet Assistant. Today, you learn the following:

☐ What the Internet Assistant is

☐ How to obtain the latest version of the Internet Assistant

☐ How to install the Internet Assistant

☐ How to use the Internet Assistant (understanding how it's put together)

What Is the Internet Assistant?

According to Microsoft, Internet Assistant is an add-on to Microsoft Word for Windows that gives you the capability of viewing pages on the Internet World Wide Web. You also can create and navigate "webs" of documents on existing local networks.

Note: The Internet Assistant for Word is not, in itself, sufficient for browsing the Web. To use the Internet Assistant for Word on the Internet, you must first use some kind of Internet connectivity program to connect to the Internet. If you don't know what I'm talking about, you probably need to buy an entry-level book about the Internet or to seek the help of a local users group.

However, there's more. The Internet Assistant is implemented as a WLL (Windows Link Library) that gets installed into your Word for Windows 6 STARTUP directory. While the Internet Assistant is enabled, it adds a number of new features to your WinWord menu to facilitate browsing the Web and creating new Web documents. For example, a Web Browse option is added to your View menu (a Web Browse is also added to your File menu) (see Figure 3.1). Moreover, the Internet Assistant enables you to create Web documents *Word-style,* using styles for headings, titles, and so on. When you save a document, the Internet Assistant adds a new item to your list of File | Save As choices: Hypertext Markup Language (HTML).

Note: The Internet Assistant requires Word for Windows version 6.0a or higher. Registered users of Word for Windows 6 can obtain the latest release from Microsoft by calling 800-426-9400. There may be a nominal charge for diskettes.

Figure 3.1. *The Internet Assistant adds a Web Browse option to Word's View menu.*

The Internet Assistant package enables you to use Microsoft Word as a Web browser, and it also includes a demo version of a separate stand-alone browser called InternetWorks Internet Assistant by Booklink Technologies (or, possibly by NaviSoft) (see Figure 3.2). In order to use it, you need not have Word for Windows. If you don't already have another Web browser to which you are accustomed, you very likely will prefer the InternetWorks Internet Assistant over Word as a browser. Although it's limited and missing some features at this time, it's still vastly superior to using Word as a browser, in terms of speed and features.

Figure 3.2. *A demo version of InternetWorks Internet Assistant comes with the Microsoft Internet Assistant for Word.*

Note: At this writing, a fuller-featured version of InternetWorks Internet Assistant is available in beta from the Macmillan Computer Publishing FTP site at `ftp.mcp.com` in the `/pub/software/Internet` directory as `beta7.exe`. The name very likely will have changed by the time you read this.

Obtaining the Latest Version of Internet Assistant for Word

The latest version of the Internet Assistant can be obtained free (except for whatever data connection charges you incur) directly from Microsoft over the Internet, or from the Macmillan Computer Publishing Web site. It also can be obtained on disk for a small fee (800-426-9400; the cost in the U.S. is $5.50 at this writing). Use these steps to obtain the Internet Assistant over the Internet using a Web browser:

1. Start your Web browser, and set the URL to `http://www.microsoft.com/pages/deskapps/word/ia/chcklist.htm`.

2. Click on Download Internet Assistant.

To obtain the Internet Assistant using an FTP client, use the following steps (I'm assuming that you're familiar with your FTP software; if you're not, consult the documentation that comes with it to accomplish these steps):

1. Start your FTP client software.

2. Log onto `ftp.microsoft.com`, specifying anonymous as the user ID and your e-mail address as the password (for example, `smith@jones.com`).

3. Change directories to `deskapps/word/winword-public/ia`.

4. Get (download) the files `README.DOC` and `WORDIA.EXE` (note that Microsoft's FTP server lists files in uppercase, which is different from most FTP servers on the Internet).

Macmillan Computer Publishing (MCP) will attempt to maintain the latest version on their FTP server as well, although it's best to use the Microsoft site if at all possible. To obtain the file from MCP, set the URL on your Web browser to `http://www.mcp.com/softlib/Internet/` and click on the item corresponding to the Internet Assistant for Microsoft Word.

Expanding and Installing the Internet Assistant

If you obtained the Internet Assistant online, you obtained a file called WORDIA.EXE. This file is a self-extracting archive file that expands into a number of files needed to install the Internet Assistant. To expand the file, you should copy WORDIA.EXE to an empty subdirectory on a disk that has at least 2.5MB of free space available. Then, at the DOS command line, type the following:

```
wordia
```

This extracts a number of files from WORDIA.EXE, as shown in Figure 3.3, including an installation program called SETUP.EXE. If you obtained the Internet Assistant on disks directly from Microsoft, you won't have a program called WORDIA.EXE and can use SETUP.EXE directly from the installation disk.

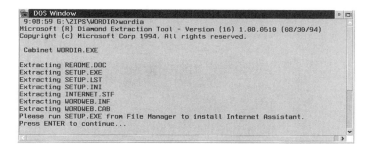

Figure 3.3. WORDIA.EXE *expands into the files needed to install the Internet Assistant.*

To install the Internet Assistant, execute these steps:

1. Start Windows (if installing in OS/2, start a full-screen WIN-OS/2 session).
2. From the main menu, choose File | Run.
3. In the Command Line box, type the disk and directory location followed by SETUP.EXE, as shown in Figure 3.4 (for example, c:\scratch\setup.exe or some other scratch directory, such as g:\zips\wordia shown in Figure 3.4), and click on OK.

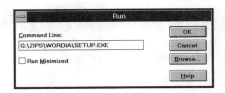

Figure 3.4. *Choose File \ Run from the menu and run the Internet Assistant* SETUP.EXE *program.*

4. The setup program now displays a copyright screen; click on OK to continue.

5. The setup program now displays the license agreement; click on Continue each time it's offered, and then click on Agree.

6. The setup program now displays the proposed location for installing the Internet Assistant. Click on the large button to accept the location (see Figure 3.5); or click on the Change Directory option to specify a different directory (you will need at least 2MB of space on the disk where the Internet Assistant is installed, as well as about 200KB or so on the disk where Windows is installed and about 100KB on the disk where Word 6 is installed).

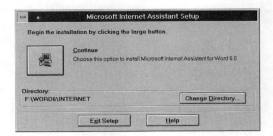

Figure 3.5. *Click on the large square button to accept the location and install the Internet Assistant.*

7. The setup program now asks whether you want to install the browsing components (the InternetWorks Internet Assistant Web browser); click on Yes to do it or No *not* to do it (see the text following this procedure).

8. The setup program now verifies that there is enough disk space and begins copying files to the proper location; when done, it prompts for you either to launch Word or exit the setup program. Make whichever selection you want by clicking on the appropriate button.

In step 7, the setup program asks whether you want to install the browsing components. The *browsing components* refers to the InternetWorks Internet Assistant program mentioned previously. Unless you are seriously strapped for disk space, at least install it and take a look at it. That way, even if you're already using something else, you can compare the InternetWorks browser and make a decision about which browser best meets your needs.

Installing InternetWorks Internet Assistant

If you *do* install the InternetWorks browser, at this writing at least, the setup program does *not* create a program item to run it. You need to do it manually. From the program group where you want the InternetWorks Internet Assistant browser to be accessible, do the following:

1. Choose File | New from the menu.

2. Click on OK.

3. Type the command line as *location*\iwia.exe, where *location* matches the disk and subdirectory you specified in step 6 when running the setup program.

4. Type a description (for example, InternetWorks Browser) in the Description box and click on OK (see Figure 3.6).

When you're finished, the icon shown in Figure 3.7 will appear in the program group. You can double-click to start the browser. To use it on the Internet, you must be logged onto the Internet with SLIP or PPP access.

Figure 3.6. *Setting up a program item for InternetWorks Internet Assistant.*

Figure 3.7. *Double-click on the InternetWorks Internet Assistant icon to start the demo browser that comes with the Microsoft Word Internet Assistant.*

Understanding the Internet Assistant

There are three major components to the Internet Assistant add-on to Word:

WORDHTML.WLL	A Windows Link Library that adds TCP/IP communications capabilities to Word
WEBVIEW.DOT	A Word 6 template used when browsing the Web with Word
HTML.DOT	A Word 6 template used to create HTML documents

Other files are added as well (such as WORDHTML.CNV for saving files in HTML format). However, the special effects you see in Word after installing the Internet Assistant are all owed to the three major components.

How Does *WORDHTML.WLL* Change Word 6?

The file WORDHTML.WLL is added to your Word 6 STARTUP subdirectory when you install the Internet Assistant. This file is a Word Link Library. It contains a number of new commands and functions that are available for use in Word when browsing the Web and when creating HTML documents. It also adds items to the Word 6 menu and to the formatting toolbar for accessing the HTML tools. Despite what some users think, the Internet Assistant installation does not actually change Word 6. It merely copies some files into directories so that Word automatically will use them.

To see exactly *how* `WORDHTML.WLL` gets integrated into Word 6, choose File | Templates from the Word 6 menu for a view similar to that shown in Figure 3.8. If you have added any other `.WLL` files or `.DOT` files for global use in Word, they have been added in the Global Templates and Add-ins list. Items show up in this list either as a result of explicitly adding them with the Templates and Add-ins dialog box, or as a result of putting the files into the Word 6 `STARTUP` subdirectory. The file `wordhtml.wll` is there because the Internet Assistant installation program put it into the Word 6 `STARTUP` subdirectory. Note that in this figure, only `wordhtml.wll` is shown, and that there is an X beside it. This means that `WORDHTML.WLL` is currently loaded into memory.

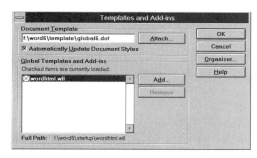

Figure 3.8. *The Templates and Add-ins dialog box reveals how Word integrates* `WORDHTML.WLL`.

Changes to Word's Menus and Toolbars

The `WORDHTML.WLL` add-on adds several items to Word's menu. To see what they are, press Esc to dismiss the Global Templates and Add-ins dialog box without making any changes. Now click on File on the main menu. Observe that one of the commands is Browse Web, shown in Figure 3.9—but don't click on it just now. Click on View from the main menu, and observe that it contains an item called Web Browse (refer to Figure 3.1)—again, don't click on it right now. These two items—Browse Web and Web Browse—are not identical. Choosing the File | Browse Web item opens an existing HTML document called `DEFAULT.DOC`. Choosing the View | Web Browse item causes Word to go into Web browsing mode while viewing the current document. You learn more on exactly what each option does a little later in today's lesson. For now, however, you're just exploring how Word gets changed by having `WORDHTML.WLL` loaded.

Figure 3.9. *The Internet Assistant adds a Browse Web option to Word's File menu.*

Now click on Insert in the menu. Observe that an item called HyperLink has been added to the bottom of the Insert menu. Click on the HyperLink option to display the dialog box shown in Figure 3.10. The HyperLink dialog box is a tabbed affair that enables you to insert hyperlinks to local documents, URLs, or bookmarks within the current HTML document (assuming you're editing one). You learn how and when to use these in a little while. For now, just know that they're there.

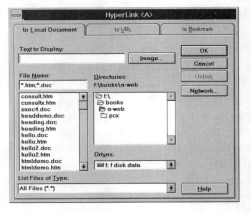

Figure 3.10. *The HyperLink dialog box added to Word by the Internet Assistant.*

Those are all the changes that WORDHTML.WLL adds to the regular Word 6 menu. Now let's take a look at what WORDHTML.WLL does to your Word 6 toolbars. If your Formatting toolbar is not already displayed, display it now. Choose View | Toolbars from the menu, click on Formatting so that an X appears beside it. While you're here, click (if necessary) to enable the Show Tooltips option. Then click on OK.

The Formatting toolbar displays (by default, but your default might be different) as shown in Figure 3.11. Note the glasses icon at the left end of the toolbar. Move your mouse pointer so that it is over the glasses icon, as shown in Figure 3.11. As you do so, a text box appears that says Switch to Web Browse View. The glasses tool corresponds to the File | Browse Web and View | Web Browse options.

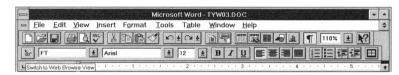

Figure 3.11. *The Internet Assistant adds a Switch to Web Browse View tool to the formatting toolbar.*

To prove that these features were added by WORDHTML.WLL, choose File | Template from the menu and click to remove the X next to wordhtml.wll; then click on OK. Now, repeat the exercises shown earlier in this heading. Under File, Browse Web is gone; under View, Web Browse is gone; and, under Insert, the HyperLink option is nowhere to be found. Moreover, notice that the little pair of glasses has disappeared from the Formatting toolbar.

Don't panic. You can get them all back simply by choosing File | Template, clicking to enable WORDHTML.WLL, and clicking on OK. See? The mystery's gone, right? One interesting feature about .WLL and .DOT files placed into your Word STARTUP subdirectory is that they are automatically loaded each time you start Word. If you turn a .WLL file off, close and restart Word, the fact that you turned it off is not remembered by Word.

Tip: If you want to be able to turn WORDHTML.WLL off and make it stay off, you can. Just put WORDHTML.WLL into a different subdirectory. Then use File | Template to add it back in. Items that you explicitly add—as opposed to items that you put into the STARTUP subdirectory—don't get automatically reloaded when you start Word unless you left the X turned on next to them in the Templates and Add-in dialog box. To provide my own setup with additional control over WORDHTML.WLL, I created a subdirectory in STARTUP called

STARTUP\ASST, and moved WORDHTML.WLL to that subdirectory. Then I chose File | Templates from the menu to add wordhtml.wll to the list.

You can do this too. First, with Word *not* running, move WORDHTML.WLL to a different subdirectory. Now start Word and execute the following steps to add WORDHTML.WLL to the list of add-ins:

1. Choose File | Templates from the menu.

2. Click on Add.

3. Use the List Files of Type control to set the file type to *.WLL.

4. Use the Drives and Directories controls, as necessary, to navigate to the location of wordhtml.wll.

5. Click on wordhtml.wll and then click on OK.

6. Observe that an X is next to wordhtml.wll (assuming you want it enabled for right now), and click on OK to close the dialog box.

Web Browse or Browse Web View

In the preceding section, you looked at how WORDHTML.WLL changes the landscape of Word's main menu bar. Now let's take a look at the Web Browse mode. You do not need to be connected to the Internet to do this, by the way. You can browse the Web while online if you like, but it's easier right now just to look at some local documents.

There are three controls for entering Web Browse view, as discussed previously:

☐ Choose File | Browse Web from the menu.

☐ Choose View | Web Browse from the menu.

☐ Click on the Switch to Web Browse View tool (the glasses on the formatting toolbar).

The first method opens a document called DEFAULT.DOC and switches into Browse Web view. Choose File | Browse Web to display the view shown in Figure 3.12. Word opens the file DEFAULT.DOC, which the Internet Assistant setup program installed in the Internet Assistant subdirectory (usually a subdirectory called INTERNET that is created on your main Word 6 directory). The Web Browse view occurs because DEFAULT.DOC uses WEBVIEW.DOT as the template.

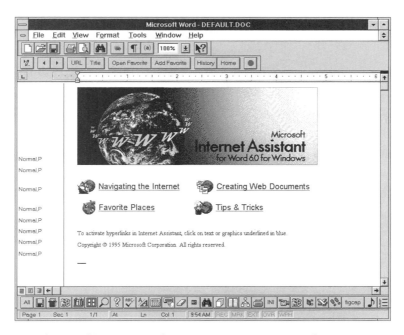

Figure 3.12. *Choose File | Browse Web to open* DEFAULT.DOC *in Web Browse view.*

If you choose View | Web Browse or if you click on the Switch to Web Browse View tool, Word does not open DEFAULT.DOC. Instead, Word switches to Web Browse view. Let's see exactly what happens. First, just so you don't get too upset, choose File | New from the menu (or click on the New tool on the Standard toolbar) to open a blank Word document. Next, use File | Template to verify that WORDHTML.WLL is loaded and that the current document template is normal, as shown in Figure 3.13. Then press Esc to dismiss the dialog box without taking any actions.

Now click on the glasses icon to go into Web Browse mode, for the view shown in Figure 3.14. Pretty weird, eh? A couple of things just happened. Before you explore what happened, click on the icon that looks like a pencil at the left end of the formatting toolbar (the icon that took the place of the glasses that were there a moment ago). Note that when you do that, the view goes back to what it was before, and the glasses icon is back on the toolbar.

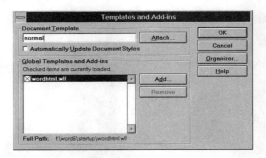

Figure 3.13. *The Templates and Add-ins dialog box shows that* wordhtml.wll *is loaded and that the current template is normal.*

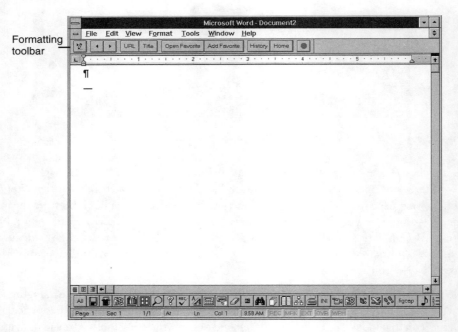

Figure 3.14. *Clicking on the Switch to Web Browse View icon displays the* WEBVIEW.DOT *Formatting Toolbar.*

Click on the glasses again to return to Web Browse view. If tooltips are not enabled, choose View | Toolbars and click on the Show Tooltips option so that an X appears in the box next to it. While you're there, click to turn on the Standard toolbar (in addition to the Formatting toolbar) if it's not already enabled. Then click on OK to close the dialog box. Now move the mouse so that the pointer is over the pencil icon at the left end of the toolbar. Note that it

says `Switch to Edit View`. With `WORDHTML.WLL` loaded into memory, any document can now be viewed either in Edit view or in Web Browse view.

Previously, you verified that the current template was `NORMAL.DOT`. Now that you're in Web Browse view, let's see whether that's changed. Choose File | Template from the menu to see the name of the current template. It's now `WEBVIEW.DOT`, and you didn't change it! When you click on the glasses icon—or if you were to choose View | Web Browse from the menu—Word automatically attaches `WEBVIEW.DOT` to the current document. When you click on the pencil icon (switch to Edit view), Word automatically reattaches the original template (usually).

> **Note:** Web Browse view is a state that you can choose for any displayed document. It is not a view that takes over all of Word 6. It's possible to have one document open in Web Browse view and another in Edit view at the same time.

While in Web Browse view, take a look at the Standard and Formatting toolbars, shown in Figure 3.15. Click alternately on the glasses and pencil tools to switch back and forth, noting the differences between the toolbars in Edit and Web Browse views. Notice that the menu changes as well. Among other things, changes in the menu and toolbars are part of how `WORDHTML.WLL` provides new features to you for browsing the Web and for creating HTML documents.

Standard toolbar —
Formatting toolbar —

Figure 3.15. *The Standard and Formatting toolbars are both changed when* `WEBVIEW.DOT` *is active.*

While in Web Browse view, move the mouse pointer over each of the tools on the toolbar to display the tooltip text. Familiarize yourself with the purpose of each of the tools shown in Figure 3.15. After you've done this, click on the Edit (pencil) view tool to return to normal view. From the menu, choose File | Templates and observe the name of the current document template. If you're still in the blank document you created earlier in this section, the current template is `NORMAL.DOT`. Press Esc to dismiss the dialog box.

Now click on the Web Browse (glasses) tool to return to Web Browse view, and again choose File | Templates to display the name of the current template. Surprise! Now it's `WEBVIEW.DOT`!

Caution: If you're like most Word users, the prospect of having a template in your current document suddenly swapped for another one might be a little disturbing. If you're careful, however, it shouldn't present any problems. If you switch into Web Browse view while editing a document that is not an HTML document, be careful *not* to save and close it. If you do, it will be saved with the `WEBVIEW.DOT` template attached to it, and it will forget the name of the original template!

For example, the current template for the document I'm creating right now is called `GLOBAL.DOT`. If I switch into Web Browse view, the template changes to `WEBVIEW.DOT`. If I switch back to Edit view, the template gets changed back to `GLOBAL.DOT`. No problem so far. If—while in Web Browse view—I save the current document, the only template information saved is `WEBVIEW.DOT`, not `GLOBAL.DOT` Even so, because I'm still editing the current document, Word still remembers that the original template was `GLOBAL.DOT`. However, if I close the current document while `WEBVIEW.DOT` is still attached—after having saved it—and then reopen it, `WEBVIEW.DOT` will still be attached. Moreover, if I then switch back into Edit view, the template changes to `HTML.DOT`, not to the original `GLOBAL.DOT`! Word's memory that `GLOBAL.DOT` was the original template is now history.

If this happens to you, you often can merely choose File | Templates from the menu and attach the original template to it, without any problems or harmful side effects. However, depending on your settings, it's possible that some formatting might get lost in the process. So, forewarned is forearmed. The best insurance policy is to avoid saving a non-HTML document if you happen to switch into Web Browse view while editing it.

The *WEBVIEW.DOT* Template

The second major component to the Internet Assistant add-on for Word is the `WEBVIEW.DOT` template. When you install the Internet Assistant, `WEBVIEW.DOT` is copied to your Word 6 `TEMPLATE` subdirectory. Any time you switch to Browse Web view, Word attaches the `WEBVIEW.DOT` template to the current document. As seen earlier, this happens even if the current document is not an HTML document. Keep this fact in mind, by the way. It's a clue that you can turn *any* Word document into an HTML document.

The `WEBVIEW.DOT` template adds some special capabilities to Word. If the standard and formatting toolbars are displayed, part of the capability is obvious. Let's take a look at the WEBVIEW toolbars to see what's there.

WEBVIEW.DOT **Formatting Toolbar**

As shown in Figure 3.16, the WEBVIEW.DOT formatting toolbar contains ten tools.

Formatting
toolbar

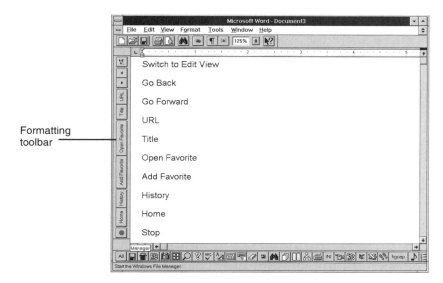

Figure 3.16. *The WEBVIEW.DOT formatting toolbar—up close and personal.*

Let's take a look at each of the tools on the WEBVIEW.DOT formatting toolbar.

Switch to Edit View

The Switch to Edit View tool has a different effect depending on the default template of the current document. If the current document is based on NORMAL.DOT or some other user template, the user's own Formatting and Standard toolbars are displayed. If the document is based on HTML.DOT, however, the HTML.DOT Formatting and Standard toolbars are displayed (as discussed later in the section).

Go Back (Ctrl+,)

When browsing the Web, the Internet Assistant browsing component keeps track of where you've been, keeping a kind of history of the URLs you have loaded. Once you have gone forward from any given URL to a link contained therein, the previous URL is available via the Go Back button. The Go Back action is also accessible from the Window item in the main Word menu.

Go Forward (Ctrl+.)

▶ When browsing the Web, once you have used the Go Back button, the previous URL (which is logically *after* your current location) can be displayed by clicking the Go Forward button. The Go Forward action is also accessible from the Window item in the main Word menu.

URL

URL Use the URL (uniform resource locator—remember this from Day 1?) button to specify a URL directly. Many users browse by clicking on links, but you also can specify a URL directly without having to find it as a link first. When somebody says, "Check out this URL," click the URL button to do it. When you click the URL button, the dialog box shown in Figure 3.17 is displayed. Type the URL name and click on OK to display the document associated with that URL. The Open URL dialog box is also accessible by choosing File | Open URL Document from the Word menu.

Figure 3.17. *Use the Open URL dialog box to specify a specific location on the Internet.*

Title

Title Use the Title button to display or specify a title for the current HTML document. Generally, you should use this option to specify a title for an HTML only when you are editing an HTML document. The title that you add is not displayed in the HTML document. Instead, it is embedded in the HTML file using the `<TITLE>` tag. This information then gets used online by Web browsers in displaying the HTML document as a Web page, usually in the title bar.

The title also gets used when someone uses a Web search tool to locate HTML documents related to a specific topic. For example, if you have a Web site dedicated to the insect world, you should choose a title that imparts that information, rather than something clever that doesn't actually mention insects. In other words, a title such as "Insects of the Americas" would be a much better title than "New World Crawlers," particularly if you want people to find your Web site.

To specify a title, click on the Title button on the toolbar (or choose File | HTML Document Info from the menu) to display the dialog box shown in Figure 3.18. Type the title and click on OK. Titles should be no more than 64 characters, because that appears to be the maximum

acceptable length for some Web browsers. Again, make the title informative so it can be useful when people search for URLs related to a specific topic. The Advanced options are discussed in Day 4.

Figure 3.18. *The Title button activates the HTML Document Head Information dialog box.*

Open Favorite

| Open Favorite | The Word 6 Internet Assistant comes with a document called FAVORITE.DOC. This document is used as a storage location for interesting or useful URLs. Use the Open Favorite button to display the Favorite Places document, as shown in Figure 3.19. The Open Favorite action is also available using Tools | Open Favorite on the Word menu.

Figure 3.19. *The Favorite Places document is used to store your favorite places!*

Add Favorite

Add Favorite Use the Add Favorite tool to add the current URL to the Favorite Places (FAVORITE.DOC) document. At this writing, when you click the Add Favorite button, Word briefly opens FAVORITE.DOC, appends the URL and its title, and then closes FAVORITE.DOC. I say "at this writing" because Word has the capability of suppressing the display of this action, making it all occur much more quickly. It's possible that the visible aspect of this action will be suppressed at some point in the future. The Add Favorite action is also available using Tools | Add Favorite on the Word menu.

History

History As indicated in the discussion of the Go Back and Go Forward buttons, the Internet Assistant keeps a list of the URLs you visit. Click the History button to display the list, as shown in Figure 3.20 (or choose Window | History from the menu). The title of the HTML document is displayed in the list, and the URL is displayed in the text box. A useful feature when creating HTML documents is to browse places you want to add to your HTML document and then use the History list as a quick way to copy those references to the Clipboard. For example, shown here is the Your Direct Line to the North Pole Web page, with the URL http://north.pole.org/santa/talk_to_santa.html. To copy this URL to the Clipboard for use in an HTML document, select the North Pole entry on the list and then click on the Copy Hyperlink button. You can now paste this link wherever you want it. Position the text cursor (the insertion point) where you want the link to appear and press Ctrl+Ins (or choose Edit | Paste from the menu).

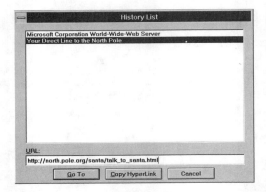

Figure 3.20. *This History List shows the individual URLs you visit during a session.*

Home

Home Use the Home button to open DEFAULT.DOC (or choose Window | Home from the menu). You can make any document your home document by naming it

DEFAULT.DOC and putting it into the Internet Assistant directory (usually the INTERNET subdirectory of your Word 6 directory). If you do this, you might want to make a backup copy of the existing DEFAULT.DOC file.

Stop

Use the Stop button to cancel downloading an HTML document or other file. For example, if you click on a GIF (image) file and decide that the download is taking too long, you can use the Stop button to cancel the download. When downloading a Web page that contains a lot of graphics, it sometimes is useful to use the Stop option once the text you want has appeared.

WEBVIEW.DOT Standard Toolbar

The WEBVIEW.DOT template also makes changes to the Standard toolbar, as shown in Figure 3.21. Let's take a look at each of the tools added by the WEBVIEW.DOT template. As shown here, the first five tools on the toolbar are also available on the default Standard toolbar associated with NORMAL.DOT. In this section, you look only at the differences. Consult the Microsoft Word Users Guide for information about the other tools.

Figure 3.21. WEBVIEW.DOT *makes a number of tools available through a customized Standard toolbar.*

Find

The Find button activates Word's Find dialog box, as does choosing Edit | Find from the menu. Actually, the Find icon is not really created by the Internet Assistant at all, because it's available from Word's Tools | Customize | Toolbar dialog box, but is not part of the default Standard toolbar. The Find feature can be useful in locating text in long Web pages.

Copy HyperLink

Use Copy HyperLink to copy the title (HTML header) and URL to the Clipboard for use elsewhere. This feature is similar to the Copy HyperLink command available from the History List dialog box discussed earlier today. After you copy the hyperlink to the Clipboard, you can then paste it into a Word document by pressing Ctrl+Ins.

How Are Hyperlinks Created in Word?

Hyperlinks are created in Word using the PRIVATE and MACROBUTTON fields. You can actually create hyperlinks manually by choosing Insert | Field from the menu, using the appropriate fields, and adding the necessary text. Let's take a look at the hyperlink for the Top support issues URL contained in the Tips & Tricks item in DEFAULT.DOC. The Tips & Tricks item actually opens a file called TIPS.DOC that is stored in your Internet Assistant directory. So, open TIPS.DOC and click on the Edit button to display the file in editing view.

Making sure that you are in editing rather than browsing view, move the mouse so the pointer is over the text Top support issues, and click once. Notice that the entire text area gets selected. That's because Top support issues is really a Word field. Press Shift+F9 (toggle field display) to reveal the contents of the field. It should display as the following:

```
{{ PRIVATE HREF="http://www.microsoft.com/pages/deskapps/word/ia/support.htm"
}MACROBUTTON HtmlResAnchor Top support issues}
```

If you have a color display, note that the words Top support issues are formatted in blue. Here is the syntax for the MACROBUTTON field:

```
MACROBUTTON macro label
```

When displayed as normal text, only the *label* displays (you can press Shift+F9 to toggle back to normal text display). When you click on it, the *macro* gets executed. In this instance, the macro (HtmlResAnchor, which is an instruction to resolve the URL listed after HREF=) then uses the HTTP protocol to resolve the URL shown.

Html Hidden

{a} The Html Hidden button really just toggles the display of field codes and field results. You can accomplish the same action by choosing Tools | Options | View and checking or unchecking the Field Codes option. Alternatively, choose Tools | Customize | Toolbars and click on the View category. Notice that the identical icon is featured in the top line of icons, third from the right. If you have need for such a tool in your other Word editing, here's where you can get it! The Html Hidden button is useful when you need to edit or otherwise see the contents of a hyperlink.

Changes to the Menu

As suggested by other discussions today, the WEBVIEW.DOT template makes changes and additions to your menus. For starters, WEBVIEW.DOT trims away menu options that aren't useful for Web browsing and adds some menu-based access points for some options that *are* useful when browsing. Let's take a quick look at what gets added and where WEBVIEW.DOT adds the commands to the menu:

File Menu

Open URL	Corresponds to the URL button on the Formatting toolbar
Close All Web Documents	Enables you to end your Web session quickly by closing all documents that have the HTML.DOT template or the WEBVIEW.DOT template attached.
HTML Document Info	Corresponds to the Title button on the Formatting toolbar

Edit Menu

Copy HyperLink	Copies the hyperlink (HTML title and URL) to the Clipboard

View Menu

HTML Edit	Corresponds to the Switch to Edit View (pencil) icon on the Formatting toolbar
Load Images (On or Off)	A toggle that tells Word whether or not to load images when browsing the Web; if you have a slow connection to the Internet, turning this option off can speed operations considerably

Tools Menu

Open Favorite Places	Corresponds to the Open Favorite tool on the Formatting toolbar
Add to Favorite Places	Corresponds to the Add Favorite tool on the Formatting toolbar

Window Menu

Go Back	Corresponds to the Go Back tool on the Formatting toolbar
Go Forward	Corresponds to the Go Forward tool on the Formatting toolbar
Home	Corresponds to the Home tool on the Formatting toolbar
History List	Corresponds to the History tool on the Formatting toolbar

Help Menu

Internet Assistant	Entry point for the WORDHTML.HLP, for Word Help which is on the Internet Assistant subdirectory
About Internet Assistant	A credits and copyright list for Word

Note: WEBVIEW.DOT also adds a collection of Web-related commands. To see the full list, choose Tools | Macro from the menu. Under Macros Available In, choose WEBVIEW.DOT and a complete list will appear, as shown (in part) in Figure 3.22. Except for AutoOpen and AutoNew, these additional commands are actually contained in wordhtml.wll. At this writing, no built-in macro documentation is provided for these commands, so you're pretty much on your own in figuring out what they do. Once you do, however, you can write some nifty macros to automate creating and accessing HTML documents further.

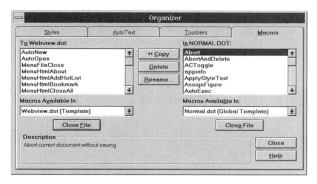

Figure 3.22. WEBVIEW.DOT *makes a number of Web- and HTML-related macros available.*

The *HTML.DOT* Template

3

The third major component to the Internet Assistant add-on for Word is HTML.DOT, the template used when actively editing or creating HTML documents. When you install the Internet Assistant, HTML.DOT is copied to your Word 6 TEMPLATE subdirectory. When you want to create a new HTML document, you should specify HTML.DOT as the template. When you want to convert a normal Word document to an HTML document, you should save the file under a new name and then attach (using File | Templates) the HTML.DOT template to it. This doesn't make a document a functional Web document. However, it's where you start.

Like the WEBVIEW.DOT template, The HTML.DOT template also makes changes to the menu and toolbars.

Toolbar Changes

The HTML.DOT template adds a number of tools to the Formatting toolbar, and just one (Html Hidden) to the Standard toolbar. As with WEBVIEW.DOT, a number of tools also are trimmed away because they have limited utility when editing an HTML document. For example, fonts and point size are controlled by HTML tags as well as by the end-user's Web browser. Therefore, those have no utility when performing HTML editing. Bold, italic, underlining, bullets, and numbering, however, *do* have a role in HTML editing, and therefore are preserved on the Formatting toolbar.

Switch to Web Browse View

Use this option to attach WEBVIEW.DOT to the current document and enable browsing. This is a useful option for testing links and other features you install into an HTML document.

Go Back

When browsing, use this option to return to the previous URL.

Go Forward

When browsing, this option takes you forward in the history list.

Style

`Heading 1,H1` When creating HTML documents, Style quickly becomes your most-used tool. Although Word's Formatting toolbar normally sports a Style tool, the styles you see for HTML.DOT are decidedly different. They are styles that translate directly into HTML tags. In Day 4, you'll learn which styles to use for which HTML tags.

Bold, Italic, and Underlining

Bold, Italic, and Underlining are acceptable HTML formatting. When you apply these formats to text, the corresponding HTML character formatting tags are created when the document is saved in HTML format.

B Use the Bold tool, as well as the corresponding keystrokes Ctrl+B, to format text.

I Use the Italic tool, as well as the corresponding keystrokes Ctrl+I, to format text.

U Use the Underlining tool, as well as the corresponding keystrokes Ctrl+U, to format text.

Numbering

Use the Numbering tool to format text as a numbered list. Word automatically numbers the items, and the numbering is exported using the corresponding HTML commands. HTML supports automatic numbering of lists.

Bullets

Use the Bullets tool to format text as a bulleted list. Bulleted lists are supported by HTML, and the appropriate HTML tags are added when you save the document in HTML format.

Decrease Indent and Increase Indent

Like bullets and numbering, indentation also is supported as an HTML attribute. When you use the Decrease Indent and Increase Indent tools to position text, the formatting is exported when you save the document in HTML format.

 Use Decrease Indent tool to move the indentation of the text to the left.

 Use Increase Indent tool to move the indentation of the text to the right. Use this tool for indenting text instead of using tabs or spaces.

Horizontal Rule

 Use the Horizontal Rule tool to insert a heavy horizontal line in the document. When you save the document in HTML format, the line is saved as the <HR> tag. Horizontal rules are good for creating separation between distinct segments in an HTML document.

Picture

Use the Picture tool to insert an inline picture into the body of an HTML document. Inline pictures are displayed as part of the Web page. Therefore, if you include them, try to use small GIF or JPEG files that won't take too long to download.

Bookmark

Use the Bookmark tool to mark locations—such as subheadings—in an HTML document. You then can insert a hyperlink to those locations elsewhere, such as in a table of contents or as a cross reference. The CREATING.DOC document that comes with the Internet Assistant (in the Internet Assistant subdirectory) uses several bookmarked areas to jump to later locations in the document. HTML bookmarks work very much like Word bookmarks, and Word's bookmarks are converted into the corresponding HTML syntax when you save a document in HTML format.

HyperLink

Use the HyperLink tool to insert a hyperlink to a local file, a remote URL, or to a bookmark in the same HTML document.

Title

Use the Title command to set the HTML Document Head Information. This information displays as a title bar in most Web browsers, and is used by some Web search tools.

Changes to the Menu

The HTML.DOT makes a few changes to the menu. The changes for the File, Edit, and View menus are the same ones that WEBVIEW.DOT makes, as described earlier today. The Insert menu makes the following changes:

Insert Menu	
HyperLink	Corresponds to the HyperLink tool on the Formatting toolbar
Horizontal Rule	Corresponds to the Horizontal Rule tool on the Formatting toolbar
HTML Markup	Inserts HTML commands directly, without any translation by Word

Summary

Today, you learned where to find the Internet Assistant and how to install it. You also learned exactly what the Internet Assistant is and how it works. You saw that it works in two ways. First, a Word Link Library adds in a number of commands to support HTML authoring and Web browsing. Second, Web and HTML-specific templates are used to implement the additional commands, and to enable existing Word commands to be used for HTML document creation.

Q&A

Q I hate using styles. Do I really have to use styles to create HTML documents?

A No, but it sure makes life a lot easier. To use Word to create HTML documents without using styles, you have to make repeated and continuing use of the Insert | HTML Markup command, and you have to learn—or look up—each HTML tag and manually type it into the dialog box window. You also could merely use Word as a text editor and create the HTML document directly, without any dialog boxes at all. However, to do so is to ignore Word's strength as an HTML editor. By using Word styles, HTML tags are handled automatically, without your having to learn or even care about HTML syntax.

Q I'm a keyboard freak. Can I assign the HTML and Web tools to keystrokes rather than using the mouse?

A Yes, but it might take a bit of work to find out what each of the corresponding macro commands are called. For example, the Insert | HyperLink command is defined in HTML.DOT, and is MenuHtmlInsAnchor. To assign this to Ctrl+Alt+H, you could do the following:

1. Display a file based on HTML.DOT, and choose Tools | Customize | Keyboard.

2. Under Categories, click on Macros.

3. Under Save Changes In, choose HTML.DOT.

4. Under Macros, choose `MenuHtmlInsAnchor`.

5. Click in the Press New Keyboard Shortcut field and press the key you want to assign (for example, Ctrl+Alt+H).

6. Click on Assign.

See? Nothing to it. *Hint:* Choose Tools | Macros and set Macros Available In to `HTML.DOT`. The `HTML.DOT` macros are now displayed in the list. As you click on each one, some descriptive text appears in the Description box, telling you a little about what that command does. If you click on `MenuHtmlInsAnchor`, for example, the description says `Insert hypertext link in document`. If doing this for each macro seems like too much work, skip ahead to Appendix C, "Web Resources," where the work is done for you.

Q Do I need to install and use the InternetWorks Internet Assistant in order to use the other components (`WORDHTML.WLL`, `WEBVIEW.DOT`, and `HTML.DOT`)?

A Absolutely not. Although the Web browsing capabilities of the windows link library (`WORDHTML.WLL`) are based on InternetWorks Internet Assistant technology, you do not need the InternetWorks browser for `WORDHTML.WLL` to work. However, unless you have Netscape, the WebExplorer, Mosaic, or some other suitable graphical Web browser standing by, you should at least take a look at the InternetWorks offering. For browsing, it's a heck of a lot faster (and uses a lot less memory) than Word.

4

Creating a Basic Web Document with the Internet Assistant

So far, you've learned about the Internet and the World Wide Web, as well as about Web browsers. You've also had a crash course in the Internet Assistant—where to find it, how to install it, and how it works with Microsoft Word. Today, you learn

☐ How to create a basic Web document using the Internet Assistant

☐ How to insert and format text

☐ About HTML tags and how to create them using the Internet Assistant

The "Hello World Wide Web" Minimum Web Page

In the classic "Hello World" approach to teaching programming, the student's goal is to write a short program that displays the text `Hello World` on a computer monitor. Similarly, the first goal today is to create a simple Web page that says `Hello World Wide Web`. There are a variety of ways to do that. Rather than get fancy, however, let's keep it as simple as possible just to show you how incredibly easy it is to create basic Web documents.

Note: In this book, when I say *Web page* or *HTML document*, I'm talking about the same thing. Because HTML *is* the language of the Web, HTML documents (documents that contain HTML formatting) are Web pages. You may have heard the term *operational definitions*. From an operational standpoint, a Web page is a page that can be properly interpreted by a Web browser, such as the OS/2 WebExplorer, Netscape, Lynx, Mosaic, or the InternetWorks Internet Assistant.

Exercise 4.1. Creating the *Hello, World Wide Web* page.

First, make sure that the `wordhtml.wll` file is loaded. From the menu, choose File|Templates, and verify that `wordhtml.wll` has an X next to it, as shown in Figure 4.1.

Figure 4.1. *When* `wordhtml.wll` *is loaded, it has an* X *beside it in the Templates and Add-ins dialog box.*

To create a new HTML document, begin by choosing File | New from the menu. Don't use the New tool on the toolbar (you can, but not right now), because the New tool uses `NORMAL.DOT` as a document template. File | New from the menu displays the New dialog box, shown in Figure 4.2. This dialog box shows a list of available templates. Type the letter **h** to accelerate to templates beginning with *h*. For most users, there will be just one: html. Click on Html, and then click on OK (or press Enter).

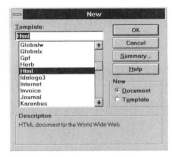

Figure 4.2. *Use File | New to create a document based on* `HTML.DOT`.

<table>
<tr><td>**DO**</td><td>**DON'T**</td></tr>
</table>

DO use File | New to create new HTML documents. Using File | New enables you to specify the Html (`HTML.DOT`) template that comes with the Internet Assistant.

DON'T use the New tool on the toolbar to create new HTML documents. Using the New tool creates documents based on `NORMAL.DOT`. If you use that approach, any convenience you gain is lost because you then have to use File | Templates to attach the Html template to the document.

Word now opens a new Document# document (for example, Document1, Document2, Document3, and so on), as shown in Figure 4.3. If your Standard and Formatting toolbars are not already on, turn them on now. From the menu, choose View|Toolbars, and click, as necessary, to put an X beside Standard and Formatting. Then click on OK or press Enter. If it didn't look like Figure 4.3 before, it should now.

Figure 4.3. *Word opens an empty Document window when you create a new HTML document.*

Now comes the hard part. Type this text into the document:

Hello World Wide Web¶

Now, if that wasn't taxing enough, choose File|Save As from the menu. Type the text **hello** as the filename—don't type an extension. Under Save File as Type, choose HyperText Markup Language (HTML), as shown in Figure 4.4. Ensure that the file has an extension of .HTM and click on OK.

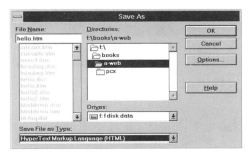

Figure 4.4. *When saving an HTML document for the first time, specify the Save File as Type as HyperText Markup Language (HTML).*

Congratulations! You've just written an HTML document. Don't you believe it's that easy? Start up any Web browser and load `hello.htm` as a local HTML document. For example, from the menu in the InternetWorks Internet Assistant, choose File | Open local file, and use the directory and disk controls to navigate to the location of `hello.htm`, then click on OK. The document should display as shown in Figure 4.5.

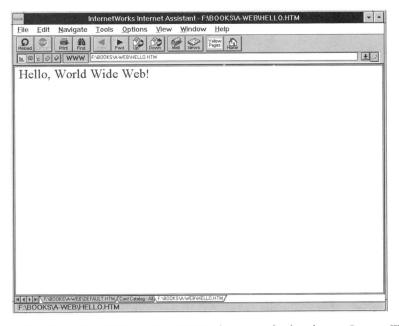

Figure 4.5. *The Hello World Wide Web HTML document displayed using InternetWorks Internet Assistant.*

Note: When you save a file in HTML format, it loses some Word formatting (see Appendix A, "HTML 2.0 Summary and Word Equivalents"). If you need to retain the formatting for other purposes, you should first save the file in normal Word format (.DOC) and then save it in HTML format.

Before moving along, take a look at the HTML document you just created. To really look at it, you're going to have to tell Word that hello.htm is something other than what it really is. First—now that you've saved it—close hello.htm by pressing Ctrl+F4 (or choose File|Close from the menu). If you reopen it, Word displays what you just saw. Instead, choose File|Open (Ctrl+O) from the menu and click on the Confirm Conversions option so that it is checked as shown in Figure 4.6. Under List Files of Type, choose All Files (*.*). Click on hello.htm and then click on OK. Word now displays the Convert File dialog box, which enables you to choose the conversion type. For Convert File From, choose Text Only as shown in Figure 4.7, and click on OK.

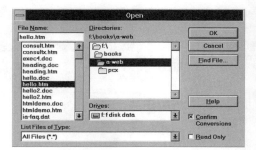

Figure 4.6. *To control what converter Word uses, choose the Confirm Conversions option.*

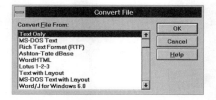

Figure 4.7. *To see a raw HTML file, set the converter to Text Only.*

Whoa! Word now displays hello.htm as shown in Figure 4.8. It looks quite a bit different now, because all the HTML tags are displayed in their native splendor.

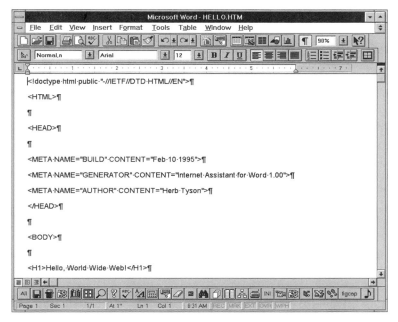

Figure 4.8. *When opened as a text file,* HELLO.HTM *displays as a raw HTML file.*

Eccentricities of the Internet Assistant

After you use the Internet Assistant for a few minutes, you might notice that some actions and keystrokes don't work as they do without the Internet Assistant. One annoying problem, for example, is the Go Back (Shift+F5) keystroke. Without the Internet Assistant, Shift+F5 toggles the insertion point among the last four locations where editing occurred. With the Internet Assistant loaded, however, Shift+F5 no longer performs that action. At best, Shift+F5 does nothing. At worst, it tries to reload the last URL. Another annoying problem is that the Internet Assistant keeps turning off the Wrap to Window option (Tools|Options|View).

Unfortunately, there does not appear to be a good solution to either of these problems, short of disabling the Internet Assistant except when you absolutely need it. You can turn it off by choosing File|Template, and clicking to remove the x next to wordhtml.wll in the Templates and Add-ins dialog box.

Elements of Web Page Style (Tags)

Formatting in HTML documents consists of tagged regions. HTML formatting tags are plain ASCII text instructions enclosed in angle brackets (<>) as shown in Figure 4.8. A tagged formatting area typically uses two tags: one at the beginning and another at the end. For example, to designate a particular line as a heading, you enclose the heading text inside tags that mark the beginning and end:

```
<H1>Hello, World Wide Web!</H1>
```

The `<H1>` tag marks the beginning of text to be considered a level 1 heading (Heading 1). The `</H1>` tag marks the end of the text heading. When using the Internet Assistant, however, you don't generally need to worry about inserting `<H1>` and `</H1>`. When you apply the Heading 1 style using Word's style controls, the `<H1>` and `</H1>` tags are inserted automatically when you save the file in HTML format.

Applying Styles

To apply styles in Word, you can use either the Style control on the Formatting toolbar, or choose Format|Style from the menu. Consult your Word manual or the Word online help system for additional information on using styles.

Note: You might need to open an HTML document in Text Only format for troubleshooting. Although the Internet Assistant is good, it's not perfect. If you don't get the results you want, it's useful to look at the raw HTML file and tags to see what the problem might be. Therefore, it pays to be familiar with what's really going on inside an HTML document.

Recall that tagged formatting areas typically use one tag at the beginning and another at the end. Note the words *typically* and *formatting*. Some tags do not need a `</tag>` counterpart. The META NAME tag, for example, encloses the entire meta text in the tag itself, and does not display in the HTML document when accessed using a Web browser. Many other tags don't have an ending counterpart, so don't worry if you see some in your HTML documents.

An HTML document typically has several parts. The entire HTML document is enclosed inside the tags <HTML> and </HTML>. When you open an HTML document as Text Only, you see those tags. The part you usually see when browsing the Web is the part contained inside the body tags (<BODY> and </BODY>). When you save a document in HTML format, the appropriate <HTML>, </HTML>, <BODY>, and </BODY> tags are inserted for you by the HTML converter. The major tagged areas of an HTML document are listed in Table 4.1.

Table 4.1. Tagged areas in an HTML document.

Area	Description
HTML	The whole HTML document
HEAD	Header information read by Web browsers
TITLE	The title of the HTML document
BODY	The body of the HTML document
HEADINGS	Major document divisions
PARAGRAPHS	Body text
COMMENTS	Internal documentation
LINK	Pointers to other parts of the HTML document, local files, and to other URLs

Head

The header region—marked by <HEAD> and </HEAD>—is automatically created by the Internet Assistant. The following is a sample header:

```
<HEAD>
<META NAME="GENERATOR" CONTENT="Internet Assistant for Word 1.02">
<META NAME="AUTHOR" CONTENT="Herb Tyson">
</HEAD>
```

Note that the META NAME tags are similar to comment tags (described later). They can be read by a Web browser that knows to look for them. Otherwise, they serve as useful internal documentation when creating HTML documents. META NAME tags are inserted only into the HEAD area of an HTML document. You can insert them directly using File | HTML Document Info, clicking on Advanced, and then clicking on Meta.

Title

The title for an HTML document is a concise name for the document. The title is placed into the HEAD area and is not displayed in the HTML document itself. Instead, most Web browsers read the title from the header and use it as the window title. For example, as shown in Figure 4.9, the title is shown in the window's title bar when using the InternetWorks Internet Assistant.

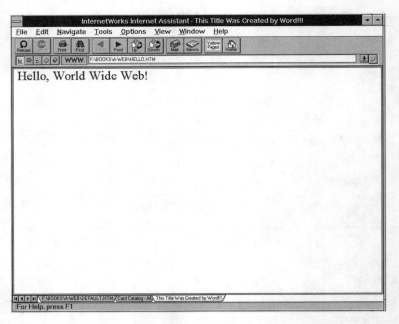

Figure 4.9. *An HTML title displays in the title bar rather than in the HTML document itself.*

Note: Strictly speaking, you do not *have* to have a title. If the title is missing, the InternetWorks Internet Assistant browser displays the underlying file or URL instead. When using the OS/2 WebExplorer, the text (Untitled) is displayed.

In addition to being more informative window designations, titles are also useful from another standpoint. Many Web search tools (tools that help you search the Web for specific content, such as Web Worm, for example) search HTML header areas for key words. For example, if you want Web surfers (that is, folks who are exploring the Web) who are looking for Web pages having to do with coins or antiques to find your Web page, it's useful to have the words *coins* or *antiques* in your HTML document title. If the Web search program

searches the entire header area, then you can use META NAME items to include additional search terms that might be useful.

To insert a title, click on the Title tool (it looks like the letter i) on the html.dot formatting toolbar, or choose File|HTML Document Info for the dialog box shown in Figure 4.10. Type the title and click on OK. The title is always inserted into the HEAD area. You do not need to position the insertion point before inserting the title. When you insert your title, it does not show up in the text of your HTML document, except when opened as a text file. When opened as a text file, the title will display inside the HEAD area, surrounded by the <TITLE> and </TITLE> tags:

```
<TITLE>How to Teach Your Dog to Yodel and Make Waffles</TITLE>
```

Figure 4.10. *The HTML Document Head Information dialog box.*

> **DO**   **DON'T**
>
> **DO** use meaningful, eye-catching, and informative titles for your HTML documents. They help others locate and identify your Web pages.
>
> **DON'T** omit titles or use obscure titles that are more cute than useful. The World Wide Web is growing by leaps and bounds. Usually, the only way someone knows about your Web page is the title.

Body

The body of your HTML document is where the action is. That's the part that the world sees. The body can contain headings, regular paragraph text, graphics, links, and comments. Today, focus on the simple parts and leave graphics and links for tomorrow and the next day.

Headings and Horizontal Rules

You can use headings in your HTML documents the same way you use headings in other Word documents. You can use *horizontal rules* in the same way. A horizontal rule is a line that creates vertical separation in your HTML document. Headings and rules divide your HTML documents into logical sections (see Figure 4.11).

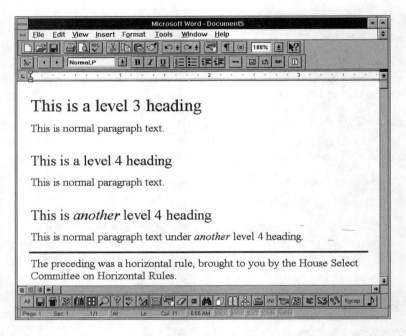

Figure 4.11. *Use headings and horizontal rules to divide your Web page into logical sections, much like a résumé.*

HTML supports six heading levels, identified by the tags <H1> through <H6>. Creating headings using the Internet Assistant is as simple as applying styles. To create a heading, the easiest way is to type the text that you want to be a heading, and then apply the appropriate heading style. For example, to create a level 3 heading called Summary, you type the word Summary on a line by itself and apply the Heading 3 style. To apply the Heading 3 style, press Ctrl+Shift+S and choose Heading 3 from the drop-down list, or click on the drop-down style arrow on the formatting toolbar.

Tip: Each of the six heading styles has an associated alias style name. This means that you can apply the style merely by pressing Ctrl+Shift+S, typing the alias, and pressing Enter. The aliases for Heading 1 through Heading 6 (<H1> through <H6>) are, quite logically, H1 through H6. To apply the H1 heading, press Ctrl+Shift+S, type h1, and press Enter. Whenever Word uses an alias for style names, the alias is the same as the underlying tag definition. For example, the alias for Heading 1 is H1, which also happens to be the HTML tag.

Horizontal rules can be created in several ways. The easiest way is to click on the horizontal rule tool on the HTML.DOT formatting toolbar, shown in Figure 4.12. You also can insert one by choosing Insert | Horizontal Rule from the menu. Note that part of this magic is accomplished by using the Horizontal Rule, HR style. You *could* manually create a horizontal rule by applying the Horizontal Rule style to a blank paragraph. By using the built-in commands, however, the Internet Assistant ensures that the necessary transition between other text and the horizontal rule is made. Note that the Horizontal Rule style has an alias of <HR>, which corresponds to the HTML tag for creating a horizontal rule. Level 3 and 4 headings and a horizontal rule are shown in Figure 4.11.

Figure 4.12. *The horizontal rule tool.*

 Tip: Sometimes a horizontal rule does not display properly when paragraph marks are displayed in your document. If adding a horizontal rule seems just to insert some paragraph marks, click on the paragraph mark on the standard toolbar to turn off the display of nonprinting characters.

Paragraphs

In an HTML document, most text is considered ordinary paragraph text, or *normal* text, if you prefer. You format ordinary text by applying the Normal style, which has the P alias. In HTML, the <P> tag is used to designate a new paragraph.

Comments

HTML version 2.0, which the Internet Assistant supports, provides the capability of supplementing your documents with comments. As the name implies, comments make statements about the insides of HTML documents. Comments are not displayed as part of the document—they are ignored by Web browsers. They are very useful for leaving yourself reminders—for example, where certain graphics can be obtained, alternative URLs (when a crucial URL suddenly stops working), and so on.

The Internet Assistant does not provide a direct mechanism for inserting comments. However, they are so useful—even essential—in some settings, that you need to know how to create them at the outset. To insert comments—as well as any other HTML tags that aren't directly supported by the Internet Assistant—you use the Insert | HTML Markup command from the Word menu. Type the exact HTML command in the text box and press Enter. To insert a comment HTML tag, for example, type the following:

```
<!If www.xyzxys.com stops working, then try www.xyzxyt.com>
```

Once you are familiar with HTML, you can insert any markup tag directly using the same technique.

Why Do <<HTML Markup>> Commands Disappear?

During the current editing session, HTML commands that you insert using Insert | HTML Markup display as <<HTML Markup>>, as shown in Figure 4.13. That's because Word uses a macro button to preserve the HTML markup command during the current session, both for editing and for conversion when you save the file in HTML format. When you double-click on <<HTML Markup>>, the Insert HTML Markup dialog box is redisplayed with the HTML Markup command displayed for you to edit.

Once you save the document as an HTML file, however, the HTML markup command is no longer displayed in that way. When you save in HTML format, the <<HTML Markup>> notation is removed and the underlying command is converted to the native HTML format. So, if you insert a comment, it is no longer visible when editing the file as an HTML file.

Similarly, when other HTML markup commands are inserted using the Insert HTML Markup dialog box, they are converted into HTML format when you save the file, and the <<HTML Markup>> macro button disappears. For example, you can insert a heading by typing the following:

```
<H1>This is a heading</H1>
```

Until you close the document, it is displayed as <<HTML Markup>> rather than as a heading. After saving as HTML and reopening the file, however, it is converted into a normal HTML heading.

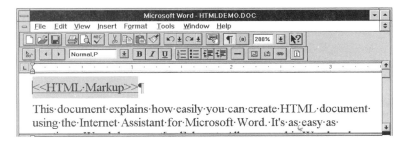

Figure 4.13. *HTML Markup commands are displayed as <<HTML Markup>> macro buttons in a Word document.*

Creating a Web Document Using Basic Tags

Now that you know what the basic HTML markup commands, you're ready to create a basic Web document.

▼ Exercise 4.2. Creating a basic Web document.

Using the skills and techniques covered in this chapter, create an HTML document suitable for posting on the World Wide Web. This document will contain a title, headings, body text, and a horizontal rule. (You'll include links tomorrow.)

First, create a new HTML document. From the menu, choose File|New. Under Templates, choose Html, and click on OK. Word opens a new Document#window. First, create a title for the document. For this exercise, call it *Teach Yourself Web Publishing with Word.* To insert the title, click on the Title icon on the HTML.DOT Formatting toolbar. It's the icon on the far right that looks like a lowercase letter i. In the Title field, type **Teach Yourself Web Publishing with Word**, as shown in Figure 4.14, and click on OK. Notice that nothing appears in the document. Do you remember why? If not, then review the Title section presented earlier in today's lesson along with the second question under Q&A.

Figure 4.14. *Type the HTML document title in the Title field.*

Next, create an in-document title that appears centered if the user is using Netscape or the WebExplorer. From the menu, choose Insert|HTML Markup for the dialog box shown in Figure 4.15. In the text box, type the following:

```
<center><h1>Teach Yourself Web Publishing with Word</h1></center>
```

Figure 4.15. *Type the entire HTML markup command in the text box.*

Now click on OK. When you do, only <<HTML Markup>>, in blue, appears on-screen, as shown in Figure 4.16. This is a macro button that you can use to access the underlying command. To edit or display the contents of the HTML markup tag, double-click on the <<HTML Markup>> macro button. Word then redisplays the Insert HTML Markup dialog box.

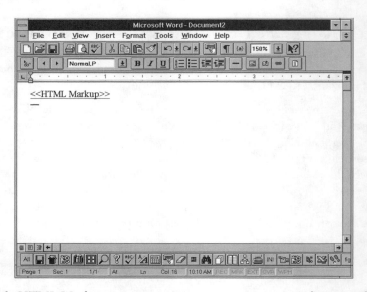

Figure 4.16. *HTML Markup tags appear as <<HTML Markup>> macro buttons, which you can edit by double-clicking.*

Now type some introductory text. Introductory text should explain very succinctly the purpose of the Web presence and what can be found there. Under the <<HTML Markup>> macro button, type the following (press Enter just after the <<HTML Markup>> item if necessary):

```
This document explains how easily you can create HTML document using the
Internet Assistant for Microsoft Word. It's as easy as creating a Word
document—almost. All you need is Word and the Internet Assistant.¶
```

Click anywhere in that paragraph and note in the Formatting toolbar that the current style is Normal,P, as shown in Figure 4.17.

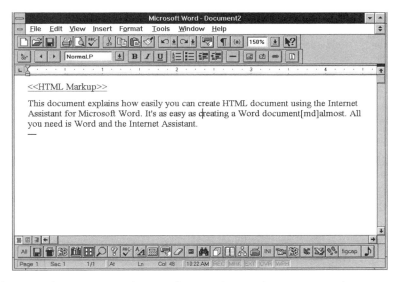

Figure 4.17. *Ordinary paragraph text is formatted using the* Normal,P *style.*

Next, insert a heading. If you didn't already do so, press Enter at the end of the paragraph you just typed—just after *Internet Assistant.* Put the insertion point in the paragraph that immediately follows. Note that the style currently is still Normal,P. Using the style control in the Formatting toolbar, apply the style Heading 3. Now type the following, and press Enter:

```
What is the Internet Assistant¶
```

Notice that when you press Enter, the style reverts to Normal,P. Now you're ready to type a description of the Internet Assistant. Type the following, and then press Enter (as indicated by the paragraph mark (¶) at the end of the last line):

```
The Internet Assistant is an add-on for Microsoft Word, available free from
Microsoft. The Internet Assistant turns Microsoft Word 6 into a powerful tool
for creating and editing HTML documents suitable for posting on the World Wide
Web. You can obtain the Internet Assistant by ftp from Microsoft at
http://www.microsoft.com.¶
```

Create another heading. In the paragraph following the one you just typed, apply the style Heading 4. Now type the following, and then press Enter:

```
How Do You Use the Internet Assistant to Create Web Pages?¶
```

Type the text that goes under that heading and press Enter:

```
It's as easy as using styles. Just create a new document in Word, using
html.dot as the document template. Type the document exactly as you want it to
appear, using Heading 1 through Heading 6 styles for different headings, and
using Normal,P as the style for ordinary paragraph text. When you're done,
first save the document as a Word document so you can come back and edit it in
Word format. Then, save the document in HTML format. The Internet Assistant
converts the document into HTML version 2.0, converting Heading styles into
<H#> tags, converting italic and bold formatting into the appropriate tags, and
so on. The resulting .HTM file is then ready for posting on the Web. It's
really that easy!¶
```

Okay, you're nearly done. Insert a horizontal rule so you can set off a final line or two at the bottom of the Web page. Click on the Horizontal Rule tool or choose Insert | Horizontal Rule from the menu. If a heavy horizontal line does not appear, choose Tools | Options | View and turn off the display of nonprinting characters. Note that after the horizontal rule is inserted, the insertion point is positioned below it, ready for the next paragraph.

Finally, insert the last paragraph:

```
This document was prepared entirely using just the Internet Assistant and
Microsoft Word version 6.0c. It took about five minutes!¶
```

Now, save your creation. First, save it as a Word document (.DOC). When and if you want to change it, always edit the .DOC version rather than the .HTM version. That preserves your capability of editing any HTML Markup tags that were inserted using the Insert | HTML Markup command. It also preserves the document's integrity as a Word document. From the menu, choose File | Save As, and type a name for the document (for example, htmldemo). Set the Save File As Type to Word Document. Note that Word automatically supplies the .DOC extension.

Next, save a copy in HTML format. From the menu, choose File | Save As. Under Save File As Type, choose HyperText Markup Language (HTML). Note that the extension changes to .HTM. Click on OK, and you're done! If you followed the directions, your finished document looks like the one shown in Figure 4.18.

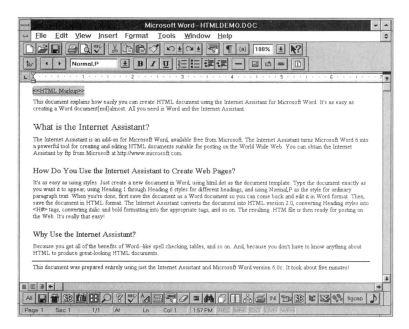

Figure 4.18. *The finished* HTMLDEMO.HTM, *viewed as a Word document.*

Take a look at the Web document you just created. If you have Netscape or the WebExplorer, you can see all the formatting, including the centered title. If you have Mosaic, InternetWorks Internet Assistant, or another Web browser that does not support the <CENTER> tag, the title is left-aligned rather than centered. Open your favorite Web browser. If you have Netscape, for example, choose File|Open File from the menu. Using the Drives and Directories controls, navigate to the location of the .HTM file you just created. Click on the file and then click on OK to open it. It should appear as shown in Figure 4.19. Using the same procedure and InternetWorks Internet Assistant, the document appears as shown in Figure 4.20.

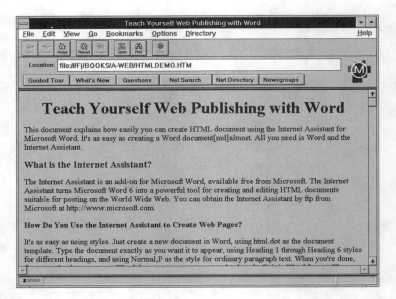

Figure 4.19. *HTMLDEMO.HTM as seen from Netscape.*

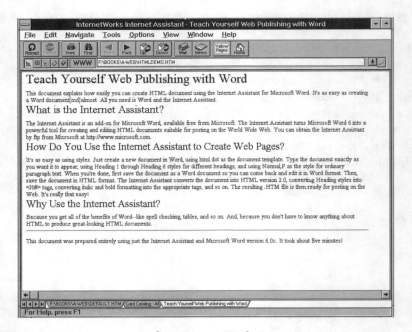

Figure 4.20. *HTMLDEMO.HTM as seen from InternetWorks Internet Assistant.*

Summary

Today, you've had a full dose of HTML. You've learned the basics of what goes into an HTML document, and how those components are created using the Internet Assistant and Microsoft Word. You learned about the <HEAD>, <TITLE>, and <BODY> tags. In the exercise presented in the Workshop, you created an HTML document using the skills demonstrated today. If you're game, you can substitute your own headings and text for those shown in the exercise.

Q&A

Q How do I keep HTML Markup commands in the <<HTML Markup>> format?

A Save the file in normal Word .DOC format. If you have an HTML document that is undergoing development or revision, it's a good idea to save the file in ordinary Word format as a .DOC file. Use Save As to create an HTML document as needed, with an .HTM extension. However, don't use that HTML document as your working document. Use the .DOC version instead. When you're ready to look at it using a Web browser, use File | Save As to create the necessary .HTM file.

If you've ever used Word to create formatted e-mail messages, it's the same principle. You use Word to do the formatting (generally spatial formatting rather than bolding and the like), and then save the file as Text with Layout. If you need to change the message, however, you return to the .DOC version of the file for any changes, and save the result as Text with Layout for the finished product. If you do the text version, you will find that formatting is very difficult to maintain because of the way spaces and paragraph marks are inserted to create vertical and horizontal spacing.

Similarly, to create HTML documents, you work on the Word .DOC version of the file (based on HTML.DOT), and then save in HTML format to an .HTM file when you're ready to *publish* (that is, go public by putting your files onto the Web). If you need to do any touch-up editing, you should return to the .DOC version and resave in HTML format when the editing is done. Note that you *can* work on an .HTM version of a file. However, you lose direct control over any <<HTML Markup>> tags. Therefore, it's better to work on the .DOC version.

Q Why doesn't the <TITLE> display in the HTML document?

A The <TITLE> is not part of the body of the document. It is part of the <HEAD> (header). Unlike Word document headers, HTML headers are not used for displaying information in the document. Rather, they provide supplemental information to Web browsers and to Web search programs. The <TITLE> is usually displayed as part of a window title bar rather than in the document itself. The

<HEAD> area is analogous to Word's document summary information, which contains the document title, subject, author, keywords, and comments. Like Word's document summary information, the <HEAD> contains information about the document rather than the document itself. That information is useful to other processes—just as Word's document summary information is useful to Word's File Find feature—but does not display in the document itself.

If you want to have a title in the document itself, use one of the heading styles (<H1> through <H6>). If you need the title to be centered, see the next question.

Q   I tried to center a heading, but it wasn't centered in the resulting .HTM file. Why not?

A   The Internet Assistant supports HTML version 2.0, which does not have a <CENTER> formatting command. Later versions of the Internet Assistant will probably support <CENTER> and other enhancements. Until then, you can use Insert HTML Markup to insert the <CENTER> tag. For example, choose Insert|HTML Markup and type the following:

```
<center><h1>This is the Title</h1></center>
```

It then displays correctly when read by a Web browser that supports higher levels of HTML. For example, using the Netscape or the OS/2 WebExplorer, that title displays as shown in Figure 4.21. When using the Internet Assistant under Word, however, the <CENTER> and </CENTER> tags display as <<Unknown HTML Tag>>. When using NCSA Mosaic or InternetWorks Internet Assistant, the <CENTER> tag is ignored, resulting in an ordinary <H1> heading without centering (see Figure 4.22).

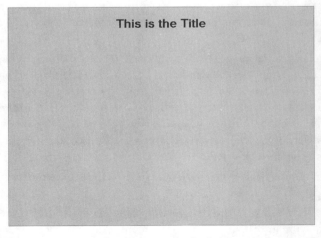

This is the Title

Figure 4.21. *Netscape and the WebExplorer correctly display text formatted with the* <CENTER> *tag.*

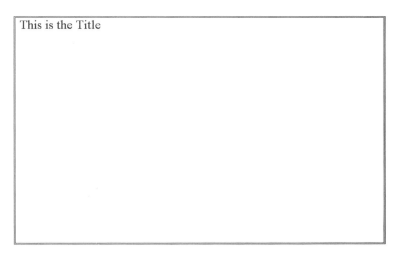

This is the Title

Figure 4.22. *Some browsers don't support centering.*

Note: Because of the way Web browsers handle spaces, it's exceedingly difficult to center text on a Web page without using the <CENTER> command. As a practical matter, you're probably better off including the <CENTER> tag using Insert | HTML Markup, knowing that most people accessing your Web page will probably be using a browser that recognizes the <CENTER> tag, either now or in the near future.

4

DAY 3

Presenting Information and Ideas with HTML

5

Tags and Styles

On Day 4, "Multimedia on the Web Pages," you learned some fundamental formatting, including headings, normal paragraph text, and horizontal rules. Today, you learn about

☐ Additional formatting options

☐ Character styles

☐ Lists

☐ Text blocks

☐ How to convert an existing Word document into an HTML document

How HTML documents appear to different users depends entirely on which Web browser they're using. For one thing, different Web browsers implement different versions of HTML. HTML version 2.0 is the current standard, and HTML version 3 is being developed. Some commands, such as the <CENTER> command, will be a part of HTML version 3, but aren't currently supported by Web browsers that adhere strictly to HTML version 2, such as InternetWorks Internet Assistant and the Internet Assistant for Microsoft Word.

Note: As you read today's lesson, you will notice that some effects can generally be accomplished by more than one method. This might create some ambiguity about what to use and when. Before tossing a coin to make the decision, read the section, "Logical Versus Physical Formatting," later in today's lesson.

Applying Formatting in Word

There are two distinct types of formatting you need to know about for creating HTML documents with Word. One is the character- or font-level formatting and the other is paragraph level formatting. There are two ways to format at the character or font level. You can format text *after* it has been typed, or you can turn formatting attributes on and off *as* you type.

Consider bold formatting, for example, which is a character (font) level format. If you want the phrase "dog's best friend" to be **bold**, you can type the phrase and then format it. To format it after it has been typed, select the phrase and then click on the Bold tool on the formatting toolbar (alternatively, you can press Ctrl+B). To format the phrase as you type it, press Ctrl+B to toggle bold on. (You can click on the Bold tool, but it's usually easier to press Ctrl+B because the fingers are poised to type anyway.) Then type the phrase. When you finish typing the part you want to be bold, press Ctrl+B again.

Tip: You can toggle bold formatting for a single word by putting the insertion point anywhere inside the word and pressing Ctrl+B or clicking on the Bold tool. For example, to make the word *dog* bold, put the insertion point either between *d* and *o* or between *o* and *g*, and press Ctrl+B. Before *d* and after *g* won't work. Other character-level formatting (italic, underlining, and so forth) works in the same way.

Both methods—selection after the fact or turning bold on and off as you type—point out the fact that bold formatting must be applied to the text you want to format. All character-level (font-level) formatting works in the same way.

Paragraph-level formatting works differently. Paragraph formatting—by definition—affects all paragraphs in the selection, not just part of a paragraph. For that reason, you can apply paragraph formatting to the entire current paragraph without selecting text. For example, consider alignment. You can turn on alignment for the whole paragraph, but not for just part of it. To center the current paragraph, put the text cursor (the insertion point) anywhere in the paragraph and click on the Center tool on the toolbar (or press Ctrl+E).

To center more than one paragraph, select all or part of each of the paragraphs you want to format and apply the Center format (toolbar or keystroke). Every paragraph in the selection will be centered. Similarly, to remove centering, select all or part of each of the paragraphs you want to center, and then either press Ctrl+E or click on the Center tool. Like character formatting, paragraph formatting acts as a toggle. Note, however, that the current version of the Internet Assistant does not support the <CENTER> HTML tag, and so you should consider this an example only of how paragraph formatting works in Word.

Character (font) formatting includes bold, italic, underlining, font, point size, and character styles. Paragraph formatting includes alignment (center, left, right, and justified), numbering, bullets, indentation, and paragraph styles. One possible point of confusion for new Word 6 users is the difference between character and paragraph styles. Both are available from the same controls, so it's easy to get confused unless you know what to look for. It's also easy to get confused because many Word 6 users don't use the character-style formatting feature. If you don't use the feature, you might not even be aware that it exists. However, by default, a character style named Default Paragraph Font is used for all text unless you specify otherwise (much as a paragraph style named Normal is used unless you specify otherwise). Even though both types of styles are applied using the same tools, the rules are different. It's important to understand the difference early because the Internet Assistant makes heavy use of character styles.

To apply a style, you can use the Style tool on the toolbar, or you can use the Style dialog box. Let's look at the Style tool first. With a document based on HTML.DOT on-screen, click on the arrow to the right of the style to display the list of styles shown in Figure 5.1. Notice that Address, Blockquote, Definition Compact, and Definition List are all shown in bold, and CITE, CODE, Default Paragraph Font, Definition Term, and Definition are all shown in regular text. The bold items are paragraph styles, and the nonbold items are character styles.

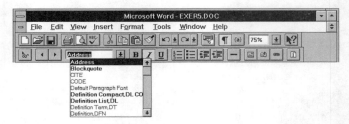

Figure 5.1. *Click on the drop-down arrow next to the Style tool to display the list of styles.*

Character- and paragraph-style formatting works the same way as other character- and paragraph-style formatting. When you apply a paragraph style, the formatting affects all paragraphs in the selection. When you apply a character style, only the selection is affected. If no text is selected, only the current word is formatted (if the insertion point is in the interior of a word) or only text you type from that point forward. If you are used to being able to format an entire paragraph without selecting it by applying a style from the Style tool, you should always note carefully what kind of style you are attempting to apply. If it's a paragraph style, then you can indeed format the entire paragraph without selecting it. If it's a character style, however, then you need to select the part of the paragraph you want to format before applying the style. To format as you type, select the character style, type the text you want formatted, and then reselect the Default Paragraph Font style.

You also can select and control styles using the Style dialog box. To display the Style dialog box, hold down the Ctrl and Shift keys and type S twice, or choose Format, Style from the menu to display the dialog box as shown in Figure 5.2. In normal use of Word, the Style dialog box is used to define styles. When creating HTML documents, however, you should resist the impulse to redefine styles in HTML.DOT. That's because the formatting and appearance of documents you publish to the Web are controlled entirely by HTML tags. The CODE format, for example, is interpreted by Web browsers in a particular way, depending on the browser you are using. Giving CODE a proportional font or a point size of 8 affects only the appearance of text formatted as CODE when you view that document from Word. When read as an HTML document, those nuances and variations you include are ignored.

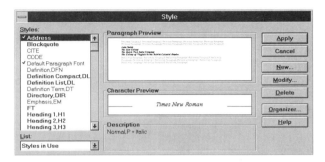

Figure 5.2. *You can also apply styles using the Style dialog box.*

For additional information on formatting in Word, or on Word in general, you should obtain the *Word for Windows 6 Super Book* (by Herb Tyson and published by Sams Publishing), available at most computer bookstores, as well as via the Internet at http://www.mcp.com.

Character Styles

As pointed out in the previous section, Word 6 supports two kinds of styles: character and paragraph. This section focuses on character styles used by the Internet Assistant. Character styles can be applied to one or more characters, within a paragraph, or spanning parts of multiple paragraphs. Word's character attributes include—among others—font, point size, bolding, italic, underlining, language, color, superscripting, and subscripting. Not all of these are supported in HTML, however, as you will see.

> **Caution:** Because of the way character and paragraph styles work, it sometimes might appear that you are unable to apply some paragraph styles. A consequence of having two kinds of styles (character and paragraph) is that two different styles can be applied to the same text. Unfortunately, the Style control on the formatting toolbar can display only one style name at a time. If you apply the Heading 1 style to a paragraph, and then apply any character style other than Default Paragraph Font to the same text area, Word displays only the character style name. However, if you apply a character style (Strong, for example) first, and then apply a paragraph style (Heading 1, for example), it might appear that the Heading 1 style did not take because the displayed style Strong is not replaced by the style Heading in the Style control on the toolbar. In fact, both styles are in effect, even though only the character style is displayed.

One solution—assuming you don't want the Strong style applied to that text—is to apply the Default Paragraph Font style. To do that, first select the text you want to format. Then, you can either apply the Default Paragraph Font using the toolbar or by pressing Ctrl+Spacebar. When you apply the Default Paragraph Font style, Word again displays the paragraph style name rather than the font style name in the style tool.

If you need to know what styles—character and paragraph—are in effect at all times, use Word's style area bar to display the paragraph styles. To do this, choose Tools|Options|View, and set the Style Area Width to about one inch. As shown in Figure 5.3, you now can clearly see that Heading 1 and Strong are both in effect for the selection.

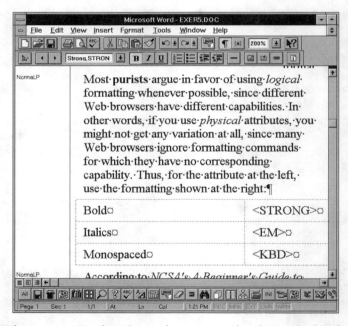

Figure 5.3. *When you use Word's style area bar, paragraph styles are displayed at the left.*

HTML also supports something akin to character styles, although the terminology used to describe this kind of formatting varies by what you read and the amount of variation you can control is rather limited compared to Word. HTML tags effectively and potentially provide bolding, italic, underlining, and monospacing (display using a fixed font rather than a proportionally spaced font). To a certain extent, using heading levels, you also can get

different point sizes. In any case, the end result is determined entirely by what Web browser is used. For example, using a text browser such as Lynx, about the only character formatting variation you can show is bold and underlining. Using graphical browsers such as Mosaic and Netscape, what the user sees is limited by the way in which the browser is programmed.

> **Note:** In addition to having varying defaults, many browsers also enable you to choose the treatment applied to different types of tags. If you choose Options|Fonts from InternetWorks Internet Assistant's menu, for example, you can specify the display of strikethrough, italic, bolding, and underlining to virtually any kind of text supported by the browser. In the discussion today, however, assume that all browsers are used according to their default setups. There's simply no way in the world to guarantee that *every* user of *every* browser will always see your documents exactly the same. You could implement your documents as .GIF or .JPG files rather than as text files. However, that would make your Web page so slow that it might not get seen at all, let alone seen equally—and there's the text browser, Lynx, which can't display graphics.

Bold

HTML provides two types of bold formatting: bold <B> (physical) and strong <STRONG> (logical). For all practical purposes, these are identical (or synonymous), as shown in Figure 5.4, which shows InternetWorks Internet Assistant and the OS/2 WebExplorer both displaying the identical HTML document. However, bold <B> appears to have a more universal implementation than <STRONG>, so I'm tempted to recommend that you use it, despite the fact that many HTML guides recommend that you use the logical strong format. To format text as bold using Word, select the text you want to format and click on the Bold tool on the formatting toolbar. Alternatively, you can press Ctrl+B to apply bold formatting. Repeat the process to remove bold formatting, because bold formatting in Word is a toggle. When you save the document in HTML format, the <B> and </B> tags are supplied at the beginning and end of the bold area, respectively.

<STRONG> is implemented as a character style. To apply <STRONG> formatting, you must apply the Strong style. That means that you can format part of a paragraph as Strong without affecting the rest of the paragraph. To apply the <STRONG> attribute, select the text you want to format and choose Strong from the Style tool.

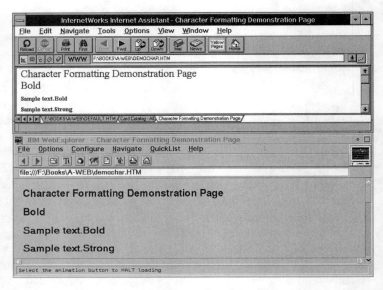

Figure 5.4. *InternetWorks Internet Assistant and WebExplorer treat* `<STRONG>` *and* `<B>` *as synonyms.*

Italic

There are four types of HTML tags that sometimes display as italics, depending on which Web browser you use:

Italic	`<I>`
Emphasis	`<EM>`
Cite	`<CITE>`
Variable	`<VAR>`

As shown in Figure 5.5, Netscape (bottom) displays all four as italic, and InternetWorks Internet Assistant (top) displays all except Variable as italic. In practice, if you want the best assurance that the text the user sees will be italic, use italic formatting, which results in the `<I>` tag. If you care more about the future and potential standards, use Cite or Variable when the kind of text being formatted is appropriate (see discussion later in today's lesson). As a practical matter, Emphasis means that viewers will use whatever means they have at their disposal to emphasize the selected text. For some text-only browsers, that might mean text is displayed in a distinct color; for most graphical Web browsers, Emphasis is displayed in italic.

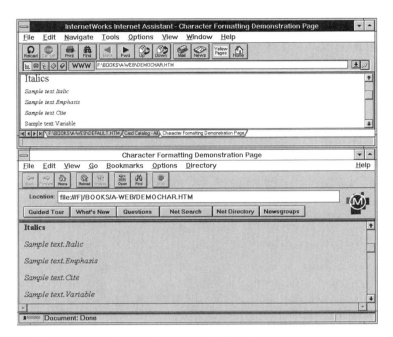

Figure 5.5. *Different viewers display formatting differently.*

Italic *<I>*

The <I> tag is achieved by using italic character formatting in Word. To format text as italic, select the text and click on the Italic tool on the toolbar, or press Ctrl+I. Alternatively, you can press Ctrl+I, type the text you want to be italic, and then press Ctrl+I again at the end of the italic section.

Note: You can format a single word as italic by placing the text cursor anywhere inside the word (after the first letter and before the last letter) and pressing Ctrl+I or clicking on the Italic tool. This is true of all character formatting, and I'll try not to mention it again.

5

Citation *<CITE>*, Emphasis *<EM>*, and Variable *<VAR>*

The <CITE>, <EM>, and <VAR> tags are implemented using the character styles Cite, Emphasis, and Variable, respectively. To apply these styles to text already typed, you must select the text and then choose the corresponding style from the Style tool or from the Style dialog box. Remember that these are character styles and affect only the text that is selected. Alternatively, you can select a style as you go along. Select the style. Then type the text. Then reselect Default Paragraph Font or some other character style at the point where you want the selected style to end.

Citation often is used when citing reference sources, as in "see J. Humphrey Winstead's *Eat your neighbor's lawn for fun and fitness,*" for example. Variable is used when specifying variable names in mathematical presentations:

```
Total Cost = Price * Quantity
```

Variable also might be used in giving computer instructions when you want to indicate a variable parameter, something that might be different for different users. For example, if you're telling someone about editing the WINWORD6.INI file, you might tell them to specify the following:

```
edit d:/windir/WINWORD6.INI
```

where *d* is the drive where Windows is installed and *windir* is the name of the main Windows directory. Both *d* and *windir* vary from system to system.

Underline *<U>*

Underlining often is used instead of italic when display or printing options are limited. Mercifully, underlined text has only a single implementation in HTML, removing the ambiguity of what to use and when. In the Internet Assistant, it is implemented by using underlining character formatting rather than by using a character style. To format already-typed text as underlined, select the text and press Ctrl+U, or click on the Underline tool.

Strikethrough *<STRIKE>*

Strikethrough often is used in draft documents to indicate proposed deletions. Note that <B>, <I>, and <U> are implemented only through character formatting and not by using character styles. Strikethrough, however, is implemented both by using the Strikethrough character style and by using the strikethrough character format. To use the style, choose the Strikethrough style from the Style tool. To use strikethrough character formatting, choose Format|Font from the menu and click so that an X appears next to Strikethrough.

When revising Word documents, strikethrough often is used to indicate deleted text. Unfortunately, if strikethrough is used as a result of revision mode, the formatting is not preserved when you save the document in HTML formatting. Instead, deleted text shown strikethrough is stripped out of the resulting HTML document. If you need to show text in strikethrough, you must use either the Strikethrough style or character formatting.

Fixed or Monospaced

When writing documents about computers, it's common (in this book, for example) to display text that is typed on the keyboard or appears on a monitor screen in a `monospaced` or "computer" font. Note that as you read this book, most of the text is proportionally spaced, but output from the command line and text you type at the command line is shown in a monospaced font.

Most graphical Web browsers default to using a proportionally spaced font such as Times Roman for most of the text in Web documents. Most also recognize the `<KBD>` tag for displaying text in a monospaced font (such as Courier). It's common to use the text contrast for showing text that you are supposed to type or that is supposed to be output from a computer screen. Potentially, HTML supports four distinct tags that often are displayed in monospace:

Keyboard	`<KBD>`
Sample	`<SAMP>`
Typewriter	`<TT>`
Code	`<CODE>`

As shown in Figure 5.6, implementation varies widely. For example, Netscape (bottom right) shows all four as monospaced. The OS/2 WebExplorer (bottom left) displays Keyboard and Sample in a proportionally spaced font, and Typewriter and Code in a monospaced font. In contrast, InternetWorks Internet Assistant (top) shows just the reverse, with Keyboard and Sample being monospaced and Typewriter and Code as proportionally spaced. Given these contrasts, there's simply no way to guarantee any particular displayed result. However, `<TT>` appears to be the most widely implemented tag at this time.

Keyboard *<KBD>* and Typewriter *<TT>*

Keyboard and Typewriter, both implemented as character styles, are used to show text that the user should type. To insert tags for these styles, select the text you want to format and choose the appropriate style from the Style tool.

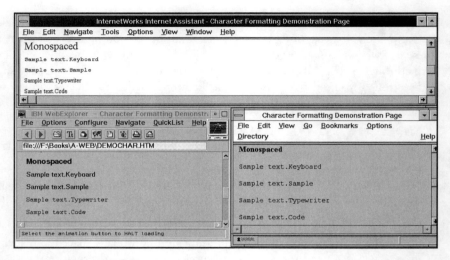

Figure 5.6. *Different Web browsers implement the* <CODE>, <TT>, <KBD>, *and* <SAMP> *tags in different ways.*

Sample *<SAMP>*

The Sample tag sometimes is used to format example text, for contrast with ordinary text. Sample is implemented as a character style. To insert the <SAMP> tag, select the text you want formatted, and choose Sample from the Style tool.

Code *<CODE>*

The Code tag often is used to format sections of computer programs or scripts. For example, suppose you need to include a batch file in the text of your HTML document. You might have the following:

```
echo off
del g:\wintmp\*.tmp
del g:\wintemp\*.tmp
del f:\books\internet\~*.tmp
del f:\books\a-web\~*.tmp
del f:\word6\template\*.tmp
```

Using the Code formatting—assuming the reader's Web browsers supports the <CODE> tag— sets the code off distinctly. Figure 5.7 shows an example using the WebExplorer.

> **Here is a code sample**
>
> In my case, I have a special batch file that I used to delete leftover .TMP files from locations they are known to habituate. Here's my batch file, which I call DELTMP.BAT:
>
> ```
> echo off
>
> del g:\wintmp\*.tmp
>
> del g:\wintemp\*.tmp
>
> del f:\books\internet\~*.tmp
>
> del f:\books\a-web\~*.tmp
>
> del f:\word6\template\*.tmp
> ```
>
> If you use OS/2, you could instead call it DELTMP.CMD.

Figure 5.7. *The <CODE> tag sets program text off from the main text.*

Paragraph Styles

Paragraph styles affect the entire paragraph. Word's paragraph-level formatting attributes include line spacing, tab definitions, borders, indentation, and alignment (centering, left, right, and justified). Within a paragraph, only one setting for each attribute is allowed. For example, you cannot have a paragraph in which some lines are centered and others are left- or right-aligned. It's all or nothing.

HTML and the Internet Assistant support a number of different kinds of useful paragraph level formatting, including lists and various kinds of text blocks. Using the Ordered List (<OL>) tag, for example, you can achieve automatic numbering in most Web browsers. Using the Preformatted (<PRE>) tag, you can cause most Web browsers to present text preserving all spacing so that the text appears exactly as you type it.

Lists

HTML version 2 supports a number of different types of lists. Most Web browsers implement at least some of the list formats. The Internet Assistant provides support for the following types of lists:

Ordered	<OL>
Unordered	<UL>
Definition	<DL>
Menu	<MENU>
Directory	<DIR>

As usual, however, implementation varies in different browsers. For example, unordered, menu, and directory lists—introduced today—seemingly are for different kinds of lists. With

WebExplorer, Mosaic, and InternetWorks Internet Assistant, the menu and directory lists are identical, but unordered lists appear with bullets. Using Netscape, however, all three list types are displayed identically. At some point in the future, it's not unreasonable to expect that Netscape will differentiate the display of the three types of lists, and that the other browsers will differentiate more than they do now.

All this leads to a suggestion. As you consider different formatting options that ostensibly produce identical on-screen results, keep the future in mind. What displays right now with bullets might not display that way a year from now using an updated browser. The current <UL> (unordered list) tag *usually* (but not always) produces bullets. What if a <BL> (bulleted list) tag is added in a later release of HTML? At that point, Web browsers might remove the bullets from <UL>. What if you use <UL>, <MENU>, and <DIR> interchangeably and special features get added to support enhanced menus or directories? At that point, you need to revise your HTML document (which you'll probably need to do anyway, long before then).

All the different types of lists—except for definition lists—have in common the <LI> (list item) tag. For the most part, when using the Internet Assistant to create HTML documents, you won't need to be concerned about the <LI> tag. It might be useful to know, however, that the general structure for lists is as follows:

```
<list tag>
<LI>list item
<LI>list item
...
<LI>last list item
</list tag>
```

How each list type is formatted is determined by the *list tag* itself (<OL>, <UL>, <MENU>, or <DIR>) and how different browsers display those lists.

Ordered or Numbered Lists *<OL>*

Use ordered lists for things that have to occur in a specific order, or which are ranked by importance. Ordered lists are commonly used for step-by-step lists of instructions. Numbering reinforces the need for a specific order. To use the <OL> formatting, use the Numbering tool on the formatting toolbar or apply the List Number paragraph style. For example, suppose you want to create the following as a numbered list:

```
North on I-75 for 50 miles to exit 56.
East on US 36 for 30 miles to SR 135.
North on SR 135 for five miles to Acacaby Road.
Right on Acacaby Road for 1.5 miles to Baca Reed Farm Drive.
Left on Baca Reed Farm Drive for .5 miles to Haney Circle.
Left on Haney Circle to 3rd house on left.
```

There are several ways. One way is to type the list, disregarding whatever style is currently in effect, and then apply the formatting after the fact. To do that, type the list and then select it. Then click on the List Number style from the Style tool or from the Style dialog box.

You also can apply the style as you go along. To do that, if the insertion point is not already on a line all by itself, press Enter to create a new line for beginning the list. Next, click on the numbering tool or choose List Number from the Style tool. Now, type the list, pressing Enter at the end of each line. Note that each time you press Enter, Word automatically keeps the style as List Number for the next line. When the list is done, if you have an extraneous numbered blank line at the end of the list, move the insertion point to the line just below the last item and choose Normal from the Style tool.

Unordered Lists *<UL>*

Unordered lists usually are displayed with bullets on most Web browsers. To create a potentially bulleted list, use the same procedure as that for ordered lists. Rather than using the List Number style, however, use either the Bullets tool on the Formatting toolbar or choose the List Bullets style from the Style tool or dialog box. For example, let's create an unordered list of HTML list types. Consider the following list:

> ordered lists
> unordered lists
> menu lists
> directory lists
> definition lists

To create an unordered or bulleted list, the easiest way is to type the list of items. Next, select all the items and apply the unordered list style, or click on the Bullets tool. Using the WebExplorer, this list displays as shown in Figure 5.8.

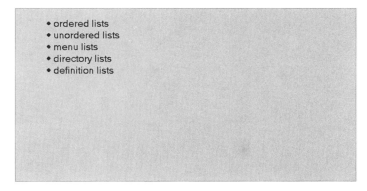

Figure 5.8. *You can use WebExplorer to display a bulleted (unordered) list.*

Menu Lists *<MENU>*

A menu list is a list of items—usually choices and usually limited to one line per item. According to the HTML specification, menu lists generally are more compact than unordered (bulleted) lists. To create a menu list, you execute the identical steps that you use to create an unordered list, except that you choose Menu from the list of styles instead of Unordered. Note also that there is no tool on the toolbar that corresponds to a menu list.

Directory Lists *<DIR>*

The HTML specification for a directory list calls for display in three columns. At this writing, none of the four major Web browsers (Netscape, Mosaic, InternetWorks Internet Assistant, or WebExplorer) supports the three-column display. In fact, only Word—using the Internet Assistant .WLL support—seems to support the <DIR> HTML version 2 specification.

A directory list typically is for displaying lists of filenames. The formal HTML specification calls for items to be no more than 20 characters long apiece. To create a directory list, type the list of items—one per line. Then select all the items on the list and apply the Directory style. A directory and menu list are shown in Figure 5.9. As you can see, the two types of lists are displayed identically.

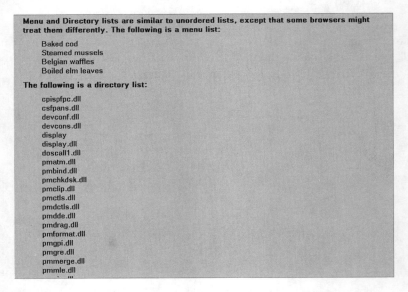

Figure 5.9. *Most browsers display menu and directory lists identically.*

Definition Lists *<DL>* and *<DL COMPACT>*

Definitions lists (also called glossaries) are a little more complex than the other kinds of lists shown so far. The Internet Assistant supports two kinds of definition lists: Definition List (<DL>) and Definition Compact (<DL COMPACT>). Most browsers do not currently differentiate between the two types of definition lists. However, at some point in the future it might be reasonable to expect <DL COMPACT> to present the list in a more compact way. Of the various Web browsers tested, only Word itself—using the Internet Assistant add-on—effectively differentiates between the two definition formats.

For an example, let's use a few entries from the glossary of this book to create a definition list. In the raw HTML file, a definition list appears as follows, using <DL> or <DL COMPACT>, depending on which one you specify:

```
<DL>¶
<DT>client<DD>A computer that obtains information or services from other
computers. Servers and clients are logical compliments.¶
<DT>FTP<DD>File Transfer Protocol. It's a method for transferring files over
the Internet.¶
<DT>Gopher<DD>A point-and-click system for accessing Internet results. In many
ways, gopher was a precursor to the Web. Gopher is still very much in use, but
is being rapidly pushed aside by the World Wide Web.¶
<DT>GUI<DD>Graphical user interface.¶
<DT>home page<DD>A home page is a starting point on the Web. From the user's
standpoint, it's where you begin your Web browsing each time you start your
browser. From a server's standpoint, it's the primary point of presence on
the Web.¶
<DT>HTML<DD>HyperText Markup Language. HTML is a system for formatting documents
for presentation on the World Wide Web.¶
</DL>¶
```

To create this kind of list, Word uses two styles: Definition Term (<DT>), a character style; and Definition List (<DL>) or Definition Compact (<DL COMPACT>). Fortunately, you do not need to apply the Definition Term style manually. To create this definition list, press Enter to start a new paragraph, and select the Definition List or Definition Compact style from the Style tool on the toolbar. Next, type the definition shown in the following example; in place of **<TAB>** and ¶, press the Tab and Enter keys:

```
client<TAB>A computer that obtains information or services from other computers.
Servers and clients are logical compliments.¶
```

Type each term and definition in the same fashion. After typing the last item, use the style tool to apply the Normal style to indicate the end of the definition list.

When you save the document as an HTML file, the Internet Assistant adds the <DL>, <DT>, and <DD> tags automatically. Displayed using the WebExplorer, this definition list displays as shown in Figure 5.10.

5

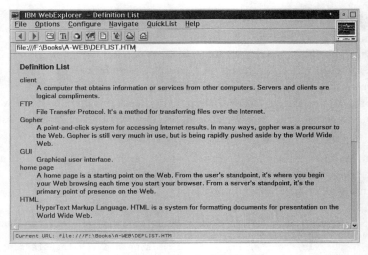

Figure 5.10. *A Definition List displayed using the WebExplorer.*

Lists Within Lists—Indentation

Occasionally, you might have a need for the following kind of list:

1. Trees
   - ☐ Oak
   - ☐ Pine
   - ☐ Elm
2. Bushes
   - ☐ Rose
   - ☐ Bay

Note that there really are two types of lists. One is a numbered list of major plant groupings (trees and bushes). The other is a bulleted list of specific types of plants within those major groupings. This kind of list is called a *nested list*, wherein different lists are nested under items within the main list.

There are a number of ways to create nested lists. To create the list shown in Figure 5.11, type the whole list. Next, apply the main list paragraph style (ordered in this case) to each of the main headings. Finally, select each group of subordinate items and apply the subordinate list paragraph style (unordered, in this case) to each of the subordinate headings. In this example, you also can click on the Bullets tool to apply the subordinate list format.

Figure 5.11. *You can nest bulleted lists within numbered lists.*

Tip: When applying the same style to noncontiguous paragraphs, you can use the Repeat keystroke (F4) to save time. In this case, for example, put the insertion point anywhere in the Trees line and choose the List Number style from the style tool. Now click in the Bush line and press the F4 key. The same formatting is applied in the cursor's new location. Note also that when applying paragraph formatting, you do not need to select the paragraph. Placing the insertion point anywhere in the target paragraph is sufficient.

The procedure described works for nesting lists of different types within an existing list. To create a nested list of the same type, the procedure is different. You use the Increase Indent and Decrease Indent tools on the Formatting toolbar. For example, suppose you want to create the following list:

Trees
- Oak
  - Red
  - Pinoak
- Pine
  - Norfolk Island
  - White
  - Australian
- Elm
  - Dutch
  - Slippery
Bushes
- Rose
- Bay

You could proceed in several ways. One way is to type the whole list, deferring indentation until you're done. Then select the entire list and apply the List Bullet style. Finally, use the Increase Indent tool to indent each of the tree and bush types. Once the list is finished, it displays using a Web browser as shown in Figure 5.12. Notice that some Web browsers, such as the WebExplorer, display different bullets at each level. Here, the WebExplorer displays a solid circle, solid square, and then an empty circle.

Bullets Nested in Bullets

- Trees
  - Oak
    - Red
    - Pinoak
  - Pine
    - Norfolk Island
    - White
    - Australian
  - Elm
    - Dutch
    - Slippery
- Bushes
  - Rose
  - Bay

Figure 5.12. *You can nest bulleted lists within other bulleted lists.*

Text Blocks

So far today, you've looked at a variety of different types of character and paragraph formatting. Another special type of text is block-oriented. HTML provides three types of text block formatting for handling certain kinds of text:

Preformatted	`<PRE>`
Quoted	`<BLOCKQUOTE>`
Address	`<ADDRESS>`

Preformatted *<PRE>* and *<PRE WIDTH=>*

Preformatted text is the only current way to achieve column-aligned tables in HTML. HTML does not support tabs or tables, as such. Instead, when working with raw HTML, you need to insert spaces to achieve a table-like layout. Unfortunately, most Web browsers are programmed to ignore extraneous tabs and spaces. Fortunately, there's an exception: Preformatted (`<PRE>`).

As its name implies, Preformatted text is text whose formatting you want to preserve. Are you ready for another *unfortunately*? Well, unfortunately, most Web browsers insist on displaying Preformatted text in a relatively ugly (by some folks' tastes) monospace text. The reason is that in order to have things line up correctly, all characters need to be the identical width. If you have ever imported text from a DOS-style bulletin board into Word, you know what happens when you apply a proportionally spaced font to text that has been meticulously aligned using the space bar.

The identical thing happens when using Web browsers. The solution is to use the Preformatted option. When the document is saved in HTML formatting, any spacing needed for producing tab alignment or table column alignment is inserted into the .HTM file.

The classic example is the large block letters you sometimes see on batch print jobs. For example:

```
#####  ######  #     #  #####
  #     #       #   #      #
  #     #####    ##        #
  #     #        ##        #
  #     #       #   #      #
  #     ######  #     #    #
```

If you have a section of text such as that, all you need to do is select it and apply the Preformatted style. It will display as shown in Figure 5.13.

Figure 5.13. *The Preformatted format preserves spaces.*

Tables

A variation of the Preformatted style is also useful for tables. For tables, however you do not need to do the work of formatting. All you need to do is create a Word table. Easy enough, right?

Take a look at the HTML.DOT Standard toolbar. Did you happen to notice a Table tool? No? Well, because tables are not supported by HTML, it was not included. Note also that the Table menu selection is missing. To make creating tables easier, one way is to put back the Table tool onto the toolbar. Unfortunately, that approach will not produce useful tables. Instead, if you want to present data in table form, you will have to do it the old-fashioned way—that is, using tabs to align the text into columns, and then applying the PRE style.

Quoted *<BLOCKQUOTE>*

Another kind of text block is used for displaying quoted text. Remember that part of the Internet arose from research establishments. Given the need for citations in academic and other research writing, it should come as no surprise that HTML's narrow vocabulary includes the <BLOCKQUOTE> tag for presenting quoted text. Block quotations are often used in conjunction with the <CITE> tag. Consider the following, for example:

> It is estimated that over 100,000 people will die from causes related to television during 1995, and that the number will top 250,000 by the year 2000. Health officials, although concerned, are unwilling to recommend putting warning labels on televisions until a precise cause and effect relationship can be established.

To prepare the preceding for inclusion in an HTML document, select the quote and apply the Blockquote style. Most Web browsers indent the block quote at the left so that it stands out from the rest of the text, as shown in Figure 5.14.

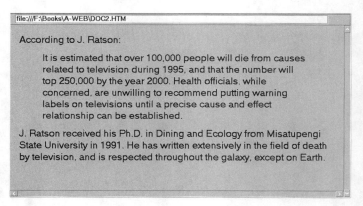

Figure 5.14. *Block quotes usually are indented so they stand out.*

Address *<ADDRESS>*

The last block format is for addresses. I saved it for last for a reason. It's a reminder that every HTML document you publish to the Web should have an address block as the last line. It shows people who to get in touch with if they have questions or comments. Later, you will learn how to make the address into a link that users can use to send you e-mail directly. Keep in mind for now, however, that we have yet to explore links, and that none of the formatting discussed today is for actually accessing other parts of the Internet. All of the formatting in today's lesson is oriented to the presentation of information only.

The <ADDRESS> tag, implemented using the paragraph style Address, is for formatting addresses, both electronic and postal. Consider the following:

```
Macmillan Computer Publishing (www.mcp.com)
201 W. 103rd Street
Indianapolis, IN 46290-1097
317-581-3500
```

To format this as an address, simply type the text into the HTML document, select the text, and apply the Address style. What could be simpler?

Consider the results, however, shown in Figure 5.15. Notice that the first instance of the address had too much vertical spacing, but the second looks about right. Why? In the first, I pressed Enter at the end of each line. In the second, I pressed Shift+Enter at the end of each line. The first results in the <P> tag (paragraph) being used for each line. The second results in the <BR> tag (line break). By explicitly using an intraparagraph line break (sometimes called a soft return), rather then a regular return, the displayed spacing between the address lines is smaller.

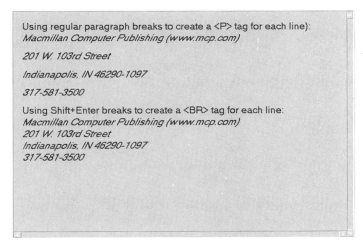

Figure 5.15. *Use Shift+Enter instead of Enter to decrease the separation between address lines.*

There is still a problem, however. Notice that there is not enough space between the line that precedes the address and the address itself. No matter how many times you press Enter, Word still inserts a single carriage return before the address. You can insert a blank line by pressing Enter, and then format that blank line as Preformatted. That way—you will recall—the actual spacing is used, suppressing the Web browser's tendency to strip out extra horizontal and vertical spacing.

Logical Versus Physical Formatting

Many of the HTML guides that exist on the World Wide Web make a point about there being two kinds of formatting. Recall that the two types are logical and physical. *Logical formatting* is formatting based on what you want to accomplish or how the text is to be used—the actual presentation method is left up to the browser. Logical formatting includes heading levels, text blocks, and attributes such as emphasis (<EM>), strong (<STRONG>), and citation <CITE>. Physical formatting refers to the specific attribute you want to apply. The physical formatting tags are bold (<B>), italic (<I>), and underlining (<U>). Some HTML gurus also consider the typewriter (<TT>) attribute as physical. The following are generally considered to be logical formatting elements:

Address	<ADDRESS>
Block quote	<BLOCKQUOTE>
Citation	<CITE>
Code	<CODE>
Definition List	<DL>
Directory	<DIR>
Emphasis	<EM>
Headings	<H1> through <H6>
Keyboard	<KBD>
Menu	<MENU>
Ordered List	<OL>
Sample	<SAMP>
Unordered List	<UL>
Variable	<VAR>

HTML purists have a saying: Trust your browser. That is, use logical formatting to indicate the intended purpose of the formatting, and then trust the browser to display it as best it can. If you use <EM> (emphasis) for text that you want to stand out from the crowd, the browser selects a display method that accomplishes that logical effect. If you use <I> (italic), however, the browser uses italic if it can, but otherwise will be forced to ignore the <I> formatting. Logically, which would you rather have happen? Would you rather use <EM> and feel confident that the text will be emphasized in one way or another if at all possible? Or would you rather use <I> and run the risk that it won't necessarily be formatted differently at all?

That's the argument. In practice, however, many HTML authors don't appear to be paying much attention to the logical versus physical debate and the guidelines. Unfortunately, neither (necessarily) are the Web browser authors paying all that much attention. The emerging result is that sometimes the physical formatting characteristics are supported better

than the logical ones. However, I say the *emerging* result because the jury is still out. My advice to you, as blossoming HTML authors, is to try it both ways and see which method yields the better results when using the browser you believe your audience is most likely to use.

Creating a Full-Figured HTML Document

Now that you've learned all about tags and styles, you're ready to put them to practical use in the following exercise.

▼ Exercise 5.1. Creating a full-figured HTML document.

Let's use the formatting techniques discussed today to create a fairly complex HTML document. The goal is a finished Web page. First, create a new HTML document. From the menu, choose File\|New. Under Template, choose Html. Word opens a new Document# window. First, insert a title for the HTML document (recall the steps from Day 4). Remember that the title is not displayed in the HTML document itself, but is used by Web browsers, usually for displaying a title bar. Click on the Title tool, or choose File\|HTML Document Information from the menu. Type the title as the following:

```
Sample HTML Document for Day 5
```

If Word is not already displaying paragraph marks and other nonprinting characters, turn them on now. It makes it easier to see exactly what's going on. From the menu, choose Tools\|Options\|View. Under Nonprinting characters, click on All and then click on the OK button.

Now, create a level 3 header. From the Style tool, choose Heading 3 to format the current paragraph, and then retype the title text. Why the same text? Remember that there is no guarantee that the browser being used will display the title in the title bar. Why Heading 3 rather than Heading 1? Heading 1 often results in headings that are much too large to be very practical. If you know that a document won't really need more than a couple of heading levels, then it's a better use of space to start at Heading 3. Also, using Heading 1 practically eliminates any chance of fitting all an HTML document on a single screen. If, on the other hand, the document is highly structured and needs all six levels, go ahead and start at Heading 1. In the end, it's a matter of aesthetics and preference.

After typing the Heading 3 text, press Enter. The new paragraph created should have the Normal,P style. Does it? If not, use the Style tool to apply the Normal style. Now, type the next paragraph, and press Enter at the end of each paragraph, as indicated by ¶:

```
This document demonstrates a number of HTML formats. It does not use graphics
or links. The purpose in days 4 and 5 are to show how to effectively format and
present information using words. Links and graphics come later.¶
There are two schools of HTML formatting:¶
```

Now, you're going to create a short definition list. Type the following two paragraphs, using the Tab and Enter keys where indicated with <TAB> and ¶.

```
Physical<TAB>Specifying the exact attribute you want presented onscreen, such
as bold, italic, or underlined.¶
Logical<TAB>Specifying the purpose of the formatting, leaving the physical
presentation up to the browser.¶
```

Once you type those two lines, select them and use the Style tool to apply the Definition List style. Now, move the insertion point to the paragraph marker following the `Logical<TAB>Specifying...` line, and ensure that the style in effect is Normal,P. If not, use the Style tool to apply the Normal style.

Type the following:

```
Most purists argue in favor of using logical formatting whenever possible,
because different Web browsers have different capabilities. In other words, if
you use physical attributes, you might not get any variation at all, because
many Web browsers ignore formatting commands for which they have no
corresponding capability. Thus, for the attribute at the left, use the
formatting shown at the right:¶
```

Note that the word **purists** is bold and the words *physical* and *logical* are both italicized. You can add the bold attribute as you type, by pressing Ctrl+B, typing the word `purists`, and then pressing Ctrl+B again. Use the same technique for italic, substituting Ctrl+I for Ctrl+B. Alternatively, you can format those words after the fact. Click anywhere inside the word `purists` (for example, after p or before t) and then click on the Bold tool to make the whole word bold. Repeat the procedure for the other two words, using the Italic tool instead.

Alternatively, you could select the word `purists` and apply the Strong style, and then apply the Emphasis style to the other two words. As an exercise, you should do it both ways, and see whether your favorite Web browser is capable of handling either way.

Next, insert a table. Insert the table the old-fashioned way by separating the different columns with tabs. Type the following, pressing the Tab key between the two entries on each line:

```
Bold          <STRONG>
Italic        <EM>
Monospaced    <KBD>
```

Now, select the three lines of the table and apply the Preformatted style to it. That way, the section will be converted into monospaced text, including the spaces, enabling the columns of the table to align correctly.

Next, set up a block quote. Move the text cursor to the paragraph just after the table, and type the following, pressing Enter at the end:

```
According to NCSA's A Beginner's Guide to HTML:¶
```

Note that *NCSA's A Beginner's Guide to HTML* is in italic. Don't use the Italic tool, however. Instead, select the phrase and apply the CITE character style. The phrase should now appear in italic.

Type the following quote, pressing Enter at the end:

```
In the ideal SGML universe, content is divorced from presentation. Thus, SGML
tags a level-one heading as a level-one heading, but does not specify that the
level-one heading should be, for instance, 24-point bold Times centered on the
top of a page. The advantage of this approach (it's similar in concept to style
sheets in many word processors) is that if you decide to change level-one
headings to be 20-point left-justified Helvetica, all you have to do is change
the definition of the level-one heading in the presentation device (i.e., your
World Wide Web browser).¶
```

Next, format that paragraph as Blockquote. Select the paragraph and use the Style tool to apply the style. The left margin of the block should move to the right a little.

Now you're going to set up a bulleted list. First, verify that the style is Normal,P, and that the cursor is in the paragraph following the block quote. Then type the following, and press Enter:

```
Just what are the logical formatting attributes? Among others, they are:¶
```

Type the following list:

```
Address <ADDRESS>¶
Block quote <BLOCKQUOTE>¶
Citation <CITE>¶
Code <CODE>¶
Definition List <DL>¶
Directory <DIR>¶
```

After typing the list, select it and apply the List Bullet style. Alternatively, you can click on the Bullets tool on the toolbar. A bullet should appear on-screen beside each item.

Next, create a numbered list of important rules to remember. Move the insertion point to the paragraph after the bulleted list and type the following, pressing the Enter key after each line:

```
In closing, remember these important rules:¶
Number every list, except for lists that should not be numbered¶
Never add numbers to lists for which numbering is irrelevant¶
Rule number 1 takes precedence over rule number 3¶
Ignore all rules¶
Rule number 4 takes precedence over rule number 5¶
```

Now, make sure that the line beginning `In closing...` is formatted with the Normal,P style. Select the five lines that follow that line and apply the List Number style. You can do that either by applying the style or by clicking on the Numbering tool on the toolbar. Each of the five lines should now appear with a line number.

Finally, type an address block. Remember that address blocks tend to get spread out (too much vertical space) if you just press Enter at the end of each one. Type the following, pressing Enter or Shift+Enter where indicated by **\<ENTER\>** and **\<SHIFT+ENTER\>**, respectively:

```
Please address all comments to me in care of the following address:<ENTER>
John Smith<SHIFT+ENTER>
The Lost Colony<SHIFT+ENTER>
The Dutch West India Company<SHIFT+ENTER>
The Colony of Virginia in the British Colonial Empire<ENTER>
```

Now, make sure that the line that begins `Please address all...` is formatted as Normal,P. Then select all four lines of the address and apply the Address style.

That's it. Save a copy of the document in regular Word format for later editing. From the menu, choose File|Save (not Save As), and change the current `doc#` name into something more meaningful, such as `ex5`, for example. Ensure that the Save File as Type option is set to Word document and click on OK. This saves the file as `ex5.doc`.

Next, choose File|Save As. Note that the HyperText Markup Language (HTML) format should already be selected, and the filename has been set to something like `ex5.htm`, depending on what you named the `.DOC` version. Now you should have `.DOC` and `.HTM` versions of the file saved to your disk. You will use the `.DOC` version for later editing, and use the `.HTM` for displaying as a Web document.

Take a look at the document using Word. First, close the `.HTM` version that's currently open. Then, choose File|Open and open the `.HTM` version of the file. It should take a little longer to open than a normal Word file because the Internet Assistant has some setup work to do. When it opens, it should appear as shown in Figure 5.16, although probably not as small!

Figure 5.16. *The finished HTML document.*

Summary

Today, you learned most of the formatting commands common to Word and HTML. You should have a good idea by now exactly what kinds of documents you can produce in HTML, as well as what formatting to use and how to use it. In the workshop, you will build a fairly complicated Web page that has no links, but which uses most of the formatting elements covered today and on Day 4.

5

Q&A

Q How can I get subscripts and superscripts into my Web pages?

A You can't. Keep in mind that HTML must function on all-text systems. Displaying superscripts and subscripts is not a capability that is built into text-only displays.

6

Hyperlinks and URLs

If you're using this book according to the two-chapters-a-day plan, you've spent the first part of today getting a crash course in HTML formatting the contents of your Web documents for presentation. Now you turn your attention to the *hyper* aspect of hypertext markup language (HTML)—how to create links. You learn how to create links to other parts of the same HTML document, to local documents (documents located on your Web server or on your own computer), and to other locations on the Internet.

Hyperlinks

A hyperlink is an active part of a document. When you access a hyperlink, the focus is transferred to another location that is referred to by the link. You usually access a hyperlink by clicking and using a graphical user interface, such as Windows, OS/2 Presentation Manager, or UNIX X Window System. You can also activate a hyperlink by pressing Enter or the spacebar, depending on how the software you are using is designed. Most of this book uses the term *clicking on the link*. If your Web browser uses some other technique, feel free to do whatever is more appropriate for you and your browser.

Hypertext and hyperlink documents are commonplace in computing now. Consider the Windows, Macintosh, and OS/2 Help systems, for example. When Help is displayed, there often are highlighted areas that you can click on to access additional information. That other information might be contained elsewhere in the same file or perhaps in another help file on your computer. The excitement of using the World Wide Web, however, is that hyperlinks can access information not only on your own computer, but on any accessible computer on the Internet (in theory). The information you access, stored in computer files, can produce words, sounds, pictures, or even action video on your own computer.

There are three types of hyperlinks:

- ☐ Links to other parts of the same HTML document
- ☐ Links to other files on your computer (or on your Web server's computer)
- ☐ Links to other computers on the Internet

In HTML, links work with a kind of tag called an *anchor*. You can use the Internet Assistant to insert the anchors automatically, but it's helpful to understand what they are and how they work.

Anchors Aweigh!

There are two types of anchor tags. One is the anchor name (NAME) and the other is the anchor hyper-reference (HREF). Anchor names are used to label sections of an HTML document so

that they can be referred to elsewhere in the document. Anchor references indicate the actual hyperlink and are used to create the clickable reference.

Suppose I want to use the main heading of this section (Anchors Aweigh!) as a hyperlink access point for use elsewhere in the document. If this were an online document, it might be useful when, any time I write about anchors, I could make the word anchors a hyperlink to this heading. That way, when I write See the discussion of anchors for additional information, you could just click on the word anchors to see the additional information.

If you're familiar with Microsoft Word, you might be thinking that this sounds suspiciously like bookmarks. Word and some other word processors have a bookmark feature that enables you to mark sections of text as bookmarks. You can then refer to those bookmarks from elsewhere in the same document or from entirely different documents. Bookmarks have other uses in Word as well. If you're thinking that anchors are similar, you are not alone. In fact, when Microsoft created the Internet Assistant, it decided to implement the anchor name by using Word's bookmark feature.

To insert an anchor name, move the cursor to where you want the document to jump when a reference to the anchor is clicked on, and click on the Bookmark tool on the HTML formatting toolbar. Alternatively, you can choose Edit | Bookmark from the menu or press Ctrl+Shift+F5 (my personal favorite). Word displays the dialog box shown in Figure 6.1. Type the name of the bookmark. Choose something succinct, logical, and unambiguous. For example, if I were bookmarking the current section of today's lesson for use as an anchor name, I might type the word anchors.

Figure 6.1. *Insert anchor names using the Bookmark dialog box.*

 Tip: When creating a hyperlink, save the HTML file first so that you link to the filename on the drive. It'll save time later on.

Tip: If the word you want to use as your bookmark/anchor name is present in the text, select it and copy it to the clipboard before displaying the Bookmark dialog box. That way, you can paste it into the Bookmark Name field rather than having to retype it. This is especially handy if the name you want to use is cumbersome to type. To copy a word or phrase to the clipboard, select it and press Ctrl+Ins. To paste the contents of the clipboard, press Shift+Ins. This tip works for any dialog box text field where the desired entry is stored in the clipboard.

To Select or Not To Select?

When creating anchor names, you do not need to select the text you want to bookmark. You can, but you don't have to, and you usually shouldn't. Just put the text cursor or insertion point (by clicking, for example) where you want the top of the Web browser window to end when you jump to that anchor name. If you select text first, however, the selection is bookmarked, not just a single point. When the anchor name is associated with a block of text rather than a single point, some Web browsers highlight the anchor when you jump to it. Sometimes, if a document is extremely busy and finding the exact reference point is difficult, you might want to make your anchor cover a selection rather than a single point. Usually, however, having text display as selected interrupts the reading flow and looks ugly. The bottom line is that you should do it only when necessary to accomplish a specific purpose. If you can't think of what that purpose is, don't do it.

If you set bookmarks to display on-screen, they appear as shown in Figure 6.2 while you are editing the document as a Word document. To display bookmarks, choose Tools|Options|View, and click on the Bookmarks item so that an X appears. When the document is saved as an HTML document, an anchor name tag `<A NAME="`*`bookmark`*`">` is inserted for you. For example, if I insert a bookmark called `anchors` next to the anchor heading for today, the contents of the saved HTML is the following:

```
<A NAME="anchors"></A>Anchors Aweigh!¶
```

If the text `Anchors Aweigh` is selected as the bookmark, instead of the point just to the left of the A, the contents of the HTML file is the following:

```
<A NAME="anchors">Anchors Aweigh!</A>¶
```

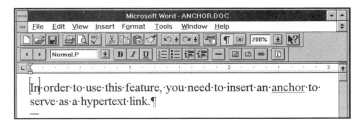

Figure 6.2. *Bookmarks display as large brackets (1).*

In this case, the closing `</A>` tag goes on the other side of the anchored text. I changed the name of the main heading from `Anchors` to the current title so that you could tell that the anchor name is controlled entirely by the text inside the `<A NAME...>` tag, and does not depend on the `Anchors Aweigh` text at all. With `</A>` used to enclose the whole title, some Web browsers highlight the title when jumping to it.

Anchor Reference (*<A HREF="reference">*)

The flip side of the anchor name tag is the anchor reference tag. Anchor reference tags, however, can be used to refer to more than just anchor name tags. Indeed, the anchor reference is the very heart of hyperlinking. What an anchor reference does is determined entirely by what you put between the quotes (`"reference"`). It can be a reference to a bookmark, to another file, or to a URL. Fortunately, you don't really need to worry about the exact syntax because Word's Internet Assistant handles it for you. However, you do need to know what you want.

Anchor Reference to an Anchor Name or Bookmark

Let's start simply. Picking up on the previous example, let's say that you want to insert a reference to the beginning of the `Anchors Aweigh` heading. I'll describe a method that uses the approach suggested in most of the HTML style guides. That is, the clickable reference should fit into the context of the discussion. First, type the text that contains a mention of anchors. Better still, if it really fits into the context, there probably already is a mention that you can use for the link, for example:

```
In order to use this feature, you need to insert an anchor to serve as a
hypertext link.¶
```

Next, choose the text that you want to use as the link. For example, you might want to use the word `anchor`. Note that you might also choose to use the word `hypertext` for an entirely different link. A well-thought-out Web presentation incorporates links as seamlessly as

possible, attempting not to insert additional text to accommodate the links. There are exceptions, of course, but it's up to you to find them and justify using them.

DO   **DON'T**

DO choose anchor reference words that fit into the context of the discussion.

DON'T write text such as `Click here for more information`.

Note that the text is not at all contrived (except insofar as it was entirely contrived for today's lesson), and that the word `anchor` is perfectly in context, following the recommendations of most HTML style guides. Now you're about to discover why you typed the text in context. Using the mouse or keyboard, select the text that you want to serve as the link, for example, `anchor`. Next, from the menu, choose Insert|HyperLink or click on the HyperLink tool on the toolbar. If it's not already displayed, click on the To Bookmark tab. The dialog box shown in Figure 6.3 appears, with the select word in the Text to Display text box, and a list of bookmarks displayed. If no bookmarks are displayed, you need to back up to the previous section and insert one someplace else in the document before you can see how the HyperLink dialog box works.

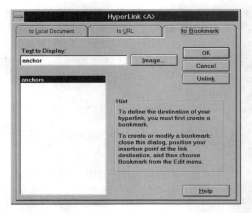

Figure 6.3. *Creating a hyperlink to an anchor name in the current document.*

Note: The selected text (the word `anchor`) is displayed in the Text to Display text box. If you display the HyperLink dialog box without first selecting text, you have to type the display text. Moreover, as you will see, you also have some additional work to do to make the display text fit into the context. Using this

approach, not only is the word `anchor` used as the link, but it replaces the original word `anchor` as well, so it doesn't end up as `anchor anchor`.

To create a link to a bookmark in the current document, click on the bookmark and then click on OK. The Internet Assistant inserts a macro button that will be used to create the hyperlink when the document is saved in HTML format. Here, for example, the word `anchor` is the display text and the word `anchors` is the bookmark. When you click on OK, the text in the document immediately changes to the following (the word `anchor`, in bold in the next line, displays in blue on your screen):

```
In order to use this feature, you need to insert an anchor to serve as a
hypertext link.
```

Now let's see what's really going on. Click on the Html Hidden ({a}) tool on the Standard toolbar to display the contents of the `anchor` link. It should display as the following:

```
{  { PRIVATE HREF="#anchors" }MACROBUTTON HtmlResAnchor anchor}
```

This is a field code for a macrobutton. The blue word `anchor` is used to display the macro button when field code results are displayed. If you click on the Html Hidden tool a second time, the field is again displayed as the blue word `anchor`. When editing the document as a Word document, you can edit the contents of the link without having to display the field code. Double-click on the display word `anchor`. This reopens the HyperLink dialog box. After you save the document in HTML format, the line is converted to the following (as viewed in raw HTML):

```
In order to use this feature, you need to insert an
<A HREF="#anchors">anchor</A> to serve as a hypertext link.¶
```

Note that the anchor reference uses the number sign (#) just before the name of the reference. In HTML, the presence of # is the instruction to search the current document for the name following the #. You don't need to use # as part of the anchor name.

Anchor Reference to a Local File

The second type of anchor reference is to a local file, which can include other HTML documents, sound files, video files, and graphics. To keep it simple, let's stick with other HTML documents for now, and save the fancy stuff for another day.

To insert an anchor reference to another HTML file, you must have another file standing by. For example, suppose you build a Web presence for the purpose of providing technical support. Many technical support providers have a number of documents that deal with specific problems, tips, and suggestions. Thus, you might have a main HTML document that serves as a point of entry, explaining the purpose of the Web presence and providing a table

of contents. Individual items referred to in the table of contents can be separate HTML files or bulletins.

As a strategic matter, you can keep everything in a single document. Indeed, you might even want to offer a separate version of the document in precisely that form. However, suppose that all your technical documents—when put together—result in an HTML file that is over a megabyte. If a user is looking for information only on a particular product, it hardly seems like a service to force them to download a 1MB+ file to find a technical bulletin that by itself is only 5KB. By keeping the individual modules separate, users download just what they need rather than the whole shebang. From your own perspective, maintenance of the site is easier as well. Rather than having to edit a huge HTML file each time a minor change is needed, the individual modules can be maintained, edited, and updated independently. This is especially useful if the different modules are created by different people.

Recall that, strategically, you might want to offer a single-volume version of your information. This enables a user to capture the entire volume for use offline. If the information is available only piecemeal, downloading the entire thing becomes very difficult. Of course, if your information is copyrighted, you might want to make it difficult to copy the whole thing. However, information providers such as those being described here usually are better served by having the information in the hands of users, rather than tucked away on a server.

Let's assume that you are creating an HTML document in which you want to be able to refer to another HTML document on the same server. First, using the *make it fit the context* rule discussed earlier, identify a likely jumping-off point in the current HTML document. In the case of a technical information server, however, you don't need to be cute or clever. Something like the following works quite well:

```
Repair and maintenance bulletins are available for the following models:¶
XG20, 750 HP tractor¶
XG25, 800 HP tractor¶
XG30, 850 HP tractor¶
XG35, 8500 HP traaaaaaaaaaactor!!!¶
```

In this case, you can make each of the XG# items hyperlinks to stand-alone files—perhaps named XG20.HTM, XG25.HTM, and so on. (Note that this also is a perfect opportunity to use an unordered list or a menu list, as described in Chapter 5 "Tags and Styles.") First, select the text you want to be used as the link—XG20, for example. Next, click on the HyperLink tool on the toolbar, or choose Insert|HyperLink from the menu. Click on the To Local Document tab to display the view shown in Figure 6.4.

Note that XG20 already displays in the Text to Display area. Now, using the Directories and Drives control, navigate to the location of the files you want to use and click on the one corresponding to the text you select. If the files are located on a network drive, click on the Network button to navigate to the desired location. Once the file you want is displayed in the list of filenames, click on the file and then click on OK.

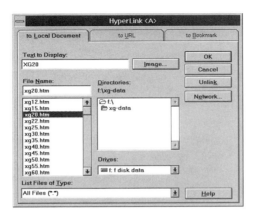

Figure 6.4. *Creating a hyperlink to a local document.*

The Internet Assistant now converts the selected text into an anchor reference to the file. In the current file, the selected text turns blue. If you click on the Html Hidden ({a}) button on the toolbar, the reference displays as follows, with XG20 in blue:

```
{ { PRIVATE HREF="../../xg-data/xg20.htm" }MACROBUTTON HtmlResAnchor XG20},
750 HP tractor¶
```

When the document is saved in HTML format, the same line becomes the following:

```
<A HREF="../../xg-data/xg20.htm">XG20</A>, 750 HP tractor¶
```

Caution: Notice that you might have a little problem here, not only when the HTML file gets placed onto a server, but even before then. The directory reference is given as ../../xg-data/xg20.htm. The location is done entirely as a location relative to the currently logged disk and directory. This is all relative to your Word and Internet Assistant working environment. What happens if your Web browser is logged to a different directory? Even worse, what if this reference (../../xg-data/xg20.htm) is posted on a server? Is it likely that the same relative directory would work on your server? (I didn't think so.)

The result is that, although you can use Word's Internet Assistant to set up the documents and links, you might have to edit the resulting HTM documents to match the setup on your Web server. Alternatively, you can set up your HTML creation environment so that its directory structure mirrors what exists on your Web server. For example, one solution is to put all your HTML documents and support files on the same directory on your server, and do the same in your work environment on your PC. If you absolutely must have subdirectories, choose

subdirectory names that are compatible with both your Web server's operating system as well as with your HTML development operating system. For all practical purposes at the present time, this means choosing directory names that are DOS-compatible.

For example, suppose your main `.HTM` file is on a directory called `\WINWORD\WEB`. If all your referenced `.HTM` (and other) files are also on that directory, the HyperLink command will not append any directory to the beginning of the filename. If your files are on one or more subdirectories of that directory— `\WINWORD\WEB\XG-DATA`, for example—only the additional subdirectory name is added (`xg-data/xg20.htm`).

Anchor Reference to a URL

The third type of anchor reference is to a URL, a Uniform Resource Locator (a Web-ese address for an Internet resource). URLs can be to a number of different types of Internet resources. For now, however, let's look at references to other Web servers (`http`). See the section, "Understanding URLs," later in today's lesson for information about other types of URLs.

Suppose, for example, that you want your HTML document to contain a link to another Web server with additional relevant information. Let's call that other server `www.tractors.xg.com`. The goal is to embed a link to `http://www.tractors.xg.com`, which is the full specification of the URL for a Web browser. One way to present that kind of URL in an HTML document is to include the name of the owner of the URL. For example, if you want to provide a link to the publisher of Word for Windows, you might include text such as, `additional information is available directly from Microsoft`. You then use `Microsoft` as the display text for the link.

Using the running example, let's imagine that your HTML document contains this text:

```
Additional information is provided by the National Tractor Farm Federation.¶
```

To use `National Tractor Farm Federation` as the display text for the link, you first select it. Then click on the HyperLink tool. If necessary, click on the To URL tab to display the view shown in Figure 6.5. As was the case when creating links to local documents and bookmarks, the selected text is automatically placed in the Display Text field. Note also that URLs you add using the HyperLink dialog box are displayed in the URL list. Each time you add a new URL, it is added to the URL list in `wordhtml.ini`, which is stored in your Windows directory.

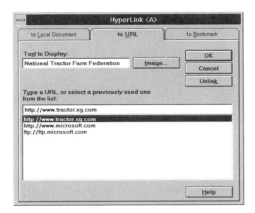

Figure 6.5. *Creating a hyperlink to a URL.*

If the link you want to use is listed, click on it. Otherwise, type the URL. Make sure you include the entire specification. In other words, for a Web page, you must include http://. When the URL is done, click on OK. The selected text turns into a blue hyperlink. In the current document, the URL is stored as a macro button. For example, using the hypothetical National Tractor Farm Federation, whose hypothetical URL is http://www.tractor.xg.com, the field inserted is the following:

```
{  { PRIVATE HREF="http://www.tractor.xg.com" }MACROBUTTON HtmlResAnchor
➥National Tractor Farm Federation}
```

Again, this is a macro button. You can double-click on it at any time later on to edit the link if necessary. To see how the link is constructed, you can also click on the Html Hidden ({a}) tool to toggle the field between code and results display.

When you save the document in HTML format, the link is converted into the following (in context):

```
Additional information is available from the <A HREF="http://
➥www.tractor.xg.com">
National Tractor Farm Federation</A>.
```

In the HTML document, viewed from a Web browser, it displays only as this:

```
Additional information is available from the National Tractor Farm Federation.
```

Sometimes, rather than linking just to a specific server, you might want to link to a specific HTML file (or other resource) on the server. If that's the case, you need to include the whole specification. Suppose, for example, that you want to refer to a document on the Tractor site called \xg\pub\xgproblems.html. When you create the link as shown previously, add that to the end of the other URL in the URL text area in the HyperLink dialog box:

```
http://www.tractor.xg.com\xg\pub\xgproblems.html
```

Now when you click on OK to insert the link (using the HyperLink dialog box), that document is referenced. Note also that on UNIX servers, the extension for HTML files usually is `.html`, rather than just `.htm`.

> **Tip:** Typing URLs is tedious and error-prone. If you are browsing the Web and happen upon a URL that you would like to include as a hyperlink, you can preserve it for later use. Add it to the history list. See the History List section under `WEBVIEW.DOT` Formatting Toolbar, and the Copy HyperLink section under `WEBVIEW.DOT` Standard Toolbar in Chapter 3, "The World Wide Web," for additional information.

Removing Links

Now that you know how to insert links, you're probably wondering how to remove them. One way—the hard way—is to click on the Html Hidden ({a}) tool, select the text used for the macro button display, copy it to the clipboard, and then paste it into the document. Then, delete the link (you have to select it to delete it because it's a field), and finally reformat the display text so that it's no longer blue.

Alternatively, you could do it the easy way. First, while viewing the file as a regular Word document (not the `.HTM` version, unless you're using version 1.02 or later of the Internet Assistant), click once on the link. Then click on the HyperLink tool. Note the Unlink button. Click on the Unlink button to convert the link back into regular text.

Understanding URLs

There are a variety of different types of URLs. First, let's review (from Chapter 1, "The World Wide Web") the syntax of a URL:

`protocol://hostaddress[:port][/directory][/filename]`

protocol tells what kind of FTP/IP (file transfer protocol/internet protocol) to use to retrieve information from the URL addressee. *hostaddress* is the name of the computer or server where the resource resides. For example, the name of the Macmillan Computer Publishing Web server is `www.mcp.com`. The name of their FTP server is `ftp.mcp.com`. Microsoft's FTP server is `ftp.microsoft.com`. The *port* number is seldom used. You use the port number

when the host computer resource is not accessible using the default port address. For example, Gopher normally uses port number 70, but under some circumstances, you might see a special port number, such as 77. *directory* is the specification of the disk location of the resource. Note that the URL does not have any distinct provision for disk drive letters. You can usually include a disk drive letter for OS/2 and DOS systems when referring to a local file. However, on UNIX systems, that doesn't work. Sometimes, different port numbers are set up to access different disks, but there's no way to know that without getting specific information from the site administrator. *filename* is just what you think: a filename.

Some URLs need just a host address name, but others need the works. One way to avoid having to learn URL syntax is to browse the Web, adding interesting URLs to your Web browser's history list. That way, you should at the very least be able to copy URLs from your browser's history list to the Internet Assistant for Word.

The following are protocols acceptable to most Web browsers:

HTTP	Web servers; for example, `http://www.ibm.net/`.
FTP	File transfer protocol servers; for example, `ftp://ftp.ibm.net/pub/games/TRICKLE.ZIP`. The protocol `file` also is used as a synonym for `ftp`.
Gopher	Gopher servers; for example, `gopher://ofs2info.gopher.ibm.com`.
News	News servers; for example, `news:comp.os.os2.apps`.
Telnet	Telnet servers; for example, `telnet://vnet.ibm.com`.
Mailto	Mail servers; for example, `mailto:tyson@cpcug.org`.

Note: The Mailto protocol enjoys less support than the other protocols, especially among DOS and Macintosh browsers. If it is supported by the browser, a window pops up for the subject and body of a message to send via e-mail to the addressee.

File Transfer Protocol

Recall that file transfer protocol (FTP) is a method for transferring files across the Internet. FTP links are popular for some Web sites for providing software updates and support. For example, as shown in Figure 6.6, the Internet Assistant is available in Microsoft's Web home page, via FTP. Here's how you would set up a link to it.

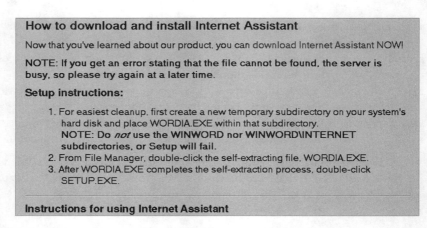

How to download and install Internet Assistant

Now that you've learned about our product, you can download Internet Assistant NOW!

NOTE: If you get an error stating that the file cannot be found, the server is busy, so please try again at a later time.

Setup instructions:

1. For easiest cleanup, first create a new temporary subdirectory on your system's hard disk and place WORDIA.EXE within that subdirectory.
   NOTE: Do *not* use the WINWORD nor WINWORD\INTERNET subdirectories, or Setup will fail.
2. From File Manager, double-click the self-extracting file, WORDIA.EXE.
3. After WORDIA.EXE completes the self-extraction process, double-click SETUP.EXE.

Instructions for using Internet Assistant

Figure 6.6. *The Internet Assistant is available at Microsoft's Web site.*

First, create the text in your HTML document for the link:

```
Download the Internet Assistant now.¶
```

Next, select that phrase (or as much of it as you think is needed to convey the purpose of the link). Then click on the HyperLink tool in the Formatting toolbar. If necessary, click on the To URL tab to display the dialog box shown in Figure 6.7.

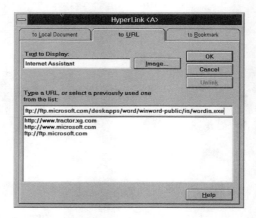

Figure 6.7. *Creating a hyperlink to FTP a file.*

Now type the URL to point to the Internet Assistant file. Note that you often need to use a Web browser or an FTP client program to obtain the necessary site, directory, and filename. To find out the exact specification for the Internet Assistant file, I started at http://www.microsoft.com and eventually found the Download... line quoted previously, which is

a suitable way to point to a filename from an HTML document. The same line informed me that the URL for the Internet Assistant is the following:

```
ftp://ftp.microsoft.com/deskapps/word/winword-public/ia/wordia.exe
```

Type the URL into the URL text area and click on OK. The selected part of the phrase turns blue. When you save the document in HTML format, that line becomes this:

```
<A HREF="ftp://ftp.microsoft.com/deskapps/word/winword-public/ia/wordia.exe">
Download Internet Assistant Now!!</A>¶
```

Gopher

Gopher is a point-and-click method menuing system for accessing the Internet, similar in intent to the World Wide Web. The intent was to make resources on the Internet accessible without having to ply the UNIX command line. For a while, Gopher servers were popping up everywhere. The much more sophisticated World Wide Web, however, has recently displaced Gopher, which appears to have stalled. Nonetheless, during Gopher's heyday, many information and support systems were created that have not yet been duplicated on the Web. Because the Web provides a URL method for accessing Gopher resources, there has not been much hurry in writing HTML documents to access some of those resources.

Gopher menus are accessible using the Gopher type of URL. One of the most well-developed and popular gopher systems is that used to support the dissemination of meteorological information. Consider the HTML document shown in Figure 6.8: (`http://galaxy.einet.net/GJ/weather.html`). This is an index of a variety of Gopher menus. Let's create a smaller version to show how it was done.

Meteorology

- American Meteorological Society
- Florida State Univ, Meteorology Department Gopher
- National Oceanic & Atmospheric Administration (NOAA)
- NCAR/UCAR Gopher (National Center for Atmospheric Research)
- North Carolina State Univ, Atmospheric Science
- RiceInfo (Rice University CWIS) (Weather Collection)
- SUNY, Albany, Atmospheric Science Research Center
- Tornado and Hurricane Research - Texas Tech
- Univ. of California - Santa Barbara (Weather Collection)
- Univ. of North Carolina - Charlotte Gopher (Weather Collection)
- Univ. of Wisconsin - Madison Space Science & Engineering Cntr
- University of Illinois Weather Machine
- Weather Processor Gopher (Purdue University)

Figure 6.8. *Some HTML pages contain a list of Gopher items.*

First, enter a heading:

```
Meteorology¶
```

Format the heading as Heading 1, which is the heading level used for this menu. Now, enter the following lines:

```
American Meteorological Society¶
Florida State Univ, Meteorology Department Gopher¶
National Oceanic & Atmospheric Administration (NOAA)¶
```

Format those three lines as List Bullet, to create an unordered (bulleted) list. Now, select each line, in turn, and use the HyperLink tool to assign the following URLs, respectively:

```
gopher://atm.geo.nsf.gov
gopher://metlab1.met.fsu.edu
gopher://gopher.ngdc.noaa.gov
```

Of course, the hard part is locating URLs to begin with. As pointed out several times elsewhere in this book, if you use the History List feature of the Word Internet Assistant browser, you can collect URLs as you go along. You can then use the Copy HyperLink command to store links in the clipboard for later pasting.

Usenet and Newsgroups

Usenet is a large and growing system for public bulletin-board-type messages. With over 10,000 newsgroups (message areas)—that are growing daily—and tens of millions of active participants, newsgroups are a primary source of information for many Internet users. They depend on newsgroups for information about software updates, UFO sightings, questions about sick goldfish, discussions about politics and religion, and much more.

Suppose you want to build an HTML document with a variety of resources related to Microsoft Word. Among those, you might want to include URLs pointing to some related newsgroups. A common way of presenting newsgroups in an HTML document is to list the exact name of the newsgroup, along with a description, using the newsgroup's name as the display text for the link. Consider the following newsgroups, for example:

```
bit.mailserv.word-pc
comp.os.ms-windows.apps.word-proc
```

One way to set up a news page is to have a definition list. You might, for example, enter the following, pressing the Tab key where indicated by <TAB>:

```
bit.mailserv.word-pc<TAB>Mixed discussion of many word processors,
most of which is about Word. Low volume, and more manageable than
comp.os.ms-windows.apps.word-proc. Individual postings get more visibility,
but less overall newsgroup traffic.¶
comp.os.ms-windows.apps.word-proc<TAB>Mixed discussion of Windows word
```

```
processors; some overlap with bit.mailserv.word-pc. High volume with less
attention to individual messages, but more overall exposure.¶
```

Next, format those (and any other) lines as Definition List so that they display as the following:

```
bit.mailserv.word-pc
```

The actual display from different Web browsers varies.

```
bit.mailserv.word-pc
```

> Mixed discussion of many word processors, most of which is about Word.
> Low volume, and more manageable than comp.os.ms-windows.apps.word-proc.
> Individual postings get more visibility, but less overall newsgroup
> traffic.

```
comp.os.ms-windows.apps.word-proc
```

> Mixed discussion of Windows word processors; some overlap with
> bit.mailserv.word-pc. High volume with less attention to individual
> messages, but more overall exposure.

Finally, first select the text `bit.mailserv.word-pc` and click on the HyperLink tool. Click on the To URL tab to display the URL page. Type the URL as `news:bit.mailserv.word-pc`. Then click on OK. Repeat the procedure for the other newsgroup. Note that the `news` protocol does not use `//`.

Terminal Access

The Telnet protocol is the oldest method for accessing Internet resources. It provides terminal access to computers connected to the Internet, requiring that you interact either with the UNIX command line, or with UNIX programs. Some searching resources are available only via Telnet. Unlike the other protocols discussed today, using the Telnet protocol requires additional software beyond your Web browser. You also need a Telnet client program, and your Web browser must "know" how to access it. For simplicity, let's assume that the person reading your HTML document has the necessary resources.

Suppose you want to make a link to the CD Connection, shown in Figure 6.9. You might have a line such as the following in your HTML document:

```
Contact the CD Connection.¶
```

To make this into a link, select the text you want to use as the display text (`CD Connection`, for example) and click on the HyperLink tool. In the URL area, type the URL as the following:

```
telnet://cdconnection.com
```

Figure 6.9. *The CD Connection is available via Telnet.*

Mail

One of the less supported protocols—at least among Macintosh and DOS Web browsers—is the Mailto protocol. For Web browsers that support Mailto, if you include a Mailto URL, the response is to provide a form for sending e-mail via the Web browser. Mailto is an excellent way to obtain user feedback. Because some of the most popular Web browsers do not yet support Mailto, however, many Web sites elect to use a form to accomplish a similar purpose (see Chapter 13, "Web Forms and Image Maps"). The difference is that information sent using Mailto ends up in your electronic mailbox, but information sent via forms must be collected from your server in a different way.

To include a Mailto URL, you use this form:

```
matilto:e-mail-address
```

For example, the following URL produces—assuming the browser supports it—a form for sending mail to me, as shown in Figure 6.10 using the OS/2 WebExplorer:

```
mailto:tyson@cpcug.org
```

If I try to build that into a Web page (which I might do to give users a more direct way to contact me), I might include a line such as the following in my HTML document:

```
Send comments to Herb Tyson (tyson@cpcug.org).¶
```

I would then use the text tyson@cpcug.org as the display text for creating a link. For users without mailto browser capabilities, the e-mail address is provided. Users with mailto can e-mail me simply by clicking on the link. To convert this into a link, first select the address, and then click on the HyperLink tool on the Formatting toolbar. When the HyperLink dialog box appears, click on the To URL tab at the top, and fill in the URL as the following:

```
mailto:tyson@cpcug.org
```

Note that—like the news protocol—the mailto URL does not use //. Why? I don't know. It's one of those little inconsistencies that make computing more challenging, I guess.

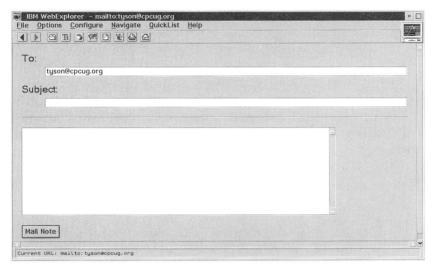

Figure 6.10. *When supported, the Mailto protocol evokes an e-mail form.*

Summary

Today, you learned how to embed a variety of types of links into your HTML documents. You explored how to create links to other parts of the same HTML document, enabling you to create a kind of dynamic table of contents and hot cross-references. You also learned how you can use links to integrate a collection of related HTML documents into a cohesive interactive document and how to create links to URLs, giving your HTML documents the potential for including information from all over the world. Today, you focused on using text and fields as links and references. In the coming days, you learn how to use graphics as clickable links and how to link to graphics, sounds, and videos.

Q&A

Q When using my Web browser, sometimes when I click on a URL, it doesn't work. But, seconds later, it does. Why?

A To connect with a URL, a number of conditions must be met—the name server has to come up with an IP translation of the address specified in the URL, all of the routes to that IP have to be working, and the Web server or other resource has to be available. There are limits to how many users can access the same site at the same time. If you happen to try during a very busy time period, it's possible that the resource simply isn't available. At this point in the technology, Web browsers aren't yet smart enough to include a computerized busy signal that works all the time. Sometimes you get a "busy—try again later" message, but not usually. To me, it's amazing how often it works and how seldom it fails. Remember those times that it doesn't work and try again later.

Q   **I used my Web browser to connect to an FTP site and to look at a directory. When I clicked on a file to download it, however, I got a message that the system was too busy. How could it be too busy if I was able to log on?**

A   Unlike FTP clients, Web browsers don't log on and stay logged on. Each time you issue an instruction to your Web browser, it goes out and quickly gets the requested resource (that is, to display a directory) and logs off. That way, servers don't get clogged by people who keep the connection going even while they're reading a long text file that's already on their own computer. FTP clients, on the other hand, remain logged on until you close the session, or until the host issues a time out (too much idle time). Usually, the result is that Web browsers use resources much more efficiently. Sometimes, however, if you are the 20th connection to a popular FTP server that allows only 20 connections, you might not get a connection when you click on a subdirectory or a file. Although it looks as if you're getting inconsistent messages from the server (there one moment and gone the next), you're not. It's simply the way Web browsers work. If it bothers you (as it does me), you might find that it's more comfortable performing FTP operations using a dedicated FTP client rather than using a Web browser.

Q   **I'm nervous about using so many URLs in my HTML document. Isn't that like plagiarism?**

A   No, it's like roadsigns. You aren't actually including the data from the other URL by using the URL in your HTML document. Instead, you're merely pointing to it. If the owner of the resource doesn't want the resource to be available that way, there won't be Internet resources for reaching it. Pure and simple. Don't be shy about using URLs. Many Web residents are electronic exhibitionists. Not only don't they mind your including their URLs, they thrive on it.

Multimedia on the Web Pages

7

Internal Images

One of the most appealing aspects of the World Wide Web is the fact that you can incorporate images and graphics on the same page. This effectively gives you the capability of publishing full-color magazines, reports, catalogs, and brochures over the Internet. Today, you learn the ins and outs of inline images, including the following basics:

☐ What kinds of images to use

☐ How to incorporate images in your HTML documents

☐ How to control where images appear in your HTML documents

☐ How to provide text equivalents for folks without graphics browsers

☐ How to use images as hot links

☐ When it is appropriate to use images

Image Formats

If you have used a Web browser for any length of time, you might have noticed that there are two ways that images (pictures) typically are presented. The most obvious way is as an *inline* image, where the picture actually appears on the Web page. The less obvious way—and one that you might not have discovered yet—is as separate *external* links that you need to download apart from Web pages. Today, you find out about inline graphics. In Chapter 8, you look at external graphics, along with other external multimedia links—audio and video.

Most of the current browsers can handle either of two image formats:

GIF   CompuServe Graphics Interchange Format (`.gif` extension)

JPEG   Joint Photographic Experts Group (`.jpg` extension)

The GIF format was developed by CompuServe. The goal was to create a file format that displays and transfers quickly and well on a personal computer, and which doesn't consume a lot of disk space. As the word *photographic* implies, the JPEG format was developed by image professionals whose primary goal was to have a relatively efficient (fast and not too huge) image format with excellent display characteristics on a personal computer. The end result is what you might expect. JPEG files are larger (usually) and consequently slower than GIF, but they look better. GIF files are more compact, optimized for electronic downloading, and lack the higher quality of JPEG files, but they usually are faster. More important than marginal differences in speed, however, is the fact that GIF enjoys more universal support for inline images among Web browsers. Although Netscape, the WebExplorer, and InternetWorks Internet Assistant all can display either JPEG or GIF files as inline images, Mosaic (at least the version I tried) cannot. Most Web browsers are capable of working with external viewers for viewing a variety of different graphics formats, so using non-GIF format images for external (linked) graphics isn't essential.

What does this mean for you? Practically speaking, it means that for your inline graphics, you probably should use GIF rather than JPEG. If you have an image-oriented Web presence in which presenting high-quality images is central to your mission, you will serve your clientele better by using GIF files when you need inline images and external links to JPEG images. One compromise is to use thumbnail GIF versions of your graphics as hot links to higher-quality JPEG versions. As long as the GIFs really *are* small (and therefore fast), you can create a very effective Web presentation using that approach.

> **Caution:** For inline images to be used in HTML documents, images stored in the clipboard will not work. As you will learn in Chapter 10, "HTML Documents for Fun and Profit," when converting existing Word documents, images that are stored only in the Word document do not work either. The image must be in a separate file, by itself, to work in an HTML document.

Using Microsoft Imager to Convert and Resize Images

So, what if all you have are TIFF, PCX, BMP, or some other format? Well, then you're out of luck.

Just kidding. Actually, if you are in the U.S. and have a telephone, you're in luck. For about $5.00, Microsoft will send registered users of Microsoft Word a program called Microsoft Imager. Imager is an image manipulation and conversion program for Microsoft Windows. It can be used, among other things, to resize graphics to thumbnail size (for example), as well as to convert images among the following file formats:

TIF	Tagged Image File Format
BMP	Windows BMP
DIB	Windows DIB
PCX	PC Paintbrush
TGA	Targa
GIF	CompuServe Graphics Interchange Format
JPG	Joint Photographic Experts Group (JPEG)
PCD	Kodak PhotoCD (read-only)

Note: Imager can read PCD formats but cannot save in that format. Imager can read and save in each of the other formats.

Suppose you have a JPEG file, for example, that you want to convert to GIF format, because GIF is a preferred format for inline images on the Web. You can use Imager to convert it. Here's how.

First, obtain, install, and open Imager. Now choose File | Open (or click on the Open tool on Imager's toolbar). Using the directory and drive controls, navigate to and select the file you want to convert. For example, suppose you want to convert `lion.jpg`, which comes with Imager. You first open `lion.jpg` for the view shown in Figure 7.1. Next, choose File | Save As, and set the List Files of Type to GIF. Type the name you want to use for the file in the File Name box, and click on OK. That's it!

Figure 7.1. *Microsoft Imager displaying* `lion.jpg`.

Now let's make a few comparisons. Recall that—in effect—there is a tradeoff between GIF and JPEG fields between file size and image quality. Simply put, more data equals higher resolution. Now let's prove half of that argument. First, close the displayed `lion.gif` (Imager displays the new filename, even though the JPEG image is still loaded.) Now use File | Open to open `lion.jpg` and `lion.gif`. First, select `lion.jpg` (click on it), and then choose

View | Zoom, and set the zoom to 800 percent. Now click on `lion.gif` and set its zoom to 800 percent also.

Compare the two views, as shown in Figure 7.2. See how much grainier `lion.gif` is, and how much smoother `lion.jpg` is? That's because the GIF file uses eight bits per pixel, but the JPEG file uses 24. That's the half of the argument I can prove.

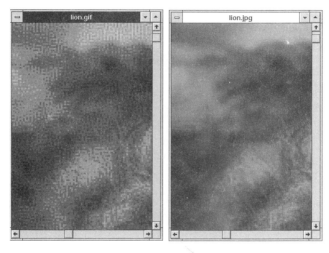

Figure 7.2. *At higher zooms, JPEG images generally are of higher quality than GIF images.*

However, when I compared the resulting file sizes, I discovered that—in addition to being grainier—the GIF files were about 50 percent larger than the JPEG versions. Viewed from the various Web browsers that I tried, the two different versions were indistinguishable in quality (to my eye, anyway) when used as inline HTML graphics.

Another nifty thing you can do with Imager is create thumbnail-sized graphics for use as clickable links to larger versions. I'll get on with how to incorporate inline images in a moment. However, remember that to incorporate them, you have to actually *have* them.

Suppose you want to create a thumbnail-sized version of the painting *Monet's garden in Giverny* (as well as small versions of other paintings) as clickable links for high-quality images of paintings. First, use File | Open in Imager to open the original file. Next—just to be safe—perform an immediate File | Save As to the ultimate filename and type so you don't accidentally save your resized creation over the original. Now, from the menu, choose Image | Resize, for the view shown in Figure 7.3. If you need to keep the height and width in the original proportions, make sure the Allow Distortion option is not selected. If you want to make your image perfectly square, however, and if the height and width are not identical, you need to allow distortion in order to make the image square.

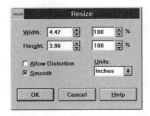

Figure 7.3. *Imager enables you to resize images for use as thumbnail pictures.*

Tip: If you have an existing GIF file that is the size you want to use, open it in Image to see its dimensions. Use View | Summary Info to read the current size. Then use those dimensions as a guide for how large to make your thumbnails. What Image calls one inch actually refers to the full printed size. A one-inch image usually produces a pretty large image in Web browsers. Images of about .4 inches by .4 inches usually work well for thumbnail GIF files.

Set the Units to inches, pixels, or centimeters, whichever you prefer. Use the Width and Height controls to reduce the size to the desired dimensions. Then click on OK. Now choose File | Save to save the image. Remember that you previously used File | Save As to save the file under a different name from the original. If you skipped that step earlier, make sure you use File | Save As *now* and change the name.

How To Obtain Microsoft Imager

In the U.S., call 800-426-9400. Outside the U.S., call your local branch of Microsoft, or try 206-936-8661 to get the telephone number of your nearest Microsoft office. At this time, Microsoft Imager is not available for downloading.

Image File Location

Before you insert the picture, take a minute to think about how your Web server directory is going to be set up. You should organize your working directory structure in Word so that it mirrors the anticipated structure on your Web server. Are all your HTM, GIF, and other files going to be on the same directory? If they are, create a directory or subdirectory and put your existing HTML files (including .DOC files based on HTML.DOT) and any needed image files

there. This saves you work both now and later. It saves work *now* because you won't have to keep navigating the drives and directories controls when opening and saving files. It saves you work *later* because you won't need to modify the directories in your HTM files quite as much. Note that you might still need to change the .htm extensions to .html, depending on your Web server, but at least you won't have to worry about the subdirectory names.

On the other hand, if your server is going to be set up so that your main index.html file (discussed later in this book), .html, and image files are going to be in separate directories, you should organize your file in the same way. Thus, any needed subdirectories can be referred to relative to the current directory, rather than your having to worry about editing the .html files after they've been uploaded to your Web server. There will be much more about this in Chapter 11, "How To Install Your Web Document onto a Web Server." For now, however, it pays to set up your working directories the right way.

Inserting Images

Now that you know where to get images and where to put them, you need to know how to insert them. First, either open an existing Word document (*.doc file, *not* an *.htm file) that's based on the HTML template (HTML.DOT), or create a new HTML document (choose File I New from the menu; select the Html template, and click on OK).

DO / DON'T

DO use the .doc version of a file (based on HTML.DOT) that was used to create an .htm file, whenever it is available. If you have only the .htm file—an .htm file that was not created by Word, or which was, but whose corresponding .doc file is not available—you can edit an .htm version. However, when the .doc version exists, it is preferred.

DON'T use an .htm version when you also have the .doc version. If you use the .htm version, you lose some controls, such as the macro buttons for HTML links.

Now decide where to put the picture. Remember that images discussed today will appear inline with text, so positioning is important. Once you have decided, click on the Picture tool on the HTML.DOT Formatting toolbar to display the dialog box shown in Figure 7.4. If you previously followed my advice, then your image files are stored in the same directory as your HTML document, and should now appear in the list of files under File Name. If they are not displayed, use the List Files of Type, Drives, and Directories controls to display the image file you want to use. Then click on the desired filename so that it is in the File Name box.

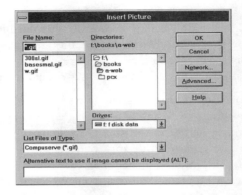

Figure 7.4. *Click on the Picture tool on the* HTML.DOT *Formatting toolbar for the Insert Picture dialog box.*

What, No Preview?

Is something missing? Note that HTML.DOT's Insert Picture dialog box, shown in Figure 7.4, lacks the preview capabilities of Word's regular Insert Picture command, shown in Figure 7.5. That's because the two Insert Picture dialog boxes are based on different commands. If you'd like to preview the pictures to see which one to use, you can open a new document based on NORMAL.DOT and use Word's regular Insert Picture command to preview. Both JPEG and GIF files can be previewed.

Alternatively, you can add Word's original InsertPicture command to your toolbar so that you can use it without having to open a new document. You have to be cautious, however, not to use Word's InsertPicture command in HTML documents. Unlike the HTML.DOT InsertPicture command (actually, MenuHtmlInsIMG in HTML.DOT), Word's own InsertPicture command does not yield the needed <IMG> HTML tag.

With this caveat in mind, you can put Word's own InsertPicture command onto the toolbar as follows:

1. Choose Tools|Customize from the menu, and click on the Toolbar tab.

2. Under Save Changes In, choose html.dot.

3. Under Categories, choose All commands.

4. Under Commands, choose InsertPicture.

5. Using the left mouse button, drag the InsertPicture command to the desired toolbar and drop it into place.

6. In the Custom Button dialog, click on an appropriate icon (the camera icon, for example), or set the Text Button Name to something you like and click on Assign.

7. Click on Close to close the Customize dialog box. As usual, don't forget to save changes to `html.dot` when and if prompted later during the current session.

Having done that, you're now free to use the new InsertPicture command to preview GIF and JPEG images. Remember—once again—that you need to use the `html.dot` Picture tool on the formatting toolbar (or the Insert | Picture command from the menu when a document based on HTML.DOT is displayed) in order to insert an inline image. Use the new tool you just added for preview purposes only!

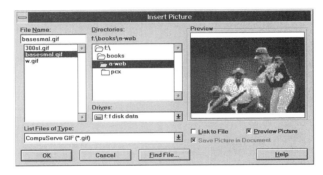

Figure 7.5. *Word's built-in Insert Picture dialog box is different from the one in the Internet Assistant.*

Next, click on the Advanced button for the dialog box shown in Figure 7.6. Notice the text alignment options of top, center, and bottom. By default, the Internet Assistant uses bottom alignment. See Figure 7.7 for a contrast of the results produced by each alignment choice. Choose an alignment that produces the aesthetic result you want. When you've made your choice, click on OK to insert the image.

Note: Regardless of your choice, when viewing the document as a Word document, all will display with bottom alignment. The top, center, or bottom alignment won't display until you view the resulting HTML document using another browser.

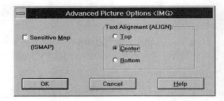

Figure 7.6. *Use the Advanced Picture Options dialog box to set the alignment.*

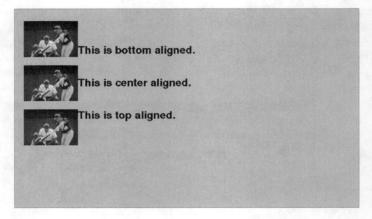

Figure 7.7. *Contrasting the bottom, center, and top alignment of inline images.*

Now let's look under the hood for a moment to see what kind of HTML tag is produced by the Picture tool. After inserting the inline image, click on the Html Hidden ({a}) tool to view the field code that's inserted. The first one (bottom alignment) should appear as follows, with the image itself just after:

```
{ { PRIVATE SRC="basesmal.gif" ALIGN="BOTTOM" } MACROBUTTON HtmlResImg }
```

Once saved in HTML format, this becomes the following (in context):

```
<H3><IMG SRC="basesmal.gif" ALIGN="BOTTOM">This is bottom aligned.
</H3>
```

Note that H3 (Heading 3) is chosen so that the text will appear larger for the screen shot. Even though the image comes within the H3 tagged section, the H3 formatting does not affect the display of the image.

If you look at all three tags for the bottom, center, and top images, you see that the only difference in the three is the words BOTTOM, CENTER, and TOP in the ALIGN= definition. In fact, if you need to use the same image more than once in the same HTML document, you can

copy the first one you insert and reuse it, rather than having to use the Picture tool again. To copy an image for use elsewhere (in the same HTML document or in a different one), click on it so that it is selected. Then press Ctrl+Ins to copy the selected image to the clipboard. Finally, move the insertion point to where you want a copy of the image to appear and press Shift+Ins. You're actually copying the field code and displayed image. If you want to change something about the copy, you can then click on the Html Hidden ({a}) tool to display the underlying field code for editing. For example, you could change the alignment from BOTTOM to CENTER.

Alternatively, if you prefer to edit via a dialog box, you can click first on the image and then on the Picture tool on the HTML.DOT Formatting toolbar. Note that even though the resulting field code is a macro button, you cannot evoke the InsertPicture dialog box by double-clicking on the image (unlike items produced using the HyperLink tool).

Providing Text Alternative to Images

Notice the text box shown at the bottom of the Insert Picture dialog box in Figure 7.4:

```
Alternative text to use if image cannot be displayed (ALT)
```

This is a very important option. When using your Web browser with graphics turned off, have you ever noticed little graphics placeholders, such as those shown in Figure 7.8? Did you ever wonder why those are there?

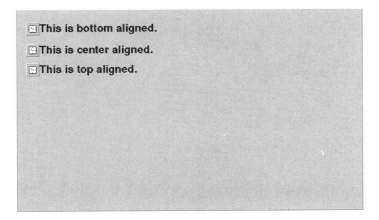

Figure 7.8. *When graphics are turned off, some Web browsers display a placeholder if ALT is not defined.*

They're there because whoever designed the underlying HTML document either did not know about or did not use the ALT option. Figure 7.8 shows what you get when you view Figure 7.7 with graphics turned off, using the WebExplorer. See those weird pictures? Mosaic, Netscape, and other Web browsers have their own cute little space fillers that they use when graphics are turned off. Although it's nice to have a space filler, some intelligent text alternative included by the HTML document's author would be much better.

To use this option when Web publishing with Word, type the alternative text in the Alternative text... text box. Consider, for example, the view shown topmost in Figure 7.9. Here, we're using a stylized *W* (borrowed from Cern, the home of the World Wide Web) to create a dropped cap effect. Cute, huh? However, if images are turned off, it doesn't look so cute, as shown in the middle view. If you include a capital *W* in the Alternative text box, however, you get the replacement effect shown in the bottom of Figure 7.9.

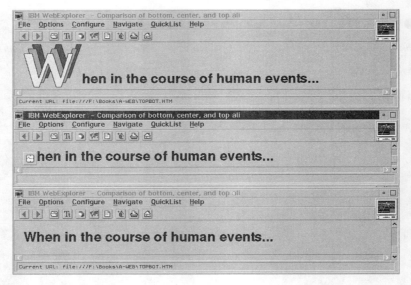

Figure 7.9. *Wise use of the Alternative text (ALT) option makes Web presentations better.*

Making an Image a Hot Link

Hot links? Sounds like some kind of sausage. Put away the cholesterol counters, I'm talking about images that serve as links in your Web pages. In Chapter 6, "Hyperlinks and URLs," you learned how to insert links into your HTML documents. In this lesson, you learned how to insert images. Now you see how to combine the two.

Why might you want to use small images as links rather than text? There are a couple of reasons. For one thing, have you ever heard the saying, "A picture is worth a thousand words?" It might be true—especially because many Web users expect to see some color and flash. If they don't see it, they might not stick around to hear your message, whatever it might be.

Don't go overboard, of course. After all, not everyone has a T1 connection (see the section following this one for a sermon about taking it easy in the graphics art department). However, there is this word called *optimal*. Some use of graphics in Web pages creates an aesthetic essence that makes the Web alluring and attracts attention.

> **Note:** A T1 line is a high-speed communication line for connection to a network such as the Internet.

A good example of the intelligent use of graphics can be found in the Web Museum. Shown in Figure 7.10 is part of the Berthe Morisot exhibit (`http://mistral.enst.fr/louvre/paint/auth/morisot/`). Here, a number of thumbnail versions of paintings are shown. You are invited to click on any that interest you to view a larger, photographic quality version.

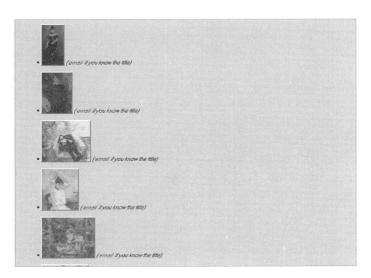

Figure 7.10. *The Berthe Morisot exhibit uses small GIFs to point to larger and higher-resolution pictures*

Another example can be found in the Branch Mall's flower shop. Shown here, in Figure 7.11, is the Hawaiian flower branch (`http://branch.com/hawaii/hawaii.html`). Here, each picture is linked to a dedicated HTML file that describes what you get and provides price and ordering information.

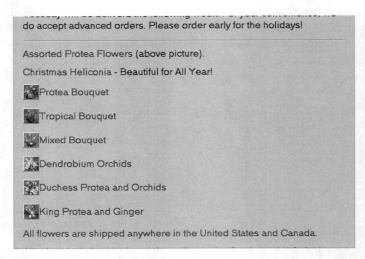

do accept advanced orders. Please order early for the holidays!

Assorted Protea Flowers (above picture).

Christmas Heliconia - Beautiful for All Year!

Protea Bouquet

Tropical Bouquet

Mixed Bouquet

Dendrobium Orchids

Duchess Protea and Orchids

King Protea and Ginger

All flowers are shipped anywhere in the United States and Canada.

Figure 7.11. *Pictures of flowers are linked to HTML documents that contain ordering information.*

Suppose, for example, that you're going to set up a car lot on the Web, and you have GIFs for a variety of automobiles you want to peddle. You might have a series of pages, showing perhaps eight (or so) thumbnail GIFs per page, with each GIF linked to additional information about the specific vehicle.

First, move the GIF to the same directory as the HTML files, or to a subdirectory relative to the directory where the HTML files reside. Unless you want to do some touch-up editing when you put the files onto your Web server, make the subdirectory names the same as they'll be on the Web server. Next, click on the HyperLink tool. Because—for this example—you're going to link to a local HTML file, click on the To Local File tab.

Now click on the Image button for the view shown in Figure 7.4, which is the Insert Picture dialog box. If you followed the suggestion about where to put the GIF file, it should appear in the file list or in a subdirectory immediately below the current directory. Use the Directories control, as needed, to locate the image file and click on it so that its name appears in the File Name text box. Next, in the Alternative text box, type alternative text to display if the image file isn't readable to the Web browser (for example, if the user has graphics turned off or is using a text browser such as Lynx). If you want a particular kind of alignment for the

image—top, center, or bottom—click on the Advanced button to select the alignment type, and then click on OK to return to the Insert Picture dialog box.

Now click on OK to return to the HyperLink dialog box, shown in Figure 7.12. At this point, nothing has been entered into the Text to Display box. You have two options. One is to go with the image and the alternative text alone by leaving the Text to Display box empty. Another option is to fill in the Text to Display area, which makes the *hot region* (the area you click on for results) include both the image and the Text to Display text. The choice is yours. However, some users might not know that the picture is clickable, because it's not underlined and in blue the way the text would be. On the other hand, other users fully expect pictures to be clickable because Web browsers are supposed to be *graphical* user interfaces to the Internet. Another consideration is whether you can conjure up some display text that fits well and that isn't redundant with the Alternative text—ALT, from the Advanced options in the Insert Picture dialog box. (Personally, I'd opt for including Text to Display; but it's *your* HTML page.)

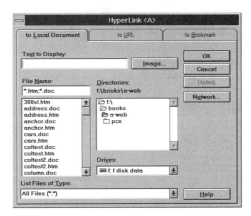

Figure 7.12. *After you choose the image, control returns to the HyperLink dialog box.*

Next, in the HyperLink dialog box, locate and click on the HTML file to which you want to link. You can link to other kinds of files as well, but let's save them for tomorrow when you learn how to include external links. Finally, click on OK to insert the finished link.

▼ Exercise 7.1. Inserting an inline image.

Here's an example with real filenames. Assume that you have a file called `300sl.gif` that you want to link to an HTML document called `300sl.htm`. You're working on a main HTML file called `cars.doc`, which you will later convert to `cars.htm`.

First, move all three files (`300sl.gif`, `300sl.htm`, and `cars.doc`) to the same directory. Next, use File | Open in Word to open `cars.doc`; or, if it doesn't already exist, choose File | New,

set the template to `html.dot`, and click on OK. Now set up the section where you want the link to appear. For example, you might have a Heading 2 header such as this:

`Mercedes-Benz Showroom`

Under that, you might have clickable links for the 1960 300SL, another for 1965, 1970, and so on. For the 300SL, you're going to insert a graphical link to a file called `300sl.htm`. Now move the insertion point to where you want the link to `300sl.htm` to appear, and click on the HyperLink tool on the Formatting toolbar. Click on the To Local File tab, if necessary. In the Text to Display box, type **1960 300SL**. In the File Name list, click on `300sl.htm`. Now click on the Image button. In the list of files, click on `300sl.gif`. Change the List Files of Type setting if necessary, to display only files matching `*.gif`. Click on the Advanced button to choose the alignment type, and make sure that it's on Bottom; then click on OK. In the Alternative text box, type some enticing text to substitute for `300sl.gif` when and if the Web browser doesn't display graphics. Type something like **Vintage 300SL**, if you can stomach the hype (after all, it is called *hype*link). Now click on OK in the Insert Picture dialog box to return to the HyperText dialog box, and click on OK to insert the link.

The link might appear in `cars.doc` as shown in Figure 7.13. In Word, a macro button is inserted, the field code for which is as follows (minus the displayed GIF):

```
{  { PRIVATE HREF="300sl.htm" }MACROBUTTON HtmlResAnchor 1960 300SL}
```

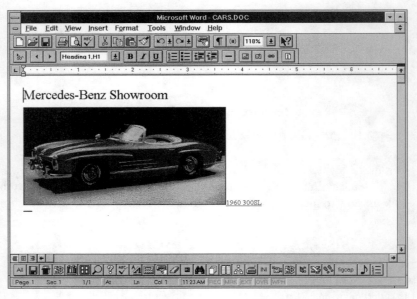

Figure 7.13. *The finished* `cars.doc`, *before saving in HTML format.*

After you save the file in HTML format, this becomes the following:

```
<A HREF="300sl.htm"><IMG SRC="300sl.gif" ALT="Vintage 300SL" ALIGN="BOTTOM">1960
300SL</A>
```

When viewed from WebExplorer, the finished version appears as shown in Figure 7.14. Can you think of any improvements you might make? For example, is the text 1960 300SL large enough? Is the bottom alignment aesthetically appealing?

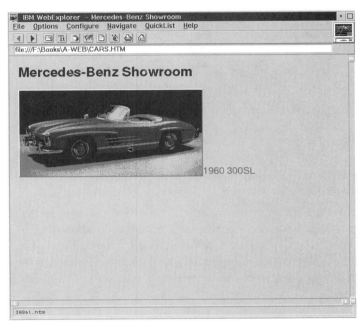

Figure 7.14. *The finished* cars.htm *viewed from WebExplorer.*

Don't Assume Everyone Has a T1 Connection

If you really want to aggravate your Web readership, consider including a number of 100KB+ inline images in your Web pages, with no text alternatives. Fortunately, examples of such creations are getting harder and harder to find. However, consider the Acura NSX home page (http://www.anes.med.umich.edu/NSX/), for example, shown in Figure 7.15. It contains a 75KB GIF file. On my system, with a 19,200-baud connection, it took over 40 seconds for the page to appear. There wasn't an ALT setting, either (see the discussion in the previous

section). If you're cruising the information superhighway, a home page with images that take that long to download might be considered speedbumps. This observation isn't meant to be critical of the effort. It might be a fine home page for Acura enthusiasts. However, a 5KB GIF would've worked just as well, with an option to download a larger GIF if the user wants a closer look.

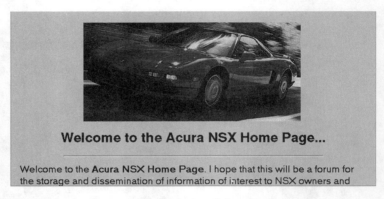

Figure 7.15. *Save heavy-duty graphics for optional downloads.*

As long as the NSX page takes to arrive, it can't hold a candle to the World Wide Web of Sports (`http://tns-www.lcs.mit.edu/cgi-bin/sports`), shown in part in Figure 7.16. This compendium of some two dozen thumbnail GIF files—many weighing in at between 6 and 10KB—took well over a minute at 21,600 baud. It reminds me of some of those megawatt Christmas light displays that seem to take over some neighborhoods during the month of December.

If your home page takes over a minute to download, there are a lot of folks with connections 28,800 baud and slower who won't hang around to see it. Here's a good rule of thumb. Your point of entry to the Web should take—at most—ten seconds to download at 14,400 baud. If it takes longer than that, you're asking too much of your viewing audience. Some users—such as those who connect using the IBM Global Network—might be paying as much as $8 per hour to connect to the Internet. If each Web page cost them a measurable amount of pocket change, they aren't going to browse very long.

Keep in mind something that the example pages cited here seem to have forgotten: the ALT option (alternative text to display when the user has graphics turned off). Numerous Web users now routinely browse with graphics turned off and turn them on selectively. Unless you make use of the ALT option, your message won't get through to many of these users.

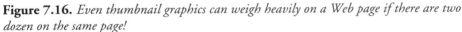

Figure 7.16. *Even thumbnail graphics can weigh heavily on a Web page if there are two dozen on the same page!*

Summary

Today, you learned how to insert inline images into an HTML document and how to align the images for controlling presentation with text. You also explored how to use Microsoft Imager to convert and resize graphics for faster and more effective Web presentations. Finally, you learned to use inline images as hot links, and how to provide text alternatives for people who don't have or don't use the graphical aspect of the Web when browsing.

Q&A

Q Why can't I use my TIF files for inline images?

A Because most Web browsers aren't set up to handle them. Web browsers, for the most part, are geared to presenting GIF, and often JPEG, images on the Web page with text. For handling TIF, BMP, PCX, and other formats, you have to use external images and place your trust in the user's Web browser.

Q   **Is there a limit to how many graphics I can put into an HTML document?**

A   Technically, probably not (except that you might exceed the file handling capabilities of your operating system if you get carried away trying to prove that my having said "probably not" is wrong). However, there are limits of reasonability, based on the patience of people who might read your Web page. I recommend that you not put anything into a point-of-entry home page that takes more than 10 seconds to download at 14,400 bps. Beyond that, however, you can include what you like in links that you include in your HTML document. However, as you'll learn in Chapter 8, you should include some information about the size of the images. Most sites, for example, now show the size of the files next to external image links so that the users know what they're getting. That way, people with T1 lines can download with abandon, and folks with slower connections can "just say no," to borrow a quote.

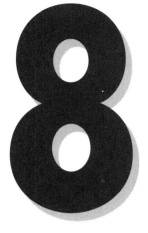

8

External Media—Images, Video, Text, and Sound

8

External Media—Images, Video, Text, and Sound

External media refers to any files that don't display on the Web page. Such files can contain digital audio, images, motion video, and text. There are several advantages to offering external media. For one thing, such files are wholly optional. They don't automatically get downloaded when you view a Web page. For another thing, using external media affords you an opportunity to offer the Web user a variety of ways to experience information.

One way to understand the Web is to think about it as a multimedia encyclopedia. Multimedia encyclopedias, such as Comptons and Encarta, have normal pages that contain text and inline graphics. Beyond that, however, there are links that you can click on to see higher-resolution graphics, hear audio clips, and see video clips. You can do the same thing on the Web.

Consider the White House home page, for example, as shown in Figure 8.1 (`http://www.whitehouse.gov`). The main page includes an image map (more about this on future days) that serves as a jumping-off point for a number of interesting exhibits. If you click on the President's Welcome message, you hear a short audio clip rendered by President William Jefferson Clinton. An audio message from Al Gore is also available. Click on the Tours option (see Figure 8.2). Note the opening screen in the Tours option, which offers three different tours. There is an icon that looks like a speaker with sound coming out of it. That icon causes a download of a 103KB AU file of President Clinton welcoming you to the White House tour. Here, the AU file is "displayed" using an external audio browser. Alternatively, the other icon shows you a written version of the welcome message.

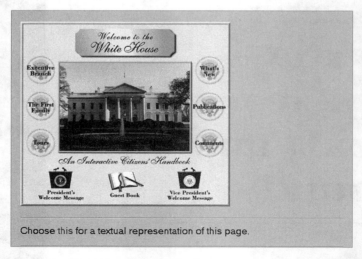

Figure 8.1. *The White House home page is the first page in an online multimedia exploration of the President's home.*

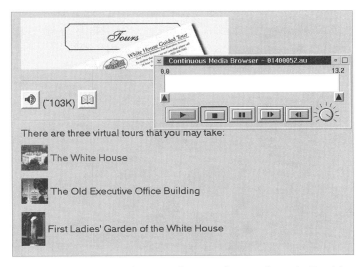

Figure 8.2. *The Tours option provides an audio introduction from the President.*

If you click on the White House tour option, you are led down a path that consists of text and images and which looks very much like an encyclopedic article about the White House (see Figure 8.3). There are a series of thumbnail GIFs, each of which you can click on for a larger and more revealing look into the White House. If you click on the Diplomatic Reception Room, for example, you download a 201KB GIF picture of the room, showing the French furniture, a tall clock, a china cabinet, and a view of the French wallpaper, which contains a panorama of 19th century landscapes titled Views of North America (see Figure 8.4). In this case, the image is displayed using an external image browser rather than as an inline image. Because this image is a GIF, it can also be viewed by most Web browsers. However, some sites contain images in other formats too, so an external image program is required.

Tip: If you don't have a good external image viewer for use with your Web browser, you might consider using Microsoft Imager. Most Web browsers provide setup options that enable you to specify what viewer to use. In Netscape, for example, choose Options | Preferences and choose Helper Applications from the pulldown list at the top of the dialog box. Many of the entries might have ????? rather than the name of a helper application (see Figure 8.5). This means that a viewer has not been specified, and that Netscape itself does

not have viewing capabilities for that particular kind of file. The listing for JPEG files shows that Netscape itself can be used as a viewer. For TIF files, however, an external viewer is needed. Here, the external viewer for TIF files has been set up as Microsoft Imager.

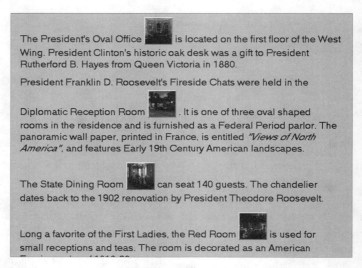

The President's Oval Office is located on the first floor of the West Wing. President Clinton's historic oak desk was a gift to President Rutherford B. Hayes from Queen Victoria in 1880.

President Franklin D. Roosevelt's Fireside Chats were held in the

Diplomatic Reception Room . It is one of three oval shaped rooms in the residence and is furnished as a Federal Period parlor. The panoramic wall paper, printed in France, is entitled *"Views of North America"*, and features Early 19th Century American landscapes.

The State Dining Room can seat 140 guests. The chandelier dates back to the 1902 renovation by President Theodore Roosevelt.

Long a favorite of the First Ladies, the Red Room is used for small receptions and teas. The room is decorated as an American

Figure 8.3. *As you stroll through the White House, a mixture of text and thumbnail GIFs illustrate the White House.*

Figure 8.4. *Detailed GIFs invite you into each public room of the White House.*

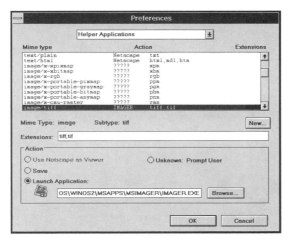

8

Figure 8.5. *Netscape and other Web browsers usually enable you to specify which external applications to use.*

Other Web sites lead you down paths that contain movies. Consider the Meteorology page in the World Wide Web Virtual Library (`http://www.met.fu-berlin.de/DataSources/MetIndex.html`), for example. Note the entry titled `Movies`, shown in Figure 8.6, which is linked to another part of the same document with the anchor name `#movies`.

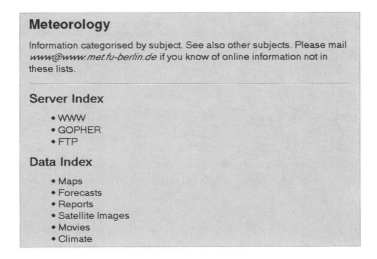

Figure 8.6. *The Meteorology page (`http://www.met.fu-berlin.de/DataSources/MetIndex.html`) even offers weather movies.*

If you click on Movies and follow the trail, you eventually come to the view shown in Figure 8.7, which offers a variety of flicks in MPG format. Movies on the Web usually have two characteristics. They are short and they are gargantuan. If you have a normal dialup connection to the Internet, you probably won't be viewing many of the 1MB+ movies offered there. For most users, the prospect of spending five minutes downloading a 15-second film clip is a bit daunting. However, the capability is there if you need it. More difficult to come by, however, is the capability of *making* the MGP files you'll offer. For that, you need a movie camera and the appropriate software (which are beyond both my budget and the scope of this book).

> • Africa Visible Image (243,693 bytes)
> • Africa Infrared Image (256,030 bytes)
>
> GMS-4 Infrared Items:
> • GMS-4 IR GIF (2,684,068 bytes) or JPEG (500,036 bytes)
> • GMS-4 IR Movie (1,150,932 bytes, ~96 frames)
>
> GMS-4 Visible Items:
> • GMS-4 Colorized Visible Image (65,528 bytes)
> • GMS-4 Visible GIF (598,749 bytes) or JPEG (401,913 bytes)
> • GMS-4 Visible Movie (620,159 bytes, ~96 frames)
>
> WorldWide IR Composite: (updated every 3 hours)
>
> The World-wide Composite is an infrared composite of the GOES, METEOSAT, and GMS satellites remapped into a Mollweide projection.
> • WorldWide IR Composite GIF (121,682 bytes) or JPEG (54,064 bytes)
> • WorldWide IR Composite Movie (734,468 bytes, ~96 frames)

Figure 8.7. *Movies usually are offered in MPG format.*

Why So Much?

So, why does the Web offer so many different kinds of data (images, movies, sounds, and so on)? If you have a telephone dialup connection, you might be wondering that yourself. If you connect at 9,600 or 14,400 bps, MPG might very well stand for *Megabyte download, Parental Guidance suggested.* The fact is, however, that a number of Internet users connect to the Internet using high-speed connections that offer nearly instantaneous access to files of 5MB and 10MB. Such users have no hesitation in viewing movies the way ordinary folks read text files. Although you might find this difficult to believe, within a few short years, you very likely will have similar capabilities at a very low cost.

Another reason is the same reason that advertising moved from printed media to active media. It sells better. If you have an idea to convey or a product to sell, the sights and sounds of your ideas and products do a better job of conveying and selling than words and still pictures alone. If a picture is worth a thousand words, a moving picture is worth a million words.

How?

Multimedia presentations are linked in the same way as HTML files. The number of considerations, however, is greater because you must make your multimedia offerings available in a variety of different formats if they are to be usable by all the members of your target audience. Thus, choosing the right audio or video format is crucial to having your message received.

The question of *how* is also a strategic question. When dealing with vastly varying bandwidths (how much data can flow over a user's connection to the Internet), it's crucial to have an informative Web site that enables users to know what each clickable link involves. You should not have a blind link to a 10MB file! Although some browsers, such as WebExplorer, inform you of the percentage completion as a download proceeds (so that you can get an idea of how much data is yet to come), not all do. Moreover, nobody wants to download a 10MB file they can't use. Thus, if the only format you have available for your movie is a format that is uncommon, information that describes the link should provide that bit of information, as well as where the user might obtain the needed viewer.

Links to External Media Located on Other URLs

You can link to external media located on other URLs (other Web sites not owned by you). However, I would caution against it for several reasons. For one thing, there is no way to guarantee that the resource will be available. For another thing, it's possible to overload other Web sites if many sites decide to "economize" on their own disk space by planting URLs to digital video files located on the other sites. As you will learn later in this book (in Chapter 11, "How To Install Your Web Presentation onto a Web Server"), each Internet site has a specified limit on the number of simultaneous connections. Without such limits, the bandwidth is narrowed so much for each user that the connection becomes unusable.

Note: In date communications, *bandwidth* has come to mean the amount of data that can be transmitted. Higher data-transfer rates result in higher bandwidth. When multiple users share the same connection, the resulting bandwidth for each user is narrower.

Images

The most common type of external media linked to HTML pages is images. There are dozens of image formats. Fortunately, much of the computing world is standardizing on GIF and JPEG images, which means that most Web browsers are able to handle most images these days. In fact, in trying to come up with home pages with examples of different kinds of images, I had some difficulty.

If images are standardizing around GIF and JPEG, why bother with anything else? For one thing, although the technology exists to convert among different image formats, information often is lost in the translation. The GIF and JPEG formats, for example, although appropriate for electronic reproduction of photographs, aren't necessarily the best format for certain drawings. Consider drawing formats such as Micrografx and Corel. There, pictures aren't a cohesive whole. Instead, each picture comprises any number of separate components that—if rendered in the original format—can be easily edited using the appropriate drawing program. A GIF or JPEG rendition of such images ruins much of the utility. After all, some pictures are for more than just viewing.

Image formats encountered on the Web include, but are not limited to, those shown in Table 8.1. If you are not a UNIX user, you might not be familiar with the X formats. They are used in the X Window System, which is a graphical user interface used in several UNIX operating systems. Note that this list is a collection of formats documented, but not automatically supported, in the popular Web browsers.

Table 8.1. Common image formats used on the World Wide Web.

Format	Extension
BMP bitmap format	BMP
Computer Graphics Metafile	CGM
Micrografx Designer/Draw	DRW
AutoCAD Format 2-D	DXF
Encapsulated PostScript	EPS
Fractal Image Format	FIF

Format	Extension
Compuserve GIF	GIF
HP Graphic Language	HGL
IEF Image format	IEF
JPEG Image format	JPG, JPEG
PBM Portable Bitmap	PBM
Kodak Photo CD	PCD
Macintosh PICT	PCT
PC Paintbrush	PCX
PGM Portable Graymap	PGM
Lotus 1-2-3 Graphics	PIC
AutoCAD Plot File	PLT
PNM Portable Anymap	PNM
PGM Portable Pixmap	PPM
RAS Raster format	RAS
RGB Image format	RGB
Targa	TGA
Tagged Image format	TIF
TIFF Image format	TIF, TIFF
Windows metafile	WMF
DrawPerfect	WPG
X-Bitmap Image format	XBIT, XBITMAP
X-Pixmap Image format	XPM
X-Window Dump format	XWD

DO

DON'T

DO include common extensions in the names of files you reference in your HTML document. Without them, many Web browsers can get confused.

DON'T use obscure extensions or omit them entirely. As shown in Figure 8.8, where extensions were not used, the WebExplorer did not know how to view the files. In fact, these files are ordinary GIF files, but the browser had no way of knowing that!

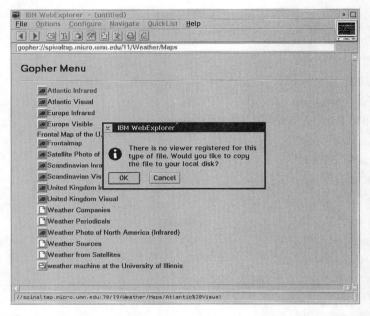

Figure 8.8. *When extensions are missing (filename is* `Atlantic%20Visual`*), the browser doesn't know which viewer to use!*

Even when and if you do a perfectly good job of documenting what formats you use, there is no guarantee that your readership will have the necessary software. However, if your Web page is named something like "Web for UNIX Users," visitors should get the idea that there might be a problem with XWD files. To ensure that as many people as possible will be able to view your external image files, you're still best off using GIF or JPG. However, if your Web page is specifically set up for Micrografx Designer users, it's perfectly okay to link to files in Designer's format.

Here are the general steps to insert an image file:

1. Decide on an appropriate image format (GIF and JPG are the most common).

2. Set up your HTML document and type the text you want to use as your link reference. Make sure you include the size of the file in the text adjacent to the reference.

3. Save the HTML document in Word format to your hard disk so that any links inserted can be relative.

4. Move the image file to the same directory as the HTML document, or to a subdirectory that is relative to that location, in the same relative location the files will reside on your Web server.

5. Select the text you want to use as your display text for activating the link.

6. Use the HyperLink command To Local Document to insert the link.

7. Save the file in HTML format.

To insert a link to an external image file into an HTML file, first copy the image file either to the same directory as your HTML file, or to the same relative subdirectory where it will reside on your Web server. In other words, if you are going to link a file, and it will be on a subdirectory called image on your Web server, create a subdirectory on your own system called images, and copy the image file to that location. For example, if your main Web server directory is the following:

```
homepage
```

and if your images will be on this:

```
homepage/images
```

and your HTML file on this:

```
html
```

create a subdirectory as follows:

```
html\images
```

References in the HTML document are relative. Linked files on `html` will not have a directory included in their tag at all. Files in the `html\images` subdirectory will be linked as being on `images`, which is relative to `html`. When put onto your server, all locations are relative to the location of your main HTML document. Thus, files on `homepage/images` will be seen as being on `images`. Because both images subdirectories are in the same relative location, the links set up will work both on your own computer and on your Web server.

 Caution: Before inserting the link, make sure you save the file as a Word document to the desired directory. This is crucial to making sure that the Internet Assistant does not insert a full path to the link. If a full path gets inserted, the resulting HTML document very likely will not work from Web browsers other than the Internet Assistant.

When linking to one or more external files, you should set up the link so that the user knows exactly what is being linked to, as well as how large the file(s) are. For example, you might set up a structure such as the following for linking to a series of pictures:

```
Photo of a UFO over Arizona (ufoariz.jpg) 127,436
Photo of a UFO over New Mexico (ufonmex.jpg) 211,112
Photo of a UFO being followed by a government jet (ufogov.jpg) 192,032
```

The preceding list might work well either as an Unordered or as a Directory list, as described in Chapter 5, "Tags and Styles." Now select as much of the first line as you want to use as the display text for the first linked image file (Photo of a UFO over Arizona, for example). Then click on the HyperLink tool on the HTML.DOT Formatting toolbar. At the top of the HyperLink dialog box, click on the To Local Document tab for the view shown in Figure 8.9. Note that the selected text appears in the Text to Display box. In the File Name box, type *.jpg, if necessary, to home in on the image files. Then click on the one you want to use. Finally, click on OK to insert the link.

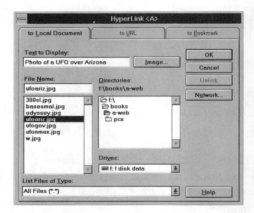

Figure 8.9. *Use the To Local Document option to insert links to external media.*

At this point, the Internet Assistant inserts a macro button field. Click on the Html Hidden ({a}) tool to display the field code, and ensure that a full path (including the disk drive) was not inserted. For example, if the field appears as follows:

```
{  { PRIVATE HREF="LOCAL:f:/books/a-web/ufoariz.jpg" }MACROBUTTON HtmlResAnchor
Photo of a UFO over Arizona}
```

you are likely to have a problem accessing the JPEG file from most Web browsers. If you follow the steps described previously to move the image files either to the same directory or to a directory relative to the main HTML file, *and* if you make sure you save the HTML file to disk as a Word document before inserting the hyperlink, you should not have this problem.

If, despite your best efforts, you do end up with a full path in the field, you should modify the field to remove the part of the URL other than the filename itself or the relative subdirectory—for example:

```
{  { PRIVATE HREF="ufoariz.jpg" }MACROBUTTON HtmlResAnchor Photo of a UFO over
Arizona}
```

or the following:

```
{  { PRIVATE HREF="images/ufoariz.jpg" }MACROBUTTON HtmlResAnchor Photo of a
UFO over Arizona}
```

You might use the latter if the file is on a subdirectory where the HTML file resides, and if that subdirectory is named images.

Repeat the HyperLink procedure for each of the images you want to insert. When you're done, choose File | Save As to save the file in HTML format. These are the resulting HTML tags:

```
<A HREF="ufoariz.jpg">Photo of a UFO over Arizona</A> (ufoariz.jpg) 127,436¶
<P>¶
<A HREF="ufonmex.jpg">Photo of a UFO over New Mexico</A> (ufonmex.jpg) 211,112¶
<P>¶
<A HREF="ufogov.jpg">Photo of a UFO being followed by a government jet</A>
(ufogov.jpg) 192,032¶
<P>¶
```

As discussed in Chapter 7, "Internal Images," you also could use inline images to click on to activate the hyperlinks for your files. Most HTML design gurus tend to discourage making Web pages excessively graphical, however. An image file here and there is okay. However, if you have an HTML file with 20 inline graphics for accessing 20 external graphics, and if each inline image is 10KB, the initial download of the HTML page takes about as long as your largest JPEG file (in this case), making the user wonder about your sense of efficiency (or lack thereof).

Video

Another increasingly popular type of external media to weave into your HTML creations is digital video, sometimes called movies. Although they technically *are* a kind of movie, I personally resist embracing that term wholesale. The problem is that the word "movie," to most people, typically means something lasting about 90 to 120 minutes. There's simply no way that the average 1995 user of the Web is going to have enough bandwidth to endure downloading a full-length feature film! In any event, the use of short (usually well under a minute) digital video clips is increasingly in popularity. As the amount and speed of data increases, you no doubt will see more and more. A particularly useful application is the

multiframe satellite sequences that you see on the nightly weather reports. Somehow, seeing the track of a hurricane or an advancing cold front brings the weather to life. Now, thanks to the magic of the Internet, you can get them on your own computer.

Of course, other uses are starting to creep in. During the writing of this book, for example, Drew Barrymore gave a startling flashdance performance for Dave Letterman's birthday—atop his desk! Within hours, someone had digitized the end of the segment and posted it as an MPG file on the Internet. Although I'm not at all certain about the legality of such postings—it's probably a copyright violation—you can expect more and more of this sort of thing in the coming years. As with images and other materials, however, before you include them in your Web pages, make sure you have a legal right to do so. After all, you don't want to be reading this book in civil court now, do you?

There are a number of digital video formats that are seen on the Web. They include the formats shown in Table 8.2.

Table 8.2. Popular digital video formats used on the Internet.

Format	Extension
MPEG Movie format	MPG
QT/MOV Quicktime	QT, MOV
AVI video format	AVI
AVS video format	AVS
MOVIE SGI movie	SGI

Including an external link to a digital video clip in your Web page requires the identical procedure that you use to include a link to an image file.

1. Decide on an appropriate video format (MPG and MOV appear to be the most popular).

2. Set up your HTML document and type the text you want to use as your link reference. Make sure you include the size of the file in the text adjacent to the reference.

3. Save the HTML document in Word format to your hard disk so that any links inserted can be relative.

4. Move the digital video file to the same directory as the HTML document, or to a subdirectory that is relative to that location, in the same relative location the files will reside on your Web server.

5. Select the text you want to use as your display text for activating the link.

6. Use the HyperLink command To Local Document to insert the link.

7. Save the file in HTML format.

Sound

What would multimedia be without sound? Sound was the first extra capability that led manufacturers to start referring to computers as multimedia systems. Sounds, like images and video clips, use up a lot of disk space and require considerable time to download. A while back, sound bytes from the "Star Trek" television show and movies were making the rounds. Here again, the copyright question comes into play. Before you include a sound file on your Web page, make sure you have the right to use it.

One sound to which you undoubtedly have the right is your own voice. Increasingly, many businesses find it a nice touch to have a welcome message of some kind in the voice of the company president. Recall that the White House home page (www.whitehouse.gov) offers several sound clips of President Clinton, Vice President Gore, and Socks (the cat). Each, by the way, also has an alternative text option that you can click on so you can read the messages rather than listening to them. My personal favorite is the text transcription of Socks' message, shown in Figure 8.10. Popular digital audio formats are listed in Table 8.3.

The First Feline

"Meow. Meow. Meow."

Figure 8.10. *So, what exactly did the cat say?*

Table 8.3. Popular digital audio formats.

Format	Extension
AU and SND audio format	AU
AIF/AIFF/AIFC Audio	AIF
WAV audio format	WAV

To include a sound clip, follow the same general procedure outlined previously:

1. Decide on an appropriate audio format (AU and SND appear to be the most popular—refer to Table 8.3).

2. Set up your HTML document and type the text you want to use as your link reference. Make sure you include the size of the file in the text adjacent to the reference.

3. Save the HTML document in Word format to your hard disk so that any links inserted can be relative.

4. Move the digital audio file to the same directory as the HTML document, or to a subdirectory that is relative to that location, in the same relative location the files will reside on your Web server.

5. Select the text you want to use as your display text for activating the link.

6. Use the HyperLink command To Local Document to insert the link.

7. Save the file in HTML format.

Text, Word, and PostScript Documents

Another kind of external link is to non-HTML documents containing text. At the moment, the most popular format is just plain ASCII. For regular ASCII files, all you need to do is follow the general steps outlined previously, using the extension .TXT (usually) for your text file. All known Web browsers handle text files without hesitation.

It is possible, however, to link to other documents that contain graphics and other formatting. One of the most popular current formats—largely because it is available on both Macintosh and PC platforms—is PostScript. For Web users to use such files, they must have a PostScript viewer of some kind, a number of which are available as shareware. Microsoft is also hoping to make Word's format a popular standard, supported by the recent freeware release of Word Viewer (see `http://www.microsoft.com/pages/deskapps/word/viewer/wordvu.htm`), a windows program that enables users to view and print (but not edit) fully formatted Word documents without having Word on their computers. Yet another emerging format that will come into play is OpenDoc. OpenDoc is a common word-processing format being promoted by most of the major word processing software publishers other than Microsoft. Another format that is popular among OS/2 sites is the INF format, which is a hypertext format used by OS/2's built-in View program. Although apparently not done yet, the Help file formats for Windows, X Window System, Macintosh, and Windows NT also would be good formats for creating attractive hypertext documents.

The advantage of using fully formatted documents is tremendous. This makes possible the instantaneous distribution of fully illustrated manuals that are always current and up to date. Using hypertext formats further enhances the utility of such documentation. Although

formatted text appears not to be getting nearly as much attention as pictures, videos, and audio, it very likely is much more important. It conveys a considerable amount of information, using disk space and download time very efficiently. I expect it to grow in perceived importance when the novelty of multimedia starts to fade.

To link to any external document, the procedure is identical to those used for other types of external media, although there are some additional considerations. One consideration—because formatting beyond plain ASCII has not been standardized in any way—is to include information in the text adjacent to the link about the needed software. For example, if you include Word documents as external links, it helps to include text describing Word Viewer, what software is needed (Windows and OLE version 2 or later), and where to find it. Better still, you can include a link to the URL where the user can download Word Viewer.

8

Another consideration is to provide an ASCII version of the file for users who don't particularly need to see a fully formatted version with graphics. There is little that is more frustrating than to have the answer to a problem in a file and not to be able to read that file.

Suppose, for example, that this book and others were online. The link to them might appear as the following:

```
Teach Yourself Web Publishing with Word    Word Format    PostScript Format
ASCII Format
Navigating the Internet with OS/2 Warp    Word Format    PostScript Format
ASCII Format
Your OS/2 Warp Consultant    Word Format    PostScript Format    ASCII
Format
For Word format, you must have Microsoft Word 6 or later, or Word Viewer.
```

In this example, each highlighted item in the first three lines becomes the display text for linking to the corresponding version of each document. In the fourth line, the word Word Viewer is used as a link to the URL for obtaining that program (`http://www.microsoft.com/pages/deskapps/word/viewer/wordvu.htm`).

Summary

Today, you learned how to create links to external media—text, pictures, audio, and video. You also explored some useful tools, such as Microsoft Imager and Word Viewer, that help you create your presentation and help others view them. You also learned a number of considerations that need to be kept in mind when setting up your links, such as the location of linked files relative to the main HTML file, and how to provide text alternatives (where appropriate) to some types of external media.

Q&A

Q When I clicked on a link to a JPEG file in Netscape, I got the message `Unable to Locate File`. Why?

A That usually happens when either too much or not enough information was included in the anchor reference. Open the Word version of the HTML file and click on the Html Hidden ({a}) tool to see the contents of the URL reference. Very often, it will contain a directory reference such as `LOCAL:f:/html/images/300sl.gif`. That URL form is not recognized by most browsers. You should instead reduce the directory information to just how much is needed relative to the location of the HTML file that contains the links. If the HTML file is on `f:\html`, and the image is on `f:\html\images`, make the reference to the file `images/300sl.gif`.

Q Is there a way to make my home page hit the ground running with a digital video and audio presentation?

A No, there is no way to force the playing of external media when a home page is summoned. Even if there were, I would not tell you how to do it—because it's a bad idea. There is simply no way to guarantee that the user has the resources or the bandwidth to use or appreciate your external media. All external media should be optional. If you ever download a 5MB movie file, just to discover that you cannot view it, you will quickly understand why such files should be strictly a user's choice.

DAY

5

Creating Web Documents that Work for You

9

Writing and Designing Web Pages: Ins and Outs

By now, you should know how to create an HTML presentation for posting on the World Wide Web. Some additional topics—such as creating an image map and using forms—still remain, which you'll learn about in Chapter 13, "Web Forms and Image Maps." Today, you focus on writing and designing Web pages in this chapter and in Chapter 10, "HTML Documents for Fun and Profit." You might find the word *design* a curious choice. However, depending on your goal, design is the perfect word for what you need to do.

Remember Your Goal

Have you ever immersed yourself in a project, only to get bogged down or overwhelmed? Or, have you ever gone off on a tangent, leaving your original task in the dust? Have you ever gotten sidetracked by a difficult chore, completely abandoning your main goal? Worse, have you ever finished something, looked at it, and then wondered why it doesn't work? All these are common problems faced by Web page designers (a term that I prefer over Web "authors").

You should always keep your goal in mind. Recall from Chapter 2, "The Basic Plan," that the most common goals for Web pages are the following:

- ☐ Advertising
- ☐ Providing information
- ☐ Public relations and building corporate image
- ☐ Collecting information and feedback
- ☐ Providing product and technical support
- ☐ Education

There are other goals that you probably should have in mind as you evaluate your finished Web presentation. Your Web presence should be noticeable (attention-getting in a nice sort of way), manageable (something the user can handle and navigate easily, regardless of connect speed), and useful (or entertaining, depending on the type of Web page). Because the Web is a competitive media (that is, numerous sites vie for attention), if you have a message to get across, you're going to have to grab your readers' attention quickly and try to hold onto it long enough for them to get the message.

Why? According to sources at the 1995 Internet World show, approximately 5,000,000 home pages had been created as of April, 1995. Here's the scary part: according to the same sources, this number is doubling every 57 days. Assuming that the five-million mark was reached on April 15, a quick projection shows that in late 1996, the number of people with World Wide Web home pages will exceed the number of people on the planet. From this, shown in Table 9.1, we can deduce one of two things. Either the rate of doubling will have to slow down, or the World Wide Web will have to expand to include other planets, thereby becoming the UWW (Universe Wide Web)!

Table 9.1. A projection of the number of World Wide Web home pages.

Date	Home Pages
April 18, 1995	5,000,000
June 14, 1995	10,000,000
August 10, 1995	20,000,000
October 6, 1995	40,000,000
December 2, 1995	80,000,000
January 28, 1996	160,000,000
March 25, 1996	320,000,000
May 21, 1996	640,000,000
July 17, 1996	1,280,000,000
September 12, 1996	2,560,000,000
November 8, 1996	5,120,000,000
January 4, 1997	10,240,000,000

Seriously, even if it isn't growing exponentially, it is growing quickly. From a practical standpoint, this means that your chances of being anything more than a face in a big crowd are diminishing daily. I point this out because, in an effort to gain and keep the attention of a Web user, there is a tendency to lose sight of the goal. In this section, let's take a closer look at the major goals and appropriate ways to make them noticeable, manageable, and useful (or entertaining, depending on the goal).

Choose an Informative Web Page Title

The best way to get attention is to have a title that states the nature of the information clearly. By *title*, I mean both the title that gets seen on the title bar in graphical Web browsers (which also gets seen by Web search programs) as well as the top heading on your Web page. Consider Web pages that provide information. The following are some examples of ineffective titles for information pages:

```
The Microsoft Home Page
Zapdoodle Fudge
The Plant Page
```

Why are these ineffective? They are ineffective because they don't really tell you what kind of information you will find. The first one just says that it's a Microsoft home page. That doesn't tell you what you'll find there. Heck, there isn't even any way to tell that this is an information site rather than an advertising site. Instead, something like the following might better tell the user what to expect:

```
Tips on Using Microsoft Products
Microsoft Product Recall Information
Using Microsoft Products to Build an Information Server
```

Zapdoodle Page is a curiosity, but it's ineffective for the same reason as the Microsoft home page. It doesn't tell you what kind of information you'll find. Moreover, if you're searching for a specific type of information on the Web, just how likely is it that your search specification will include any part of the word Zapdoodle? Instead, try something like the following:

```
Zapdoodle--How to Interpret Weird Drawings or Doodles
Zapdoodle--Soup Recipes Using Noodles
Zapdoodle--How to Combat Addiction to Cheese Doodles
```

Similarly, The Plant Page doesn't tell the potential reader anything. If you see the title embedded in a listing of URLs and titles, would you be intrigued? You have no way of knowing just what type of information to expect. Instead, you should use something more informative, such as the following:

```
Plants for a Greener Planet--How to Grow Anything Anywhere
Diagnosing Plant Diseases and Problems
How to Recognize Corporate Plants or Spies
```

Now let's take a look at some real titles from the World Wide Web. Consider the titles shown in Figure 9.1, which is a listing from the World Wide Yellow Pages (`http://www.yellow.com/cgi-bin/SearchWWYP?idxName=short`). Do you see a problem with the names? Do any of them leap out at you? Just one? Is it AMETHYST GALLERIES- the First Internet Rock Shop!? You won't see its home page here. However, you'll find it interesting. Set your Web browser to `http://mineral.galleries.com/mg_wwyp.htm`.

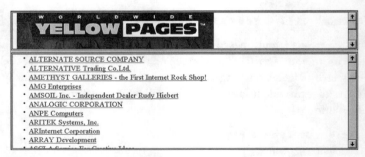

Figure 9.1. *What's in a name? Everything!*

One problem—and yes, it really is a problem—is that many businesses believe that their names alone are sufficient titles for their Web presence. Unfortunately, although your business name might be well respected and might be a perfectly fine business name, it's usually not going to be a sufficient title. I say *usually* because there probably are some businesses whose names are sufficient attention grabbers, such as a fish shop in the Boston area called *The Age of Aquarium* or a restaurant in South Carolina named *Drunken Jack's*.

However, a company named ALTERNATE SOURCE COMPANY needs something more. A quick look at its URL (`http://mfginfo.com/mfg/altsource/alternate.htm`) tells you what it is (see Figure 9.2). You also learn that it needs an effective title (REPLACEMENT PUMP PARTS FOR INDUSTRY). A quick look at the title bar—which shows the URL instead of a title—reveals that this Web page is untitled. The inside title works just fine. However, it would work even better as a formal HTML title so that you can see a little about the business before you click on the URL. Without an effective title that's visible in the link, however, most users won't even click on the company name.

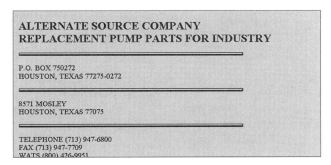

Figure 9.2. *Untitled Web pages are not a good way to attract attention.*

How about AMSOIL, Inc. - Independent dealer Rudy Hiebert? Would you guess that it sells car care products? A look at AMSOIL's home page (`http://www.xmission.com/~gastown/amsoil/`) reveals the same title that you see in the WWYP listing. The following title might get more attention:

AMSOIL, Inc.--Car care products that work!

Let's take a look at one more: ARITEK Systems, Inc. Care to guess what ARITEK does? They make, among other things, a Windows-based toolkit for developing CAD (Computer Assisted Design) applications. Looking into its Web site (`http://www.paladin.com/aritek/aritek.html/`), shown in Figure 9.3, you can tell that it has a message (even though some of

its pages are too image-intensive for the average user). If ARITEK wants to be noticed by the right people, it might consider changing its format HTML document title to something like this:

```
ARITEK Systems--Computer Assisted Design Tools
```

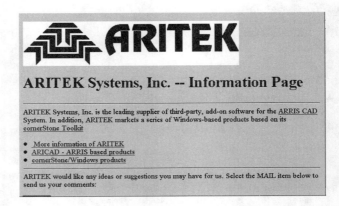

Figure 9.3. *You should include more than your business name in the title page.*

Coming up with a good title isn't really very difficult. All it takes is knowing how titles are used and how many users base their browsing decisions on title alone. Usually, it's just a matter of taking the heading from the home page or a key phrase from a business card and including it in the HTML document title.

Choose Manageable Formats

A second major consideration is manageability. Some Web pages overdo it with images and graphics. Others bunch text together so much that you have difficulty finding what you're looking for. For example, the Shopping2000 home page (`http://shopping2000.com/`), shown in Figure 9.4, contains a clutter of store names, all bunched up so that they're difficult to sort out. The probable intention was to present information together so you wouldn't have to scroll the screen to get to it. One alternative might be to present such as list as a table. Although not as compact as the listing shown in Figure 9.4, the listing shown in Figure 9.5 is a bit easier to sort out.

Figure 9.4. *Don't pack text together so tightly that it's difficult to read.*

9

800-FLOWERS	800-GIFTHOUSE	800-TREKKER	Allstate Motor Club
Ambrosia	Arthur Thompson	Artistic Greetings	ArtRock Gallery
Authorized Electronics	Barnes & Noble Direct	Best Care	Beverly Hills Motoring
California Best	Chef's Catalog	Color Me Natural	Current
Discovery Networks	Doneckers	GEnie	The Gift Attic
Golden Gate-Rebecca Raggs	Hand in Hand	Hanes, L'eggs, Bali, Playtex	Harry and David
Homestyles	JCPenney	Just My Size	Lens Express
Marshall Field's	MD Electronics	Museum of Fine Arts	National Wildlife
NordicTrack	NorthStyle	Pecans plain & fancy	Pet Warehouse
Plymouth Neon	REI	The Right Start	Ross Simons
San Francisco Music Box	Sears HealthCare	Sears Tools	Teleflora
Thoroughbred Racing	Tower Records	UpperDeck	Venamy Orchids, Inc.
World Book			

Figure 9.5. *Try to use tables or bulleted lists to organize data more clearly.*

Even so, the designers of the page shown in Figure 9.4 were on the right track about one thing: trying to get the Web page to fit on a single screen. Having to scroll through multiple screens makes it more difficult to get a clear idea of all that is available, as well as where to find it.

Another possibility for this site might have been to organize the different establishment by types of stores, using links to later points in the same document, table-of-contents style. Many real malls organize store directories by function. For example, the following categories might work, with `Potpourri` being used as a catchall for everything else:

- ☐ Electronic and Computers
- ☐ Clothing
- ☐ Recording (CD, Tapes, and Records)
- ☐ Department Stores
- ☐ Household and Hardware
- ☐ Books
- ☐ Food and Restaurants
- ☐ Potpourri (Pets, Flowers, and more)

Headings could appear below each store, perhaps using another bulleted list, along with a brief description of the store. As it is, you have to click on the individual store to find out what's inside. However, the Electronic item might be something like this:

Authorized Electronics	Complete home entertainment
Discovery Networks	Computer networking for large and small offices
MD Electronics	Electronic supplies for electronic professionals
GEnie	G.E.'s dialup computer network

Actually, I don't have the foggiest idea whether or not these labels really apply. Regardless, there certainly is *some* descriptive text that describes these establishments. The idea is to present the information in some organized way that helps users key in on their particular needs or interests. By organizing the HTML document hierarchically, users can see at a glance what the mall has to offer (categories) as well as what's in each category. By keeping users in the same HTML document until they know which stores to visit, they are spared the agony of having to visit multiple URLs.

Include Useful or Entertaining Information

A third challenge is to make the Web presence engaging, either by being truly useful or—barring that—entertaining. Finding a way to accomplish this goal without overusing graphics is indeed a challenge, but it can be done. Recall from Chapter 2 how sites such as

Macmillan Computer Publishing and CBS manage to gain the reader's attention by including contests and access to popular features (such as Dave Letterman's Top Ten lists).

Remember Your Audience

Audience might seem like an odd word to bandy about in talking about computers. However, with the World Wide Web now in so many homes, it's useful to think about the Web readership as an audience. It's also increasingly important to consider what audience you would like to reach, as well as how to reach it. Part of this, to be sure, includes how to publicize your Web presence by leaving electronic flyers and electronic business cards in places frequented by your target audience or clientele. See Chapter 12, "Publicizing Your Web Presence," for more about publicity.

When designing an HTML page itself, you should include items of interest to the target audience. For example, if you are creating an information site for C programmers, you might include things such as FTP-accessible sites for source code and program libraries, the URLs for related programming magazines and journals, if they exist, and links to related newsgroups that discuss programming topics. If you are creating an advertising site for a line of automobiles, you might include a database of articles about the cars, links to car club sites, links to automobile-related newsgroups, or even an image library of new and vintage models.

To summarize, it's really quite easy to make a Web site useful or entertaining (or both). Despite that, most Web pages you encounter are lackluster and boring. It's as if the parties that placed the items on the Web had a Web presence alone as the goal. That should never be a goal. If it is your only goal, or appears to be so, your home page won't get visited very often, and most certainly won't get picked up in any of those "Interesting Web Pages" displays that you see as you surf the Net.

Knowing When To Link

Links to external URLs can be underdone or overdone. Sometimes they are appropriate, and sometimes not. There are several valid reasons for inserting links into your HTML documents:

☐ *Reference.* Some Web pages are collections of URLs only, such as the World Wide Web Virtual Library (`http://info.cern.ch/hypertext/DataSources/bySubject/Overview.html`), shown in Figure 9.6.

☐ *Access to Related Resources.* This access is often used in Web pages as points of reference for users, as shown in Figure 9.7.

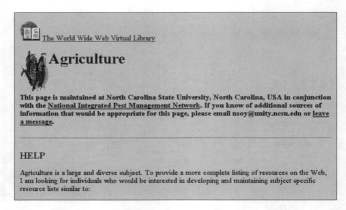

Figure 9.6. *The World Wide Web Virtual Library: Subject listing.*

- North Carolina Cooperative Extension
- Center for Integrated Pest Management

Table of Contents

- Managing the Home, Garden, and Yard
- Agricultural Integrated Pest Management and Crop Production Information
- Professional Urban Integrated Pest Management
- Directory of National and Regional Servers and Participating Institutions

What's New

The National server for the National IPM Network is now on-line, thanks to Mike Spencer and USDA/CSREES.
Have you seen the developing Florida Agricultural Information Retrieval System (FAIRS). Also look over our Mosaic version of the EPA "Worker Protection Standard for Agricultural Pesticides - How To Comply" and other safety documents
Just for fun... butterfly pictures.

Figure 9.7. *It's common for subject-oriented Web sites to point to related sites.*

☐ *Avoiding Plagiarism.* Sometimes, even though something on another URL is relevant and fits well into your plan, you link to the URL rather than copying wholesale. This effectively gives credit to the other site while still making the resource readily available.

☐ *Organization.* Sometimes, even though you, or your company, *own* all the resources mentioned in your links, you link to different areas to reduce clutter. It also can help if different personnel or departments maintain the different pages (for example, Sales, Product Support, Customer Feedback, Public Service Programs, and so forth). IBM—with its large international structure—uses this kind of organization in many of its Web pages, as shown in Figure 9.8.

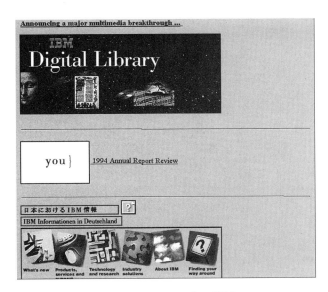

Figure 9.8. *IBM's home page points to numerous other URLs.*

There also are some ways and reasons *not* to link. For example, you should never link to a URL owned by someone else without acknowledging the owner of the link in your HTML document. You should also make an effort to annotate links that have special considerations. For example, if a link contains a 20MB digital video clip, the text next to the link should say so. If the link contains a document that works only for users with particular software (such as X Window System or Microsoft Word, and so forth), the text should say so.

Although it probably goes without saying, you should avoid links to offensive URLs—such as pictures of decaying bodies—without explicit text stating what the viewer is about to see. Free choice works only when the user knows what the choices are and the consequences of the next click. You should also avoid linking directly to very large directory listings in FTP sites. For example, Microsoft's MSLFILES subdirectory contains thousands of files and consumes tons of FTP server time and resources if you try to view it on-screen. An introductory message admonishes you not to display the directory (see Figure 9.9). Some Web browsers and FTP client programs can't handle directories over a certain size. That might mean that you get just files starting with *a* through *k*. If you want a file that starts with *w*, you've wasted your time and everyone else's. Provide a link to a key index file that contains the names and descriptions of the files and directories on the server, and get users to download the lists instead. That way, they'll be able to provide the filename for FTPing, rather than having to deal with the directory online.

```
The files are located in the MSLFILES directory (one directory below).

Please do not do a 'DIR' in that directory as it contains a great number
of files, and will take several minutes to display. The INDEX.TXT file
mentioned above lists all of the files, and is kept in synch with the
contents of the MSLFILES directory automatically.

The MSL files are either text files, zipped files (pkzip v1.1) or
self-extracting files and can *only* be obtained by their Filename
and not by their Snumber.
All Mac files are converted to BinHex format (.HQX)

=======================================================

To toggle change directory (cd) messaging on and off
        enter the following:

        ftp> quote site ckm

To toggle the directory display style from DOS (dir)
        to UNIX (ls -l) enter the following:

        ftp> quote site dirstyle
```

Figure 9.9. *Microsoft's FTP directory is too large to display.*

The Twelve Rules for Good Web Presentation Design

Depending on where you go and what you read, you get a lot of Web design advice. The following sections give you more.

Always Include a Descriptive Title

Recall that "title" means the format HTML title that you insert using the Title tool on the HTML.DOT formatting toolbar or using File | HTML Document Info from the menu. The title is not visible within the HTML document itself. The lack of visibility sometimes lulls HTML authors into thinking it doesn't matter. However, on the Web, the HTML title is seen *before* the HTML document itself. In the great Web directory in the sky, your title is listed.

So, use the title tag. However, use it well. Don't just include your business name. Add a few words to make the title say something about what you do. If the name of your business is *The Strip Joint*, then the title The Strip Joint--Nobody Under 18 Allowed says something entirely different from The Strip Joint--Antique Furniture Refinishing.

Don't Tweak Your HTML Documents for a Particular Browser

When you load your HTML document into a browser, it's very tempting to go back and fine-tune it so it looks better. What plays well on one browser, however, doesn't necessarily play well on the others. Although it is true that the most popular browser in use today appears to be Netscape, it is by no means the only one. That's one of the reasons many of the screenshots in this book were taken from the WebExplorer, Mosaic, InternetWorks Internet Assistant, and from Word itself.

Use Logical Formatting

When given a choice between using the Emphasis and Italic attributes, choose Emphasis instead. When you have some text that you want to emphasize, what's more important, achieving italics or getting the text to stand out? Not every browser can display italics. In fact, some browsers simply ignore tags they don't understand. Worse, a few even include text such as `Unrecognized formatting command ignored` just to prove that it knows something is there, but it doesn't know what. See the discussion of logical and physical formatting in Chapter 5, "Tags and Styles," for additional information.

Sign and Date Your HTML Documents

Anonymity doesn't play very well on the Web. Web surfers want to know the source. If you've done an especially good job, a reader might want to shake your electronic hand and congratulate you. If the International World Wide Web Page Design Committee wants to award you top prize, it needs your e-mail address so it can wire you your $1,000,000 award! If a Fortune 500 company wants to hire you to move all its advertising accounts to the Web, based on your Web page design, you certainly want it to know who you are.

So, use the address tag to make sure they know. It's a nice touch to use the address tag as a Mailto link so the reader can send you immediate feedback. You want to get comments such as `Nice webbery, dude, I've added you to my cool sites list`, and `We're gonna sue your pants off!` as soon as possible.

Another important tidbit to include in your HTML documents is the date. The Web is fluid. It changes daily. One problem I encounter in writing a book like this is that URLs keep changing, along with the information in HTML documents. It makes it exceedingly difficult to proofread URLs to see whether they are what I typed. I can't tell the difference between a typo and a site that's simply moved on or moved out.

I once spent a fair chunk of change downloading what purported to be the latest update for a major piece of software. Imagine my surprise to discover that the "latest update" was actually older than what I already had. Then I went back to the Web page from which I had done the download, and discovered that the authors had indeed included a date at the bottom of their HTML file next to their e-mail address: `Last Updated December 2, 1993`. Whoops! Of course, I should have looked at the date *before* doing the download. Since then, I've learned to look, and I'm constantly surprised at how often dates are missing.

Provide Text Alternatives to Images

An image map is of no use to a user without a graphical Web browser. You should use text alternatives in two ways. First, near the top of your HTML document, you need something like the following:

`We also have a `**`text version`**` of this Web page.`

Second, any time you have an inline image, you should use the alternative text option. Although a picture might be worth a thousand words, a blank picture is positively mum. "Unmum" it by including a text alternative.

Keep Your Home Page Under 10 Seconds at 14.4Kbps

Nobody wants to spend a minute downloading images just to find out that they're in the wrong location. Keep your entry point to the Web sweet, short, and simple. If you *must* use lengthy HTML documents, include local links to them and be sure to list the file type and total file size so that the user knows what to expect. Total file size means the sum of the number of bytes in the HTML document plus all the inline images. Something like the following would be especially appropriate for heavy-duty links:

```
Stroll through the streets of Paris (JPG file, 118K)
Take a gondola ride through Venice (JPG file, 238K)
Sample tapas in Madrid (MPG file, 522K)
Smell the sewers in (fill in name of your least favorite city) (MPG file, 1.1M)
```

The HTML document that contains these links, however, should itself load in under 10 seconds when using a 14.4Kbps modem connection.

Put Your Links into Context

Avoid using out-of-context text merely for creating links. Screen space on a Web page is scarce real estate and shouldn't be squandered. If you want to include a link to a definition, then don't do this:

Firewalls are important for some computer sites. Click **here** for a Firewall definition.¶

Instead, do this:

Firewalls are important for some computer sites.¶

Keep Heading Levels Small, Logical, and Consistent

Choose heading sizes that are economical in terms of space used, and appropriate for the presentation. If, for example, you have an HTML document that has to be scrolled a number of times, you should take a look at your heading levels, working from the bottom up. If you use only three different heading levels, you might consider using levels 4, 5, and 6, rather than levels 1, 2, and 3. As shown in Figure 9.10, depending on the browser, the 4, 5, and 6 headings use a lot less space while still having the impact of headings.

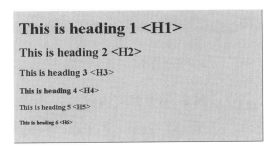

Figure 9.10. *Use lower level headings (4, 5, and 6) to economize on display space.*

You should also use levels that are consistent. For example, don't follow a Heading 3 with a Heading 5. Use Heading 4, instead. Some browsers are set to show a lot of contrast between different levels. Additionally, you should use parallel heading levels. If you have a Heading 1 followed by a Heading 3, and later use a Heading 2 that's logically parallel to the Heading 3 level, you will confuse your readers. For example, consider the following:

```
<H1>Books
<H2>Computer Books
<H3>Macintosh Books
<H4>Windows Books
<H3>OS/2 Books
<H4>UNIX Books
<H3>Nature Books
<H3>Photography Books
```

In this list, it appears that Windows Books are a subheading under Macintosh books, UNIX is an OS/2 subheading, and Nature and Photography books are Computer book subheadings. Use heading levels to indicate and reinforce the logical levels:

```
<H1>Books
<H2>Computer Books
<H3>Macintosh Books
<H3>Windows Books
<H3>OS/2 Books
<H3>UNIX Books
<H2>Nature Books
<H2>Photography Books
```

Don't Use Heading Levels for Body Text

As HTML becomes increasingly standardized, you can count on logical formatting—such as heading or body—to be treated in a logical way. You will do yourself and your Web readers a favor by not using HTML style tags for inapplicable text. It's not uncommon to see someone using an `<H5>` level heading tag for body text so that it will stand out. Instead, use a `<STRONG>` tag. Don't use body text with `<STRONG>` for headings, either. You'll get better and more consistent treatment by Web browsers if you use the styles for their intended purposes.

Always Include a Trailing Slash (/) on URLs that Point to Directories or Sites

Have you ever browsed the Web and suddenly come upon a local (local to the server) link that didn't work? Your Web browser might say something like `The Nameserver gave us garbage` followed by the name of the URL. The problem often is an inappropriate specification of a preceding link. When specifying a link to a directory or to a site, it's important to use a trailing slash (/) at the end of the URL so that any embedded local links are referenced correctly. Although some servers are smart enough to figure out the problem, not all are. That's sometimes why you see the lack of a trailing slash causing a problem sometimes, but not at others (on different servers). Of course, it's also possible that the server might be busy.

For example, in referring to Microsoft's FTP server, use the following:

```
ftp://ftp.microsoft.com/
```

Don't use this:

```
ftp://ftp.microsoft.com
```

Use a Universal Format that Works on All Browsers

Sometimes, something that looks fine on one browser doesn't look fine on others. A chief problem is what some browsers do with tags they don't recognize. They either ignore them, or worse, they include error messages on the screen. From a practical standpoint, this means that you should find the best common format that works on all browsers, instead of a format that displays wonderfully on Netscape, but poorly on other browsers. This might mean *not* using the <CENTER> tag, because support for it is not universal. It might also mean warning users that a Mailto URL might not work, or that forms might not work, and providing alternative instructions.

Beta-Test Your HTML Presentation

You might not have thought about it this way before, but an HTML document is really a high-level computer program. It's a set of instructions that are interpreted and followed by Web browsers. As with other computer software, you cannot just assume that your HTML will work well for everyone else just because it works well for you. Therefore, you should beta-test your HTML documents. You do so by creating a directory structure and a set of files that simulate how your HTML collection—including any links—works on a Web server. Working with your system administrator, you can probably set up your Web presentation on a LAN.

Once you do post your Web presentation on the Internet, you would do well to have others check it out before you start advertising its presence. You might deliberately post it with a cryptic URL until it's been thoroughly debugged. What kinds of problems might you encounter? Well, you might find that some URLs you link to don't work after 6 p.m. in Melbourne, Australia. You might find that some FTP sites are virtually unreachable during certain hours of the day. Either finding might lead you to list alternative links or to include a note in your HTML document about the times of availability. You might discover that a newsgroup you believed was universal isn't carried by most other news servers. That might lead you to include a different newsgroup, or to find a different solution (for example, maintaining a database of articles from the newsgroup so that others can see the messages even if they aren't connected to your server).

Summary

Today, you learned some of the major DOS and DON'TS of HTML document design. Much of it's common sense, but it never hurts to reinforce common sense a little. Another major DO, implicit in this discussion, is to browse the Web yourself, using something like the World Wide Yellow Pages, Yahoo, or the World Wide Web Virtual Library as a jumping-off point. Look at hundreds of home pages and you will develop a good sense of what works and what doesn't.

Q&A

Q **Doesn't using the Internet Assistant for Word implicitly mean that my Web pages will be optimized for the Internet Assistant?**

A No. The Internet Assistant is based on a very strict implementation of HTML level 2.0. Using the Internet Assistant for Word means that your documents will be strictly HTML level-2.0-compliant. How well your HTML documents are optimized for various browsers depends on how well or how strictly those browsers stick to HTML version 2.

Q **I've written some URL links, and the title from the HTML document isn't necessarily what gets used for the link's title. It's up to the HTML author. Why do you emphasize titles so much?**

A It's true that it's up to the author. However, if you use the Internet Assistant for Word's Copy HyperLink feature, the title will indeed be copied. Moreover, when writing HTML documents, where do you think HTML authors look to see how to describe a link? They look at the title page. It's to their advantage to use the descriptive title to make their own HTML documents more useful. So, although there is no guarantee that they'll use it, you can be sure that if you *don't* have a title, there is an absolute guarantee that they *won't* use a title of your choosing.

10

HTML Documents for Fun and Profit

Until now, you've learned about most of the pieces that go into a Web page. You have also explored a number of design considerations. Today, you learn how to convert an existing Word document into an HTML document. You step through the creation of different types of Web presentations, such as résumés, catalogs, product support, and an online manual or report. To create such documents, you can start from scratch or you can use an existing Word document. When you use an existing Word document, there are several kinds of formatting that don't have an HTML equivalent in html.dot and which must be modified or eliminated to work.

Converting a Word Document into an HTML Document

As you've probably guessed by now, converting Word documents into HTML documents is mostly a matter of choosing the correct formats and saving them as an HTML document. Some types of formatting, however, do not survive the conversion. In other cases, you need to use the preformatted option to gain better control. Unfortunately, when you do that, you lose the capability of using proportional spacing. For the most part, however, the HTML conversion is direct and practically automatic.

First, the bad news. Table 10.1 shows the kinds of Word formatting that do not have any HTML equivalent—either in HTML itself or in the Internet Assistant. This does not mean that you cannot accomplish the same effects through other means, but Word's built-in features won't take care of matters for you in the same way that Word's Heading styles automatically take care of headings. In addition, although you can convert existing Word tables, the end result might not be to your liking. That's because tables are reformatted using the <PRE> tag, which displays only in monospace on most Web browsers.

Table 10.1. Formatting that is not preserved when converting a Word document into HTML format.

Formatting	Effect When Saved as an HTML Document
Annotations	Completely removed from document.
Borders and shading	Removed, except for top and bottom lines, which use <HR>.
Centering	The <CENTER> tag is supported by some browsers and can be inserted manually with the Insert I HTML Markup command; text using Word's center attribute is not converted automatically.
Drawing elements	Completely removed from document.

Formatting	Effect When Saved as an HTML Document
Embedded objects	Completely removed from document.
Field codes	Usually, the field result is preserved but the field code itself is not. For example, the field {DATE} is converted into the displayed date and loses any capability of being updated in the HTML document. Field codes such as GoToButtons are not preserved or converted.
Footnotes and endnotes	Notes and reference marks are completely removed.
Frames around graphics and text	Frames are used for exact positioning in normal Word documents; they have no effect in HTML documents.
Headers and footers	Completely removed from document, including page numbers.
Indented paragraphs	All paragraph indentation (for example, set using the ruler or using the paragraph dialog box) is ignored. You usually can achieve indentation by using one of the HTML list formats, but the display of the effect is controlled entirely by which browser is used.
Index entries	Completely removed from document.
Justification	Ignored.
Page breaks and section breaks	Completely removed from document.
Paragraph spacing using the before and after options	Ignored.
Revision marks	Revisions are processed as if they have been accepted (deletions are removed and insertions are kept).
Newspaper (snaking) columns	Ignored, except for lists formatted using the <DIR> tag, which displays as snaking columns in some browsers; doesn't work for paragraph text other than lists, however.
Tables	Converted to <PRE>.
Tabs	Ignored, except in text formatted in <PRE> and <DL> tag areas.
Table of contents entries	Completely removed from document (although an unlinked table of contents will be preserved).

10

As a practical matter, what does all this mean? It means that if you rely on any of the formatting shown in Table 10.1 for a document you want to convert to HTML, you have to make other arrangements. In other words: do it yourself.

The following are the general steps for converting an existing Word document into an HTML document:

1. Open the document you want to convert and immediately choose File | Save As and give the working document a new name (for example, CONVERT.DOC). This preserves the existing document.

2. From the menu, choose File | Templates and click on the Attach button. If necessary, navigate to the directory where HTML.DOT resides and click on it so that it's highlighted in the File Name area. Click on OK to return to the previous dialog box (Templates and Add-ins). Next, ensure that the Automatically Update Document Styles option is selected and click on OK.

3. Next, from the menu, choose Tools | Options and click on the View tab. Use the mouse to set the Style Area Width to about one inch (large enough to display styles), and then click on OK. A style bar should now appear along the left edge of the document, as shown in Figure 10.1.

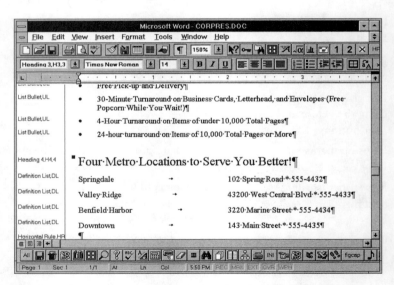

Figure 10.1. *The style area shows you the paragraph styles along the left margin.*

4. Compare the styles being used (as shown in the style area on the left) with the style names shown in Table 10.2. Any that are different must be changed to some equivalent style from `html.dot`. For example, if you use style names such as HA, HB, HC, and so on for headings, you change them to Heading 1 through Heading 6, as appropriate. Format any numbered lists to use the `List number,OL` style, and so on. Table 10.2 provides applications for the various styles listed.

5. Examine any other text that needs to be changed, making sure to convert any internal cross-references to the appropriate type of link, applying the appropriate list styles, and so forth.

6. Save the document in Word format using File | Save (as `CONVERT.DOC`, for example).

7. Choose File | Save As and save the file in HTML format (as `CONVERT.HTM`, for example).

8. Close the HTML document in Word (because some Web browsers won't enable you to open it if Word already has it open), and open it using several different Web browsers to see how it "plays." Make sure that it looks and works the way you want it to work (for example, test the links). Take notes about anything that needs to be fixed or changed, and then close the HTML document (Word might not be able to save over the `.HTM` file if it's still open).

9. Using Word, open the document you saved in step 6 (`CONVERT.DOC`) and fix anything you noted in step 8.

10. Repeat steps 6–9 until the document looks good in all the different browsers you have on hand. Keep in mind that you have at least two browsers by virtue of having the Internet Assistant: InternetWorks Internet Assistant and Word itself, both of which exhibit some display differences.

Table 10.2. Styles used in `html.dot` for converting from Word to HTML.

Style	Use	Type
Address	Use for formatting addresses, especially the address of the author of the HTML document, usually at the very end of the document.	Paragraph
Blockquote	Use for formatting whole paragraph quotes.	Paragraph
CITE	Use for formatting book titles and so forth within a paragraph.	Character
CODE	Use for formatting programming code within a paragraph.	Character

continues

221

Table 10.2. continued

Style	Use	Type
Definition,DFN	Use for formatting the definition part of a definition list (automatically applied when you use the DL or DL COMPACT style).	Character
Definition Compact,DL COMPACT	Use for formatting a definition list (supposed to consume less horizontal space in Word than plain DL; the effect varies across different browsers).	Paragraph
Definition List,DL	Use for formatting a definition list.	Paragraph
Definition Term,DT	Use for formatting the terms in a definition list (automatically applied when using DL or DL COMPACT style).	Character
Directory,DIR	Use for formatting a listing similar to what you get in DOS when you use DIR /W and the items are shown in columns across the screen (implementation varies by browser).	Paragraph
Emphasis,EM	Use for emphasizing text, usually results in italics.	Character
Heading 1,H1	Top heading level.	Paragraph
Heading 2,H2	Second heading level.	Paragraph
Heading 3,H3	Third heading level.	Paragraph
Heading 4,H4	Fourth heading level.	Paragraph
Heading 5,H5	Fifth heading level.	Paragraph
Heading 6,H6	Sixth heading level.	Paragraph
Horizontal Rule,HR	Creates a heavy horizontal dividing line in the HTML document.	Paragraph
Hypertext,A	Use for formatting links and hyperlink references (automatically applied when you use the HyperLink or Bookmark tools).	Character
Keyboard,KBD	Use for formatting text within a paragraph to indicate what a user should type. Usually displayed in monotype.	Character
List Bullet,UL	Use for formatting a bulleted list.	Paragraph
List Number,OL	Use for formatting a numbered list.	Paragraph

Style	Use	Type
Menu	Use for formatting a menu of selectable items.	Paragraph
Normal,P	Use for formatting everything not otherwise covered. Text is usually proportionally spaced, except in text-only browsers.	Paragraph
PRE WIDE	Identical to PRE in the Internet Assistant implementation.	Paragraph
Preformatted, PRE	Formats text as monospace and observes all vertical and horizontal spacing inserted by the user.	Paragraph
RestartList	Use to separate distinct lists.	Paragraph
Sample,SAMP	Use for emphasizing special or example text.	Character
Strikethrough, STRIKE	Use to indicate text that has been deleted or proposed for deletion.	Character
Strong,STRONG	Use as logical formatting for bold.	Character
Typewriter,TT	Use to indicate text typed manually, usually displayed in monospace. Often used to indicate text displayed on a terminal.	Character
Variable,VAR	Use to indicate that the text is a variable to be replaced by the user with an actual value. For example, type dir x: /s to display all subdirectories on drive x.	Character
z-Bottom of Form	Automatically inserted by the converter.	Paragraph
z-HTML Tag	Automatically inserted by the converter.	Character
z-Top of Form	Automatically inserted by the converter.	Paragraph

Converting Cross-References

Some features that make sense in a Word document might not make sense in an HTML document. For example, not included in Table 10.2 is cross-references. If you bookmark an area on a page, and then use Insert | Cross-reference to insert a reference to the corresponding page somewhere else (See page 27, for example), the cross-reference is preserved when the document is exported, and the page number is converted into a hard number rather than a floating reference. What's *not* converted, however, is any header or footer that might tell you

what or where page 27 is. So, you might have to change your referral strategy for cross-references to make sense in an HTML document. In this case, rather than saying `See page 27`, you insert a bookmark on page 27 and then include a link to that bookmark everywhere you want to refer to it:

```
Next, we'll look at the digestive system of worms. Worm reproduction will be
discussed later.
```

If readers are really interested in worm reproduction, they can click on the link to go directly to it.

This kind of construction is similar to the GoToButton field. Unfortunately, GoToButtons are not converted into links when a document is converted into HTML. You need to find them and convert them manually. You can do this by finding the location in the text where the GoToButton is located, and then using the HyperLink tool to replace the GoToButton with a hyperlink.

Note: Usually, when you select the text that you want to display for a hyperlink, that text is automatically placed into the display text fill-in area in the HyperLink dialog box. When the selected text is a field, however (such as the GoToButton field), the selected text is *not* put into the display text area. You need to type the text directly. However, select the GoToButton field anyway. That way, at least Word automatically deletes the (no-longer-needed) GoToButton field when the hyperlink is inserted.

Converting Annotations, Footnotes, and Endnotes

As indicated in Table 10.1, annotations are not preserved when converting a Word document to HTML. Furthermore, given the way annotations are implemented in Word (appearing at the end of the document when printed, like endnotes, rather than in context), you might not want that format duplicated in your HTML document anyway. If you have annotations, footnotes, or endnotes, you need to convert them to some other kind of text if you want them to display in your HTML documents. Although footnotes might seem like an expendable luxury to some users, they are neither expendable nor a luxury when trying to present technical and scientific reports online.

Virtually every approach is tedious. One approach is to save the entire document as a text-with-formatting document. Then import it into an HTML document and use the PRE (preformatted) option. Any footnotes, annotations, or references are shown as they appear

in the text document. Of course, you lose the capability of displaying the file in a proportional font, as well as the autowrap capabilities of many browsers. However, it is one approach.

Another approach is to convert each footnote, annotation, or endnote separately by copying to the Clipboard and then pasting back into the document body. A third approach is to use only endnotes and to enclose the references in square brackets—[2] refers to note 2. You can then laboriously link each note reference to the note at the end of the HTML document, using the HyperLink to Bookmark option. The advantage of this approach is that all end-notes, annotations, and footnotes can be viewed at one time by choosing View | Footnotes or View | Annotations from the menu.

To copy all endnotes to the end of your document, choose View | Footnotes to display the footnote area, as shown in Figure 10.2. Whoops! The View | Footnotes command is missing from your menu? You can temporarily change the template back to Normal.dot when you need commands that are missing from the html.dot menu. To do that, choose File | Templates. If the Automatically Update Document Styles option is enabled, click to disable it. Then click on Attach, select Normal.dot, click on OK, and then click on OK again to close the Templates and Add-ins dialog box.

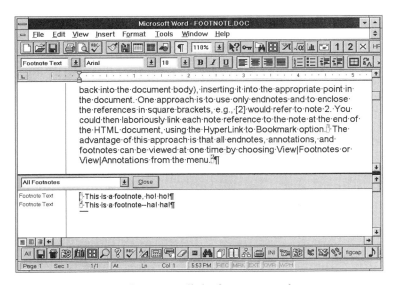

Figure 10.2. *The footnote area shows you all the footnotes together.*

Now, choose View | Footnotes from the menu for the view shown in Figure 10.3. Use the pulldown list at the top of the footnote pane to select All Footnotes or All Endnotes, as appropriate. Press Ctrl+A to select everything in the footnote area, and press Ctrl+Ins to copy them all to the Clipboard. Click on the Close button to close the footnote pane. Finally, click

in the document where you want the notes to appear and press Shift+Ins to paste the contents of the Clipboard. Don't forget to switch back to `html.dot` when you're done!

Figure 10.3. *Use the pulldown list to choose what kinds of notes to display.*

 Tip: When converting numbered footnotes or endnotes for an HTML document, start at the end and work your way backward. Otherwise, the subsequent notes are renumbered each time you delete a note reference.

Next, replace each footnote reference mark (superscripted numbers, in most cases) with bracketed replacements, such as [1], [2], and so on. Then find the superscripted reference marks in the body of the document and replace those with bracketed references. You can use Edit | GoTo and the Footnote option to find the references in the text. (Footnotes are necessary sometimes, but this seems like an awful lot of work!)

 Tip: Rather than go through all this, merely put the document online in several formatted versions (for example, Word and PostScript) and let them download. They then can use Word or WordView for Word files, or they can use a PostScript reader for the PostScript version. See Chapter 8, "External Media—Images, Video, Text, and Sound," for more about this alternative.

Converting or Creating a Table of Contents

Table 10.1 shows—among other things—that table of contents entries are eliminated from the document upon export to HTML. This does not mean that you can't have a table of contents. However, it does mean that you can and should have a different strategy. Here's one approach.

Use Word's table of contents feature (Insert | Index and Tables) to set up and generate your table of contents. If you use Heading # styles, you don't have to insert any table of contents entries. For example, suppose you want to convert today's lesson into an HTML document, and you want to put all the headings up front as a hyperlink table of contents. Here are the steps:

1. Move the insertion point to where you want the table of contents to appear; do this by clicking the mouse at the new insertion point.
2. From the menu, choose Insert | Index and Tables and click on the Table of Contents tab for the view shown in Figure 10.4.

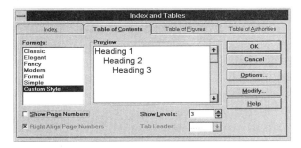

Figure 10.4. *Use Word's Table of Contents feature to create a list of links for the top of your HTML document.*

10

3. Click to remove the Show Page Numbers option.
4. Click on Custom Style and then click on Options to display the Table of Contents Options dialog box shown in Figure 10.5.

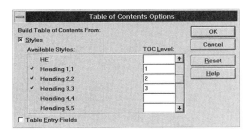

Figure 10.5. *Use the Table of Contents Options dialog box to indicate which levels to include.*

5. Use the TOC Level scrollbar to scroll down to the level 1 option, which should show that Heading 1 is going to be used for level 1, Heading 2 for level 2, and Heading 3 for level 3. Remove the TOC level number that appears for each level you do not want to appear in the table of contents. Assign the highest logical level (lowest number) you want to appear in the table of contents to the corresponding TOC level numbers. For example, if you want to show only Heading 3 and Heading 4 levels, make sure a 3 appears next to Heading 3 and a 4 appears next to Heading 4, as shown in Figure 10.5. Click on OK to return to the main Index and Tables dialog box.

6. Click on OK to insert the TOC field, which displays as a table of contents.

7. Move the insertion point anywhere inside the table of contents and press Ctrl+Shift+F9 to convert the table of contents into text. (The Ctrl+Shift+F9 keystroke executes the Unlink Fields command, which has nothing to do with hyperlinks.) Until you do this, the table of contents really is just a field. If you plan to edit the heading levels further, don't perform this step until all headings have been finalized. Once your headings structure has been finalized, you can update the table of contents by moving the insertion point into it and pressing the F9 (UpdateFields) key. Then you can press Ctrl+Shift+F9 when you're ready to convert the table of contents into hard text (as opposed to a field code).

8. At this point, each of the heading levels has been assigned the styles toc1, toc2, and so on. Select the table of contents and assign an HTML style appropriate for the table of contents. An unordered list, for example, might be attractive, so you might consider applying the List Bullet,UL style.

You can now proceed to link each item on this list of headings with each corresponding heading in the body of the document, using the Bookmark and HyperLink to Bookmark technique described in Chapter 6, "Hyperlinks and URLs." This effectively gives you a hyperlink-style table of contents without your having to gather the headings manually.

Note: You have to create the table of contents before attaching html.dot to your document, because the table of contents features are not in the html.dot menu. Of course, you can modify the menu, make assignments to the toolbar or make key assignments, or use Tool | Macros and run the Word commands directly. However, those options are even more tedious than temporarily switching the template (File | Templates, Attach) to normal.dot and then back to html.dot when you're done.

Example 1: Corporate Résumé or Display Ad

One common use for World Wide Web home pages is to display a corporate résumé. A corporate résumé basically tells the following:

☐ What the company does (including work samples, if relevant)

☐ Who the company's clients are (corporations, end users, accounting professionals, and so forth, including references, perhaps)

☐ Where the company is located

☐ How the company can be reached (including a form or a Mailto link, perhaps)

You can, of course, embellish these areas to include as much information as you deem appropriate. A good place to start is with the World Wide Yellow Pages, which contains links to a number of company home pages, many of which are really online corporate résumés. You will find some really good (and not-so-good) examples.

If you already have a corporate résumé, you can convert it using the guidelines presented earlier today. Use this section as a guide for how to format and what to include. Otherwise, you can build a corporate résumé from scratch. Consider the corporate résumé of The Smith Company, a full-service stationer, whose home page is shown in Figure 10.6. The style area is turned on in the figure so that you can see what went into this particular page. The same page is shown using Netscape in Figure 10.7.

Notice that some of the items in the bulleted list—Letterhead, Résumés, Business Cards, Invitations, Annual Reports, Brochures, and Newsletters—are shown as links. Each of these is linked to a medium-sized GIF that shows samples of that item. The e-mail address at the bottom is a Mailto link, inserted using the HyperLink tool. The URL was specified as
`mailto:printing@smith.com`.

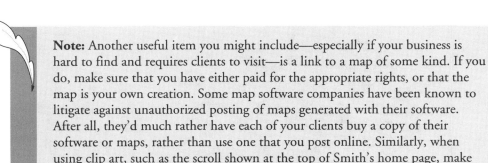

Note: Another useful item you might include—especially if your business is hard to find and requires clients to visit—is a link to a map of some kind. If you do, make sure that you have either paid for the appropriate rights, or that the map is your own creation. Some map software companies have been known to litigate against unauthorized posting of maps generated with their software. After all, they'd much rather have each of your clients buy a copy of their software or maps, rather than use one that you post online. Similarly, when using clip art, such as the scroll shown at the top of Smith's home page, make sure you aren't violating anyone's copyright or trademark. You usually can tell by looking at the software agreement that came with the clip art.

10

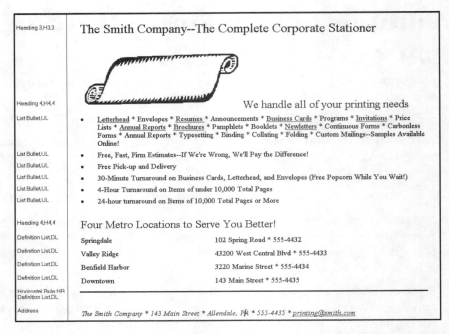

Figure 10.6. *The style area shows what Word styles were used to create The Smith Company's corporate résumé.*

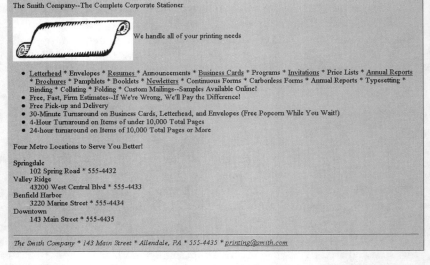

Figure 10.7. *On the Web, a corporate résumé might look like a yellow pages display advertisement.*

Example 2: Employment Résumé

An emerging use for home pages on the Web is as a vehicle for telling the world about yourself. Many use this as an opportunity to tell about their interests rather than their professional aspirations. Soon legions of résumés will appear on the Web, perhaps with some central coordinating organization (similar to the World Wide Yellow Pages, for example, but for individuals) that indexes résumés by subject, geography, and qualifications. When all this happens, you most certainly will want to be prepared.

Figure 10.8 shows the basic outline of a business résumé (using Word in outline mode). Although the contents of this particular résumé aren't recommended for anyone to follow, the general outline is pretty good. Another area frequently included in résumés is a list of references. The usual advisable practice is to write `Available upon request`. That way, you can tailor the references to the specific employer. You can—if your potential references are agreeable and online—include your references as Mailto URLs. That way, the employer can send a note to them. Alternatively, if you have written letters of reference, you can link to them.

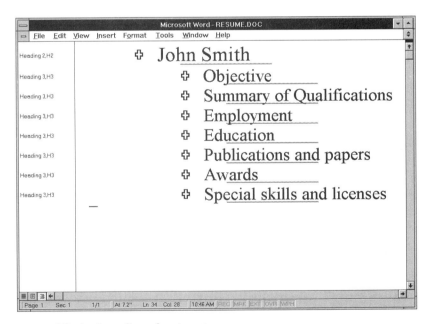

Figure 10.8. *The basic outline of a résumé.*

Figure 10.9 shows the finished document in Word format, with the paragraph styles off to the left in the style area. What you can't see is the fact that the word `except` in the Objective paragraph is formatted with the `Emphasis` character style. Other formatting of interest here

231

is the fact that to conserve vertical space, Normal,P style was used for each of the employment date periods and educational degrees. Many browsers add vertical spacing when you use the heading tags. Although use of headings as headings is usually recommended in HTML style guides, résumé style guides tell you to keep the résumé down to a page. When two style guides conflict, something's gotta give! The Strong style was applied to make the items stand out, and the CITE style was used for each of the citations under Publications and Reports.

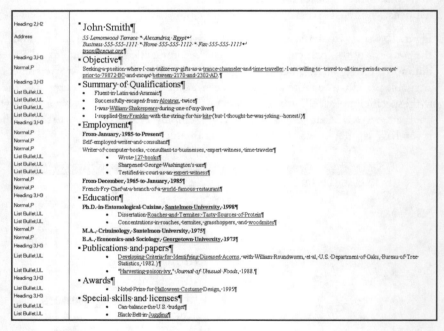

Figure 10.9. *A finished résumé in Word format.*

Figure 10.10 shows the finished document as viewed from a Web browser. One possible problem is the different treatment of HTML tags by different browsers. InternetWorks Internet Assistant was used to produce the figure because it's the only browser I have that enables you to split the view of a single Web page so that you can see the entire page. In its default configuration, however, heading levels were not set up to display in bold. This feature is entirely under the control of the browser. This emphasizes just how difficult it is to control the exact way in which your HTML ultimately is viewed by the public. You can play the odds and try to make it look good for Netscape, of course. However, by doing that, you run the risk of having it not look very good on whatever browser a prospective employer is using. As pointed out in Chapter 9, "Writing and Designing Web Pages: Ins and Outs," it pays to try your Web presentation on as many browsers as you can find, and find a happy medium that works acceptably on all of them.

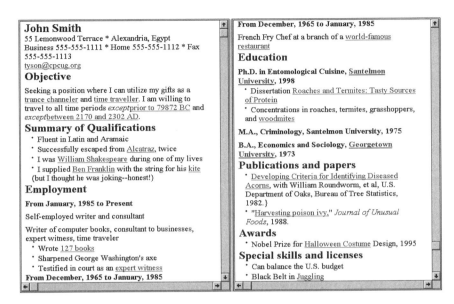

John Smith
55 Lemonwood Terrace * Alexandria, Egypt
Business 555-555-1111 * Home 555-555-1112 * Fax
555-555-1113
tyson@cpcug.org
Objective

Seeking a position where I can utilize my gifts as a
trance channeler and time traveller. I am willing to
travel to all time periods *except*prior to 79872 BC and
*except*between 2170 and 2302 AD.
Summary of Qualifications
   * Fluent in Latin and Aramaic
   * Successfully escaped from Alcatraz, twice
   * I was William Shakespeare during one of my lives
   * I supplied Ben Franklin with the string for his kite
     (but I thought he was joking--honest!)
Employment

From January, 1985 to Present

Self-employed writer and consultant

Writer of computer books, consultant to businesses,
expert witness, time traveler
   * Wrote 127 books
   * Sharpened George Washington's axe
   * Testified in court as an expert witness
From December, 1965 to January, 1985

From December, 1965 to January, 1985

French Fry Chef at a branch of a world-famous
restaurant
Education

**Ph.D. in Entomological Cuisine, Santelmon
University, 1998**
   * Dissertation Roaches and Termites: Tasty Sources
     of Protein
   * Concentrations in roaches, termites, grasshoppers,
     and woodmites

M.A., Criminology, Santelmon University, 1975

**B.A., Economics and Sociology, Georgetown
University, 1973**
Publications and papers
   * Developing Criteria for Identifying Diseased
     Acorns, with William Roundworm, et al, U.S.
     Department of Oaks, Bureau of Tree Statistics,
     1982.}
   * "Harvesting poison ivy," *Journal of Unusual
     Foods*, 1988.
Awards
   * Nobel Prize for Halloween Costume Design, 1995
Special skills and licenses
   * Can balance the U.S. budget
   * Black Belt in Juggling

Figure 10.10. *A finished résumé as seen on the Web.*

Note: This résumé used a formal HTML title: John Smith—Entomology,
writing, and the occult. Because the name of InternetWorks Internet Assistant is so long, however, the last part of the word *occult* is clipped off. Although
you want to choose an effective title, you don't want it to be so long that it gets
shortened.

Having a résumé online as a Web page gives you some interesting opportunities that you
don't usually have on paper. As mentioned before, rule number one is to keep the first page
of the résumé short. Résumé services also point out that most folks seeking qualified job
applicants scan (not *read*) the résumé for relevant key words. If you don't have the key words,
your résumé probably won't get past first base. If you have a lengthy résumé, the only ones
finding it useful might be the people at the paper recycling factory.

Rule number two is to make the first page of the résumé shout out the relevant qualifications.
With an online résumé, however, you can link up to optional information and pages that also
might be of interest, assuming you get to first base. For example, in the résumé shown in
Figure 10.10, links are included to items such as a complete list of books written by the subject

of the résumé, complete texts of reports and dissertations, and other items potentially of interest to the reader. Under the list of books, if you're really enterprising, you can include GIFs of the front cover and sample chapters. In this résumé, there are also links to GIFs (a picture of woodmites, a juggler, and so on), and relevant URLs (to universities where you got your degrees) can be included as well. (If you do a good enough job, someone might hire you as a Web page designer!)

Two other items to note are the title of the HTML document and the location of the address. Normally, addresses on HTML documents come at the end. In this case, because of the traditional structure of résumés, the address—including the e-mail address—was included nearer the beginning. A date is missing also, so that you don't announce to prospective employers just how *long* you've been looking for a job. You can, of course, put these items at the end of the document, as is customary with HTML documents. The problem, however, is to try to balance résumé customs against HTML customs. When it comes to job search, err on the side of résumé customs.

Example 3: Online Catalog

Honest Herb's Electronics and Photo is one of those places that advertises in the camera magazines. Perhaps you've seen similar ads in the *New York Times*. Honest Herb wants a Web presence, and has decided to create an online catalog. So, he revs up Word and cranks out the catalog shown in Figure 10.11.

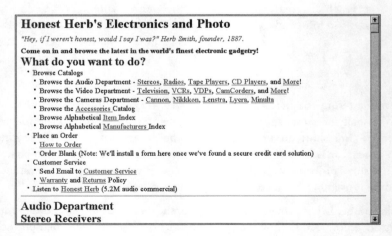

Figure 10.11. *Don't trust this guy even though his catalog looks pretty good.*

Creating and maintaining an online catalog is one of the best but most labor-intensive marketing applications for the World Wide Web. It's especially useful because of the multimedia aspects. Not only can you include bright and colorful pictures of the items you want to sell, but also video clips of your wares in action. Perhaps you'd care to include audio clips of testimonials from satisfied customers. Of course, Honest Herb Smith doesn't have any satisfied customers, so you can't listen to testimonials. However, you can listen to a 5.2MB digitized version of his latest radio commercial.

Why is maintaining an online catalog labor-intensive? It is primarily because of the tedious job of maintaining updates. If you've ever used Microsoft Access, you might have seen how you can create and maintain an online multimedia catalog. If you have Access as your browsing engine and have the database available locally, it works quite well. It's still a pain to update, however. You can also set up a Web page to access information from a database, as you will learn in Chapter 11, "How To Install Your Web Presentation onto a Web Server." Getting it all coordinated and working, however, can be quite a chore. For the example catalog in this chapter, assume that Honest Herb has done it all the old-fashioned way, with HTML and GIF files corresponding to all the text he needs—prices, item descriptions, warranty information, product pictures, and so on.

Under the Browsing section, each link item is linked to various versions or subsets of the catalog. Most of the catalog is in the main HTML document you see in Figure 10.11. However, you don't see it on-screen right now. That's because it's below (that is, you would need to scroll the Web browser down to see it). Each of the categorical links—Stereos, Camcorders, and so on—is linked to a heading below (later in the same HTML document). The alphabetical indices also are contained in the main document. The Warrant and Returns policies, however—the latter of which is shown in Figure 10.12—are maintained by Herb's legal department and change weekly. Thus, they are kept in separate HTML files.

10

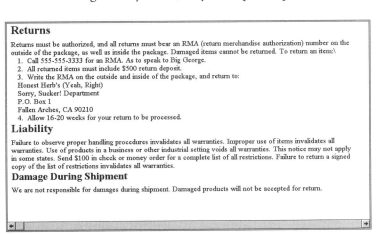

Figure 10.12. *Using separate HTML documents enables you to delegate different parts of a large Web site.*

Example 4: File and Information Server

An increasingly popular application for Web pages is as support sites for products. Web pages are a vast improvement over plain FTP sites in that they enable you to display a combination of text and links. Often, users download files from FTP sites without reading the fine print (various `readme.txt` files containing warnings, installation instructions, and so on). Using a Web page, you can put support files into context, improving the odds that users read all the warnings and admonitions. You also can include items such as product literature, special offers, and FAQs (*frequently-asked-questions* lists).

Figure 10.13 shows the product support page for Spread 'Em, which is an imaginary spreadsheet for police departments. This support page combines support, news, updates, frequently asked questions, tips, and promotional information, all in a single HTML document. Notice how the file update information is presented. Rather than scratching your head about filenames, the items clearly state what you're going to download. You don't even have to worry about filenames until and unless your own computer prompts you for a name and destination.

Spread 'Em - The Spreadsheet for Police

Welcome to the **Spread 'Em** Support Page. We're here to serve those who serve the rest of us. Recognizing that police have special needs, we created **Spread 'Em**, the revolutionary new spreadsheet just for police.

You have the right to:
- **Remain silent**. Sit back and read what's new and different about **Spread 'Em**
- **An attorney**. Learn why lawyers wish every police department used **Spread 'Em**.
- **Free updates**. Download the latest updates for **Spread 'Em**.
- **Enhancements**. Learn about Spread 'Em Wide, the enhancement that gives you up to 32 million columns!
- **Ask questions**. Enquiring users of **Spread 'Em** want to know the answers to frequently asked questions.
- **Anonymous Tips**. Get hot tips arriving daily, or give us your own hot tips on our 800 line or via email.

What's New?

Spread 'Em, that's what. **Spread 'Em** is the revolutionary new spreadsheet just for police. **Spread 'Em** includes links to national fingerprint databases, a national wants and warrants database, and **Find 'Em**, the new culprit tracking system that find 90% of suspects within 24 hours! Best of all, **Spread 'Em** does your paperwork for you, making sure that all legal formalities are covered. Now, you'll never have a case rejected by the DA for "insufficient evidence."

Latest Updates

Version 1.3 is now available. You can read what's new or download it now.

Version 2.0 beta is now available. You can read about the new features, or download it now. **Remember: this version is not for production use.**

Find 'Em data modules for June, 1995 are now available for the following regions: Northeast, Northwest, Southeast, Southwest, and Pacific.

District Attorneys' Association Polls Members about Spread 'Em

"It's amazing. The cops who bring me cases tracked with **Spread 'Em** always have their i's dotted and t's crossed." Steven A. Smith, D.A. of Southbeach.

Figure 10.13. *The Web is ideally suited to some kinds of product support.*

The links for each of the major bulleted items—news, lawyers, updates, and so on—are all linked to bookmarks later in the same document. The links for the files are to an FTP server. For example, the URL for the imaginary version 1.3 is actually `ftp://ftp.spreadem.com/spred1p3.exe`. The e-mail link uses a Mailto URL.

Summary

Today, you learned how to convert a Word document into an HTML document. You saw how easy it is to apply the Internet Assistant tags using Word styles. You studied a number of typical Web page applications, as well as what goes into making them work.

Q&A

Q We have an online catalog that works with a compiled version of dBASE. Can we put it onto the Web?

A Perhaps, but probably not using a Web browser directly. The problem is that the data display tool that users will use is a Web browser. Your data display tool is some form of dBase. If you're using a compiled, distributable executable, you can probably make that and the database available for download. However, the user might use the Web only to obtain the software, not to use the catalog. Assuming that you have the necessary software on your Web server (a program that works in the operating system supported by your server, which usually is UNIX), you can set up your Web site so that it reads and writes data to and from a database. The setup is not trivial, however. See Chapter 11 for more (but not much more) information.

Q Once I get my catalog written and posted onto the Web, how can I attract potential customers?

A See Chapter 12, "Publicizing Your Web Presence," in which methods of attracting attention (publicity) are discussed.

Q It's an amazing coincidence, but our department really wants to find an evaluation copy of Spread 'Em. We searched all the police trade magazines, and checked for the `http://www.spreadem.com` URL, but we can't find it. Where do we find more information?

A Didn't you see the word *imaginary* in that section? Spread 'Em doesn't exist, except in my own warped imagination. However, for a sufficiently large fee, I'm sure I could put you in touch with a developer.

DAY
6

Going Public

11

How To Install Your Web Presentation onto a Web Server

Today, you learn how to install your Web presentation onto a Web server. Recall that this book refers to a Web presentation rather than a Web document or a Web page because—for many of you—your Web creation involves more than a single document and because your Web presence is a way of presenting information, much as you would if you were making a formal, in-person presentation to a client.

> **Note:** Some aspects of installing your Webware—such as setting up data retrieval for search programs and setting up to write forms-retrieved data to databases—cannot be fully covered in a book such as this one. For one thing, you haven't learned about forms yet (see Chapter 13, "Web Forms and Image Maps"), or about how to set up a search program on the Web. For another, much of what you do is heavily dependent on your Web server, what operating system it uses, how it is set up, and what software is installed there. In most cases, you need to enlist the help of your Web server administrator for proper and complete setup. For yet another, this book is really about Web publishing, that is, how to create your Web presentations using Microsoft Word. The topic of setting up a Web site really has nothing to do with Word, although the basics are here so that you know generally how to proceed.

Choosing a Server

The most important aspect of setting up a Web presentation is choosing a server. Most folks reading this book probably already have an Internet provider. In many instances, your current provider might also be a logical candidate for being a Web server. In other cases, not. Some providers, for example, don't even have Web facilities. Others might have restrictions that limit what you can do. For example, my Internet access is through the Capital PC Users Group (CPCUG), which is a nonprofit organization. It has a strict rule that prohibits use of the system for commercial purposes. Hence, if I wanted to set up a yellow-pages-type interactive multimedia display ad on it, I'd be out of luck.

Another consideration is how much disk space you need. Some Web servers are servers only as a sideline, and don't have tons of disk space available for Web presentations. Some, for example, limit you to a half-megabyte (500KB) of disk space. Others might give you 5MB. Still others might allow whatever you need, provided that you pay for it.

Yet another consideration is whether or not you will be using forms in your Webware for collecting data. Data collection introduces issues of access security, indefinite or varying amounts of space for incoming data, and making sure that the necessary software is installed.

The following are key considerations:

- [ ] Is the provider a Web server?
- [ ] How much disk storage do you need?
- [ ] Will you be installing forms in your Web presentation for data collection?
- [ ] Will you be using FTP links?
- [ ] Does the Web server have any restrictions about the type of material you can post?
- [ ] Will you need, and does the Web service charge for, technical support in setting up a Web page?
- [ ] How much does the server charge for server services?
- [ ] Is the server online 24 hours a day?
- [ ] Will you have direct access to your HTML directory, or do you have to go through server personnel?
- [ ] What World Wide Web server software can be used?

What Is a Web Server?

A Web server is a computer program that runs all the time and waits for Web clients (such as Netscape, InternetWorks Internet Assistant, Mosaic, or the OS/2 WebExplorer) to request data. Recall that the URL for all Web sites begins with http, which stands for HyperText Transfer Protocol. HTTP—like FTP and gopher—is one of many TCP/IP (Transfer Control Protocol/Internet Protocol) data handling methods. It's similar in concept to Zmodem, Kermit, and Xmodem, which are file transfer protocols with which many computer users are more familiar. Basically, it's a way of sending data between a server and a client so that both programs know what to send, where to send it, when to send it, and how to send it.

Note: Web servers are also called *HTTP daemons*, or *HTTPD servers*. A daemon, (with the archaic spelling of *demon*) is a subordinate deity or spirit, sometimes called an attendant spirit. Unseen, it sits there in the dark, waiting to serve your needs or waiting to spook you. In most literature, demons are hardly something to link to. In the great world of the Internet, daemons are essential.

Web servers work by sending files to a Web client. When you specify the HTML protocol, the type of file is an HTML file. Recall that HTML files have a special kind of format called *tags*. Most of these tags are used by the Web client (or browser) to determine what to do with

the data. Other tags, such as the IMG tag, are used to tell the Web server what file to send and what type of file it is. On the receiving end, the same tags tell the Web browser what it needs to do with the information from the server.

Web servers also can be set up to run special programs on the server called *gateway script* programs.

> **Note:** When you see the word *script* in reference to a computer program, it means a set of instructions that are run by some kind of controlling program or interpreter. Scripts differ from other kinds of programs in that they are interpreted rather than compiled. Interpreted or script programs—such as batch files (.bat in DOS and .cmd in OS/2) and UNIX script files (.src)—generally are easy to understand and modify, but run more slowly than interpreted programs. In the case of gateway scripts, however, speed isn't really an issue. Gateway script programs are more accessible to the user and easier to set up and maintain.

Finding a Web Server

If you already have an Internet provider, often the easiest course of action is to use your existing provider as your Web server, assuming it provides Web facilities. Even if Web facilities aren't included in the schedule of services you might have received from your provider, call and ask anyway. Many providers offer a wide range of services, tailoring packages of services to different kinds of customers. As a shell, SLIP, or PPP customer, you might not be on the kind of customer list they usually assume would want Web server services. In addition, as the Web skyrockets in popularity, many providers who didn't offer Web server services a year or even six months ago, might today. They might be tallying demand, preparing to set up a server when and if people such as you come asking.

Many Web services have setup fees. If you buy server privileges with your existing provider, there might be a one-time setup fee for establishing your subdirectory on their server. Others might also charge additional monthly fees as well as a charge for disk storage. Find out all the charges before making a decision. If the fees are significant, it pays to shop around. Try also to project your future needs and see what the costs will be over a two- or three-year period. In shopping around, compare the two- or three-year cumulative costs of different providers.

 Caution: Look before you leap. Some providers make you a deal: a flat fee for a six- or twelve-month period, offering a substantial discount over the month-by-month arrangement. If you are tempted by that arrangement, however, try to find out first how reliable the server is. You might try accessing Web pages on that server at various times during the week over a several-week period. Once your URL is propagated throughout the net, it's sometimes difficult to get a change of address to "take" if you change servers. Many users find that they have to leave an older account in place with a Moved to... notice. Thus, the cost of choosing the wrong server initially may mean having to pay for *two* servers at the same time later. What's that old saying? *Sign up with the wrong server in haste, repent at leisure?* Well, it's something like that.

Have you ever seen those self-storage rental companies? They usually have hundreds of garage-like bays in which you can store furniture, boxes, tires, and so on, for as long as you need, for a monthly rental fee. In urban and suburban areas, such companies are commonplace. Similarly, commercial Web service providers are springing up all over the place. Even if your Internet provider *does* provide a Web server, it might be that the capabilities are more limited than a company that specializes. You might have to be more of a do-it-yourselfer. Because the Web service specialty shops recognize the competition in the marketplace, you might find that you get a better deal from them than from a full-service Internet provider. Check the business and computer ads in your local newspaper. You might be surprised to discover how many Web server outfits there are and the rates they charge. If you need to set up gateway scripts for forms and image maps, you will also find that such companies have considerably more expertise in helping you get set up correctly and quickly.

Another alternative for some users is to establish their own Web servers. When you take this approach, you gain the flexibility of setting up your software exactly as you need to, and there are no limits on storage space (except, of course, for the amount of money in your bank account). For this kind of plan to fly, you need a computer to run it on, software, and a full-time connection to the Internet. None of this is cheap, and setting up your own server is seldom cost-effective for most users. It generally is cost-effective only if you already have an existing full-time Internet computer and connection and/or if you plan to sell server services to others or provide server services to a number of different entities within a company or other institution. You also need the knowledge to set up and maintain the equipment and software.

Installing Your Webware

Next to finding the right server, installing your Web presentation on your Web server should be a piece of cake. For most users, setup is not a particularly lengthy or tedious process. You can save time and repetition, however, by knowing what is required and why. Don't transfer any files to your server until they are set up for your server. The general steps are discussed in the next sections.

Directory and Subdirectory Setup

The first step is to set up the required directory and subdirectory structure on the server. At least part of this—setting up the initial directory—usually must be performed by your Web server administrator. You also probably need shell account access (access to your account from the UNIX command line) to your server. Without such access, it can be difficult to move your files to where they need to be. If you can't access your account using a UNIX shell account, you'll need to prepare a precise list of instructions for your administrator to follow.

It's generally easiest to put all your Web-related files into a single directory. If you have a lot of files of different types, administration and maintenance sometimes are facilitated by having dedicated subdirectories for each type. For example, you might put all your HTML files into the main directory, all your GIF files into another, your JPEGs into another, files for FTP transfer into another, and so on. The important point, however, is to set all this up and to have a list of all the locations where files will reside and what they will be named. The next section tells you why.

File Preparation

Before transferring any files, you must prepare them for use on the Web server. A good way to proceed is to first make a copy of all your HTML files into a new Web-oriented subdirectory on your own system. Maintain these apart from the setup you used to write and test your Web presentation from Word. Once set up for the Web server, they no longer will work locally within Word (although they might work using a Windows NT browser under NTFS or using an OS/2 browser under HPFS). So, to make changes, you need to go back to your Word set and make the changes there. Then recopy the changed files to your Web-oriented subdirectory and prep them for copying to the Web server.

Armed now with the information on what your subdirectories will be called, use Word, as shown in the lessons of this book, to edit each of the links to local HTML, GIF, JPEG, AU, MPG, and other files to match the filenames and relative subdirectories where they will reside on the server. For example, if a file presently is named support.htm, it usually must be

renamed with the extension `.html` in order to work on a UNIX-based Web server. Thus, a link in your main HTML document probably referred to `support.htm` internally as you were testing on your own system. The link now needs to refer to `support.html` for your Web server. Once you rename the file in the link, it no longer works on your own system (unless you are using a system that supports long filenames). Talk to your Web server administrator to find out what other kinds of extension-name requirements exist.

Note: Usually, case counts. In UNIX, directory and filenames usually are case-specific. When naming files on a UNIX Web server, the case of the file referred to in the link must match the case of the file's actual name. If the file's actual name on the UNIX system is `Support.Html`, any links that refer to that file must use the exact same capitalization. Most subdirectories and files on UNIX systems are named with all lowercase letters.

To modify the links to work on your server, you have two choices.

☐ Use Word to modify the original `.DOC` files, and then save in HTML format.

☐ Use Word or a text file editor to modify the `.HTM` files directly (but use Word only if you open the files as *text only*).

If you use Word to modify the `.HTM` files, they must be opened and saved as text-only files, not as HTML files. To do this, you must click on the Confirm Conversions option in the Open file dialog box, shown in Figure 11.1.

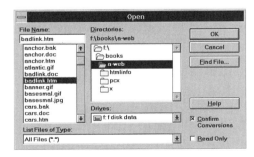

Figure 11.1. *To edit* `.HTM` *files directly with Word, you enable the Confirm Conversions option in the Open dialog box.*

When the Convert File dialog box appears, change the Convert File From type from HTML to Text Only (see Figure 11.2).

Figure 11.2. *To edit* .HTM *files directly with Word, choose Convert File From Text Only, not HTML.*

Caution: Why can't you use Word to open files in HTML format? You can, but you probably won't like the result—that is, corruption of the document. If you open the files, converting from HTML, and save them the same way (in HTML format), the modified files often have extra paragraph marks inserted, along with other formatting. For some reason, however, the resulting .HTM files are corrupted, and don't work as HTML files anymore. Because users need to enable the Confirm Conversions option, and then choose Text Only, there is a good chance of accidentally opening such files as HTML files if you use Word as the editor. Use Word to edit only the .DOC versions. If you want to edit the .HTM versions, use something other than Word, such as any text file editor (for example, Windows NOTEPAD, OS/2's System Editor, or QBASIC /EDITOR). Mind you, you *can* use Word to open as text-only and save the .HTM versions as text-only, but you have to be careful.

To modify a link, open the original .DOC file in Word. Select the link you want to modify by clicking once on it—don't double-click! First, let's talk about what *not* to do. One tempting method is to choose Insert | HTML Markup from the menu. The HTML command will be displayed in a dialog box, as shown in Figure 11.3, and you make the change in the text area. Here, the change is made merely by adding the letter l after htm. Then click on OK to save the change. Look at the end result carefully. The display text gets changed to <<HTML Markup>>. Whoops! That's probably not what you had in mind, right?

Figure 11.3. *Don't use the Insert | HTML Markup command to modify links.*

Another tempting way is to use the HyperLink tool. You can't use that method, either. The following sidebar tells you why.

Why Can't You Use the HyperLink Tool?

You can use the HyperLink tool only to make the change if the file you're changing exists on your system and is recognized by Word. For example, suppose you want to change warranty.htm to htmlfiles/warranty.html. First, you click to select the link, and then click on the HyperLink tool. Next, you delete the displayed filename and replace it with htmlfiles/warranty.html. So far, so good. When you click on OK, however, you get the error message box shown in Figure 11.4. Whoops! That's why you need to use either the Insert | HTML Markup command or to modify the field directly.

Note that the subdirectory and file htmlfiles/warranty.html really do exist on my system—I'm using OS/2's HPFS (high performance file system). However, Word was unable to see that subdirectory or that file because Word is a DOS program. Once the modification is made and the file is saved in HTML format, however, it works fine in place on my hard disk, using OS/2's WebExplorer. Having this additional capability helps verify changes. Otherwise, you have an additional round of testing once you install files on your Web server. Using a 32-bit Windows NT browser under Windows NT and the NTFS file system, you have the same capability.

Figure 11.4. *You can't use the HyperLink tool to point to a file that Word can't see.*

The correct way to change the references from .htm to .html is to modify fields directly. Here, you have two choices: manual and automatic. Let's look at the manual way first, to show you the goal and how to accomplish it. Then you'll learn a shortcut. For the manual method, first click on the link to select it. Next, press Shift+F9 to toggle the field code display on for that link. A link to warranty.htm might appear as the following:

```
{  { PRIVATE HREF="warranty.htm" }MACROBUTTON HtmlResAnchor Warranty}
```

Modify the htm extension so that it is html.

```
{  { PRIVATE HREF="warranty.html" }MACROBUTTON HtmlResAnchor Warranty}
```

Then press Shift+F9 to toggle the field back to display the result. You don't need to press F9 to update the field. The PRIVATE field is automatically converted to the proper <HREF...> tag when the document is saved in HTML format.

Repeat the process for all links in your HTML document, using either the Insert | HTML Markup command or by modifying the field codes directly. Make sure in each instance that the filename is what it's supposed to be.

There usually is a faster and more automatic way to change the .htm occurrences to .html, however. Notice that each of the file references that you want to change ends in .htm". That provides a fairly effective way to identify all the .htm occurrences that need to be changed. You can change them all using Find and Replace. First, click on the Html Hidden ({a}) tool on the Formatting toolbar to reveal the contents of all the fields. Next, from the menu, choose Edit | Replace, or press Ctrl+H. In the Find What field, type .htm". In the Replace With field, type .html", as shown in Figure 11.5. If you're exceedingly confident that there are no .htm" occurrences that you *don't* want changed, click on Replace All. Otherwise, you can alternately click on Find and then Replace for each occurrence you find that you want changed.

Figure 11.5. *You can use the Replace (Ctrl+H) dialog box to change all* .htm *occurrences to* .html.

You also need to make sure that subdirectories point to where they should. For example, if all GIF files are going to be kept in a subdirectory named GIFs, make sure those links appear with that subdirectory. The field code for a link you've been testing might appear as the following:

```
{ { PRIVATE SRC="atlantic.gif" ALT="The Atlantic Ocean!" ALIGN="BOTTOM" }
➥MACROBUTTON HtmlResImg }
```

Change it to this:

```
{ { PRIVATE SRC="gifs/atlantic.gif" ALT="The Atlantic Ocean!" ALIGN="BOTTOM" }
➥MACROBUTTON HtmlResImg }
```

DO	**DON'T**

DO use a forward slash (/) for subdirectory references in Web pages.

DON'T use the backslash (\) when referring to subdirectories in HTML documents.

(Now you see why, when doing the original .DOC version, I implored you to set up your subdirectory structure to duplicate, as much as possible, the same subdirectory structure that exists on your Web server computer. If you did that, much of the work is already done for you.)

Another thing to watch out for when adjusting links for your Web server are URLs of the following form:

```
{   { PRIVATE HREF="LOCAL:g:/www/help/help_glo.htm" }MACROBUTTON
HtmlResAnchor Help}
```

This kind of link will not work on the Internet. You must replace the `LOCAL:g:/www/help/` reference with something that will work on your Web server. You cannot include disk drive references. Moreover, to work properly, it's best if the references are all relative to the location of your main HTML home page document (usually called `index.html`). If `index.html` is on `/webpages/www/smith`, and if there is a directory on your server called `/webpages/www/help` where `help_glo.html` is stored, the following are acceptable references:

```
/webpages/www/help/help_glo.html
../help/help_glo.html
```

In the first instance, the whole directory, minus any disk drive reference, is used. In the second instance, a relative directory is used. The `../` structure refers to the parent directory. Thus, `../help` refers to a sibling subdirectory, parallel to the current subdirectory.

Go through your HTML document, changing all links as needed. If your main HTML document refers to other HTML documents, they need to be edited similarly. When all changes have been made (remember that you're editing the .DOC file), save the changes first in Word format. Next, choose File | Save As and save the change in HTML format. Don't try to assign the .html extension just yet—because it won't work! Repeat the process for all HTML documents that need to be modified.

Transfer Your Files

The next step is to copy all the files needed for your Web presentation to your Web server. In most cases, this is a fairly straightforward matter. You usually can use FTP to transfer the files. If you don't know what FTP is, you'll need to consult your Internet software documentation. If you don't have an FTP client, and if your Web server system supports other protocols—such as Zmodem, Kermit, or Xmodem—you can use one of those methods.

Caution: To save download time and trouble, many computer users are accustomed to using PKZIP, InfoZip, or some other file archiving program to collect and compress files for transfer. InfoZip, for example, can be used to collect hundreds of files—including subdirectory structure—into a single .zip file that can be transferred all in one fell swoop. You can then unzip the files at the destination, which causes that single file to expand into all the original files, using the same subdirectory structure that existed on the source computer.

All that's fine when transferring between systems that support ZIP. Does your Web server have an unzip program? Before going to all that trouble, make sure that zipping is a supported option. Often it is not, and you need to transfer the files—one at a time—to your Web server system or find an archiving program that is supported both on your own platform and on that of your server.

On the other hand, if you want to store zipped files on your Web server (for FTP access via your Web page) for others to download, there is no problem with the ZIP format (ZIP is an archiving and compression format for storing a number of files within a single file, using less disk space than the original files). Just make sure that the file is transferred to your Web server using a binary protocol.

Using FTP or some other supported protocol, transfer the needed files to your Web server. Recall that transferring files from your system to another system is called uploading, and transferring files from another system to your system is called downloading. In addition to the possibility of not being able to zip and unzip, another issue to consider when FTPing is the question of binary versus text mode transfers. Use binary (image) transfer mode.

Most FTP client software enables you to choose either ASCII text or binary transfer mode. Although HTML files themselves can be transferred as text files, other files, such as JPEG and GIF files, cannot be correctly transferred that way. Many FTP client programs default to ASCII text transfers. They enable you to transfer files merrily all day long, stripping out the eighth bit without warning you (some older computers allow only seven-bit data transfer). It isn't until the files don't work that you realize that something has gone wrong. (One poor fellow transferred over 100MB that way at 14.4Kbps. He's due to be released soon, and will probably need only a few months of outpatient treatment.)

Put Files Where They Need to Be

The next step is to move the files to the appropriate locations on your Web server. If you aren't conversant in the operating system supported by your Web server, you probably need to consult with your Web administrator. Many UNIX systems, for users' convenience, alias UNIX commands with DOS-like names, including COPY and DEL. If your files are FTPed to

a subdirectory called /homeb/smith, and you want to be on /webpages/www/smith, you might be able to move them by copying them and then deleting the originals.

> **Note:** What's your *alias*? An alias simply means a substitute name. If you're a DOS user, you might have used the DOSKEYS command to create aliases. For example, the command doskey ed=qbasic/editor $* often is used in a user's AUTOEXEC.BAT file so that ed can be used to invoke the text editor component of QBASIC.EXE. Similarly, aliases can be used in UNIX to create DOS-like command names for executing UNIX commands.

Once moved into place, your last step is to give them the appropriate names. If the server is on a UNIX system, for example, your first step is to rename all .htm files as .html. Again, you might need to talk to your Web administrator to find the appropriate command. Your main HTML document—called your home page—should usually be given the name index.html (although it should sometimes be named default.html; check with your server administrator). This enables most Web browsers to refer to your home page merely by using the name of your server and your directory, rather than having to include the name of your home page HTML document. Common extensions used on the Internet are shown in Tables 8.1, 8.2, and 8.3 in Chapter 8, "External Media—Images, Video, Text, and Sound." In addition, formatted PostScript files usually use the extension .ps, and text files use .txt.

Testing, Testing

The next step is to test your installation to see how it plays. First, you need to find out your URL. The easiest way to find out is to ask your Web administrator. If you'd rather find out yourself, it's usually not very difficult. In fact, if you name your main HTML document (home page) index.html, your URL is http://servername/directory, where servername is the machine name of your Web server and directory is the location where you copied your index.html file.

Web server names usually begin with www, but don't have to. Recall that the Web server name for Macmillan Computer Publishing (the umbrella publisher that owns Sams.net) is www.mcp.com. In some instances, you might find that machines are referred to by their IP numbers (164.109.215.16, for example). IP (Internet Protocol) numbers are the nitty-gritty addresses of hosts on the Internet. For each name such as www.webserve.com, there is a corresponding IP number. If you install your Web presentation on www.webserve.com, in a directory called webpages/smith, and your home page is named index.html, your URL is the following:

```
http://www.webserve.com/webpages/smith
```

If you name your home page `index.html`, most Web servers point to it automatically. Otherwise, you need to include the name of your home page as well. Here is an example:

```
http://www.webserve.com/webpages/smith/smith.html
```

What Are All the Tildes (~) For?

As you cruise the Web, you might notice that a number of URLs contain the ~ character. On UNIX provider systems, your home directory usually is aliased as ~. For example, my home directory might be something like `/pub/users/homeb/tyson`. Moreover, some Internet providers enable you to put your `index.html` files in your home directory. That being the case, rather than having to refer to my home page by using `/pub/users/homeb/tyson`, I can refer to it with just ~, and others can refer to it with just `~tyson` . Thus, my URL might be `http://cpug.org/~tyson`.

Common Gateway Interface

You're probably wondering by now how some of the searches and forms work on the Web. No? Well, you should be. Most of them work using something referred to affectionately around the Web as the Common Gateway Interface, or CGI. The CGI is a way of using a Web browser to activate programs or scripts on the Web server. Recall that because many such programs are controlled by scripts, they often are called gateway scripts.

Gateway scripts are used to handle information requests from a Web browser. They get activated when a user sends data from a form or a search. What happens depends entirely on how the script is written. CGI scripts take some kind of data and/or request, process it in some way, and then return a result to the Web server. In the case of forms data, the user sends data, and the result usually is an indication that the data was received. On the receiving end, the CGI script contains instructions for what to do with the data. It might be something as simple as appending it to the end of a text file. Some CGI scripts activate database programs that take the data from specific form fields and file the data in a database. The owner of the database periodically retrieves it. In the case of a search program, the CGI script processes the search request, often looking up something in a database of some kind or performing some kind of search on the Internet. When it retrieves a result, it then formats it in some way and sends the data to the Web browser (that is, back to you), along with some kind of formatting instructions.

Gateway scripts can be written in any language supported by the Web server. This includes languages such as C, Perl, TCL, Bourne Shell, and C Shell. Gateway scripts can be very simple, or they can be very complicated. In this book, you learn only enough to get you started. If you need something complicated, you might invest some time and energy in learning as much as you can about gateway scripts. One very good source is available at `http://hoohoo/nsca.uiuc.edu/cgi`.

A Basic Gateway Example

Gateway scripts sound a lot more complicated than they are. A simple example might put your mind to rest. The Web page shown in Figure 11.6 contains a link called Who's On. Many UNIX servers have a command called who, which tells you what users are on the server. In this case, the Who's On link is set up to execute the following simple C shell script:

```
!/usr/bin/sh
echo Content-type: text/plain
echo
who
```

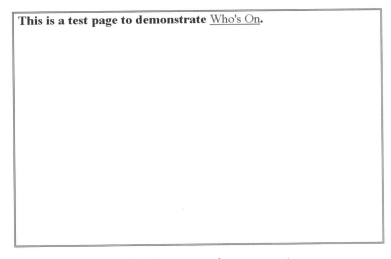

Figure 11.6. *The Who's On link will run a simple gateway script program.*

First, a program on the /usr/bin directory, called sh is run. Next, the commands following that are fed into the sh program. The program sh carries out the commands shown. First, it echoes (sends) the text Content-type: text/plain. The echo command following that produces a blank line. Finally, sh runs the who command. When this script runs, the output normally displays as shown in Figure 11.7. The first line, Content-type: text/plain, is a header. It is interpreted by the Web browser as instructions for formatting the text that follows. The output of the who command follows, and it appears in the Web browser as shown in Figure 11.8. Note that scripts *must* be stored on the server computer and cannot be tested without your being connected to a server.

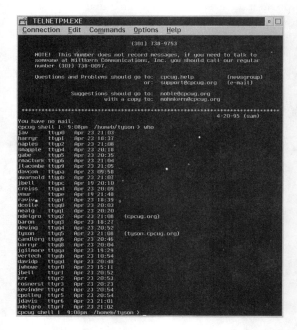

Figure 11.7. *The output of the* who *command when run from the UNIX command line.*

```
jav       ttyp0   Apr 23 21:03
harryr    ttyp1   Apr 23 18:37
naples    ttyp2   Apr 23 21:08
smapple   ttyp4   Apr 23 20:18
gabe      ttyp5   Apr 23 20:35
rmacturk  ttyp6   Apr 23 21:04
jlacombe  ttyp9   Apr 23 21:05
davcom    ttypa   Apr 23 09:58
awarnold  ttypb   Apr 23 21:07
jbell     ttypc   Apr 19 20:10
creiss    ttypd   Apr 23 20:09
enur      ttype   Apr 19 21:48
raviv     ttypf   Apr 23 18:39
dcoile    ttyq0   Apr 23 20:03
nealg     ttyq1   Apr 23 20:20
ndelgro   ttyq2   Apr 23 21:08   (cpcug.org)
baron     ttyq3   Apr 23 16:27
dewing    ttyq4   Apr 23 20:52
tyson     ttyq5   Apr 23 21:08   (tyson.cpcug.org)
candlerg  ttyq6   Apr 23 20:46
barryr    ttyq8   Apr 23 20:04
jgilmore  ttyqa   Apr 23 19:29
vertech   ttyqb   Apr 23 10:54
davidp    ttyqd   Apr 23 20:48
jwhowe    ttyr0   Apr 23 15:11
jbell     ttyr1   Apr 23 20:52
krr       ttyr2   Apr 23 20:53
rosnerst  ttyr3   Apr 23 20:23
kevinder  ttyr4   Apr 23 20:54
cpolley   ttyr5   Apr 23 20:54
jdavis    ttyr6   Apr 23 21:01
ndelgro   ttyr7   Apr 23 21:02
```

Figure 11.8. *The output of the Who program when run by a Gateway script and sent over the Web.*

Who Can Use CGI?

Some Web servers limit their users' Web pages to one-way presentations and do not permit the use of CGI. The reasons cited often include the following:

Security   Allowing the execution of programs creates the potential, at least, that hackers or others can penetrate the server by running programs you don't intend for them to run, or running them in ways you didn't anticipate.

Space   Allowing CGI processing and storage of data can generate unexpected results, leading to flooding the hard disk with data.

Performance   Allowing CGI processing might cause degradation of the service to other users (for example, if some users run heavy-duty programs, or if many users use CGI scripts).

You might find that many system administrators have firm ideas about what they will and will not allow. If yours doesn't permit gateway scripts, and if you need to set up searches, forms, or some other CGI application, your only recourse might be to find a provider who allows what you want to do. Most commercial Web servers do allow CGI—in fact, that's why they're in business!

Summary

Today, you explored the basics of selecting a Web server and installing your Web presentation. You also had a basic introduction to gateway programs, including a little about how they work. You learned that if you plan to use forms, searches, or other data retrieval from your Web setup, you need a Web provider that allows the use of CGI (that is, a CGI script is needed for interactive communications).

Q&A

Q   **Can a Web presentation be just a single HTML file, or do you have to have all that other stuff (external links, JPEGs, CGI, and so forth)?**

A   It can be just a single HTML file. In fact, most Web pages are just that. A Web presentation can be just as simple or just as complex as you want to make it.

Q   **Once I set my Web page up, how difficult is it to make changes?**

A   Most Web servers provide as much access as you want. The area where your Web files reside is open to you, so you can change or replace any of the files as needed. When you make changes, however, be sure to test everything to make sure nothing got broken.

Q   **For URLs and directories, do I use forward slashes on UNIX servers and backslashes on Intel-based (DOS, Windows, OS/2) servers?**

A   No, you always use forward slashes for HTML documents. It's true that HTML uses forward slashes because the Web has its roots in UNIX. However, the conventions built into HTML have now been incorporated into virtually all Web browsers and servers, so they all use forward slashes.

12

Publicizing
Your Web
Presence

Now that your Web page is installed and online, why isn't anyone showing up to use it? Maybe they don't know about it. Today, you learn how to get your Web page seen (and possibly heard). It's usually a matter of knowing where to leave your calling card, so to speak. There are a number of central sources—such as Yahoo, the World Wide Yellow Pages (WWYP), and the World Wide Virtual Library—whose primary claim to fame is the fact that they include links to lots of URLs. Other sources are various .announce newsgroups that welcome information about new and interesting Web pages. Still another way is to let interested people know directly about your link. One of the best ways is to make your Web page as interesting and useful as possible. Such pages quickly become popular on the Web, and are passed along eagerly by word of...er...fingers.

Product Literature and Advertisements

The most obvious and overlooked way of publicizing your Web presence is through your product literature. I just looked through a new box containing Microsoft Office, and—although I might be mistaken—I couldn't find anything in or on the box that might tell me that Microsoft has a home page on the Web (http://www.microsoft.com). Considering how accomplished Microsoft is in advertising, that's a bit surprising. How about OS/2 Warp, whose advertising singularly focuses on the Internet? Nowhere in IBM's advertisements do I see any mention of IBM's various Web home pages, which might be of interest to potential purchasers. Once you install the WebExplorer, of course, it defaults to an IBM home page. However, the most visible part of a product seems to include no clues.

There are dozens of brochures, boxes, disks, manuals, press releases, and the like around my office, and none of them tell me about the dozens of Web pages that exist. It would be simple to include it on the box with something such as "Connected? Visit us online at http://www.bigcompany.com."

Perhaps it's too soon to expect companies to start lacing their products with URLs but it shouldn't be—especially when you consider the number of individuals who now have their own home pages (five million and growing quickly). URLs should also be included on business cards along with e-mail addresses. People like the immediacy and spontaneity of the Internet. It's much faster than mail and often faster than the phone.

Getting into Yahoo and Other Major Indexes

There are many major indexes on the Web, the primary purpose of which are to catalog the thousands of Web home pages. If you are an individual, your chances of getting listed in many of these are nil. However, if you have a business or are connected to a government information provider or any other kind of public service (museums, libraries, charities, and so forth), your chances are good. If you do meet these criteria and aren't listed yet (assuming you have a Web address), either the organizations that maintain listings are overwhelmed or you haven't made the proper request through the proper channels. For the most part, the more valuable and useful the information in your Web presentation, the more likely that it will get listed on one of the resources discussed in this chapter.

Getting Listed in the WWYP

The WWYP offers both free and paid yellow page listings. To obtain a free listing, point your Web browser to `http://www.yellow.com/cgi-bin/online` and fill out the form shown in Figure 12.1. You need a forms-capable browser, such as InternetWorks Internet Assistant, Netscape, or the WebExplorer. If you don't have such a browser, there also is an ASCII-text version of the form. You can download it by clicking on ASCII Template and then e-mailing the completed form back to `listing@yellow.com`.

WW P™ Listing Submission

For a limited time, all businesses that have a World Wide Web presence can have a **free** listing in the World Wide Yellow Pages. It's the simple and easy way to attract new customers who don't know how to find you already.

Information about the form

There is also an ASCII template that you can fill out and email to listing@yellow.com.

Fields denoted with a ⬛ are required, otherwise you will get one of those "you forgot to fill in field xxx messages".

One of the requirements that you might think is a little odd is that you must provide a geographical location. While we realize that the web is independent of location, but most business have some geographic specifics. Fred's Florist can place telephone orders anywhere in the world, but if you want to drop in and chat with Fred you might want to know where he is.

```
Business Name⬛:  [                              ]

Street Address:  [                              ]
City/Town⬛:      [                              ]
State/Province⬛: [                              ]
Zip/Postal Code⬛:[                              ]
Country:         [                              ]

Telephone number⬛:[                            ]
FAX number:      [                              ]
Tollfree phone:  [                              ]
URL⬛
```
If you want better tracking of just how useful it is to be listed in the WWYP you should specify a unique URL link to your homepage. So that when people go from your WWYP listing to your homepage you can see just how effective listing here is.

Figure 12.1. *For a "limited time," you can get a free listing in the World Wide Yellow Pages by filling out this form.*

The free listings include just your URL and a snippet of information about your company, such as the examples shown in Figure 12.2 (`http://www.yellow.com/cgi-bin/SearchWWYP?heading=accountants+tax`).

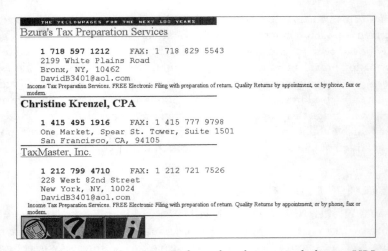

Figure 12.2. *Free listings aren't necessarily fancy, but they can include your URL, which can be as fancy as you like.*

Paid listings range from looking like display ads in the telephone yellow pages to being online catalogs and brochures, such as that shown in Figure 12.3.

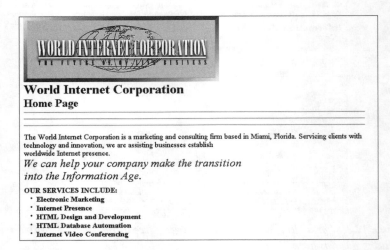

Figure 12.3. *Some Web servers do the job of posting and maintaining your Web page for you.*

Getting Listed in the World Wide Web Virtual Library

The World Wide Web Virtual Library is a voluminous collection of Web information. The heart of the Virtual Library is a massive listing by subject, the top of which is shown in Figure 12.4 (`http://www.w3.org/hypertext/DataSources/bySubject/Overview.html`).

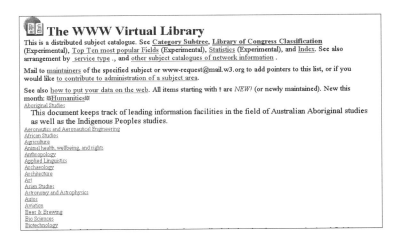

Figure 12.4. *The World Wide Web Virtual Library boasts a detailed subject list and tens of thousands of entries.*

Different subject categories are maintained by different volunteer maintainers—scattered all over the planet—so the style of presentation varies, depending on where the maintainer learned HTML. Many of the subject areas are subdivided into even more categories, such as the Astronomy and Astrophysics area shown in Figure 12.5 (`http://www.w3.org/hypertext/DataSources/bySubject/astro/astro.html`).

To get listed in the World Wide Web Virtual Library, you must contact the subject area maintainer in the areas that apply to your Web presentation. It's not uncommon for some sites to be listed in multiple areas. To see a list of all of the areas and maintainers, set your Web browser to `http://www.w3.org/hypertext/DataSources/bySubject/Maintainers.html`, which is a complete list of all of the maintainers (see Figure 12.6). The links shown are Mailto URLs. If your browser supports the Mailto protocol, you can click on any of the links to compose and send an e-mail to the respective maintainer, as shown in Figure 12.7.

12

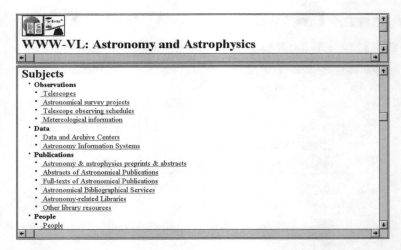

Figure 12.5. *Most of the subject headings in the World Wide Web Virtual Library have additional subheadings.*

Figure 12.6. *To get listed in the World Wide Web Virtual Library, send e-mail to the maintainer of the subject area.*

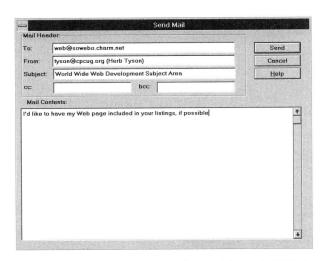

Figure 12.7. *The Mailto URL enables you to send e-mail from the Web browser.*

Getting Listed in Yahoo

Yahoo is an amazing list of mostly Web pages. As I write this, the list is approaching 40,000 entries. Shown in Figure 12.8, Yahoo (`http://www.yahoo.com`) is maintained by David Filo and Jerry Yang at Stanford University. The main subject listings are more manageable than the categories in the World Wide Web Subject Library. Once you get inside the categories, you will find additional categories to help pinpoint areas of interest (see the Education area in Figure 12.9). The listings in Yahoo seem to have fewer blind alleys than others.

Yahoo provides a form for adding entries to Yahoo (see Figure 12.10, `http://www.yahoo.com/bin/add`). The form enables you to specify the subject area under which you want to add your URL. You can get to the Add page by clicking on the Add link in any of the various subject listing pages.

12

Yahoo
[What's New? | What's Cool? | What's Popular? | A Random Link]
[Yahoo | Up | Search | Suggest | Add | Help]
• Art(829) [new]
• Business(10597) [new]
• Computers(3627) [new]
• Economy(1084) [new]
• Education(2032) [new]
• Entertainment(11201) [new]
• Environment and Nature(303) [new]
• Events(66) [new]
• Government(1321) [new]
• Health(737) [new]
• Humanities(309) [new]
• Law(264) [new]
• News(387) [new]
• Politics(242) [new]
• Reference(573) [new]
• Regional Information(5715) [new]
• Science(3817) [new]
• Social Science(145) [new]
• Society and Culture(1206) [new]
There are currently 38751 entries in Yahoo.
Some Other General Internet Directories:
[WWW Virtual Library * EINet Galaxy * University of Michigan Clearinghouse]

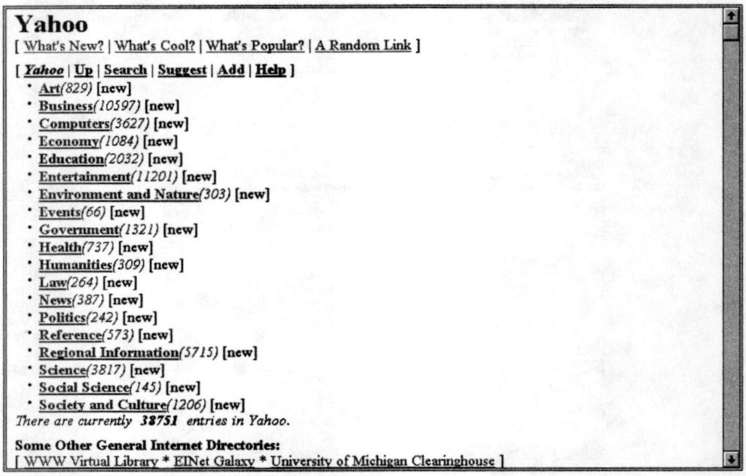

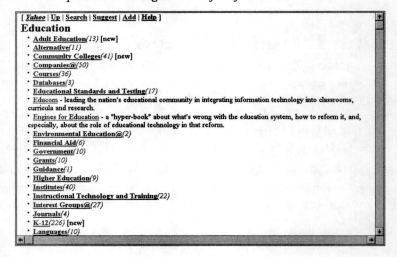

Figure 12.8. *Yahoo provides a manageable list of subjects.*

[Yahoo | Up | Search | Suggest | Add | Help]
Education
• Adult Education(13) [new]
• Alternative(11)
• Community Colleges(41) [new]
• Companies@(50)
• Courses(36)
• Databases(3)
• Educational Standards and Testing(17)
• Educom - leading the nation's educational community in integrating information technology into classrooms, curricula and research.
• Engines for Education - a "hyper-book" about what's wrong with the education system, how to reform it, and, especially, about the role of educational technology in that reform.
• Environmental Education@(2)
• Financial Aid(6)
• Government(10)
• Grants(10)
• Guidance(1)
• Higher Education(9)
• Institutes(40)
• Instructional Technology and Training(22)
• Interest Groups@(27)
• Journals(4)
• K-12(226) [new]
• Languages(10)

Figure 12.9. *Subject areas in Yahoo are subdivided even further.*

Add to Yahoo
[*Yahoo* | Up | Search | Suggest | Add | Help]

If you have URLs that you like to see in our hotlist, please fill in the form below. This form is for **adding URLs only**! To send comments to *Yahoo*, use this *form*.

· We ask you to check first whether your URL is **already in Yahoo**. The easiest way is to do a search on the URL you want to submit. If it doesn't exist, or if it is incorrectly entered in *Yahoo*, please let us know below.

· Please check our recommended submission suggestions before doing an **Add**
· Once you have submitted the URL, we will verify it, and find the best place for it in the hierarrchy. We will try to notify you via email when the entry has been added.

You may also suggest/change the category from the default
Category:

Title:

URL: http://
Optional Info:
Additional Categories:

Geographical Location of Resource (If applicable):
City: State/Province:
Country: US

Figure 12.10. *Use the Add form to add yourself to Yahoo.*

Getting Listed in Your Provider's Web Page

Another likely place to publicize your Web page—especially for individuals—is on the main Web page for your server. It's common for the home page for many Internet providers to list the home pages of individual subscribers. One such set is shown for my main provider in Figure 12.11.

CPCUG Groups' Pages
Find out about our activities....
◾CPCUG MIX BBS (*Michael Kane, sysop*)
◾CPCUG *Monitor* (*Eldon Sarte, Editor*)
◾ CPCUG Training Activities (*Greg Smith, Director*)
Find out about our SIGs....
●Beginners SIG (*Paul Shapiro, Chairman*)
● Investment SIG (*Harry Rood*)
● Windows SIG (*Pat McVeigh, Chairman*)
● Your SIG here

Members' Pages
Enjoy the creative whims and fancies of 30 of our members....
●Bob Ackerman
●Jack Aubert
●Harry Bacas
●Rob and Carol Bruce
●Thor & Velvet D. Bunny
●Bill Burch
●Ned Cahill
●William Erskine
●Bill Feidt
●Aric Finucane
●Jack Fong

Figure 12.11. *Many Web servers automatically list all Web pages on the server.*

12

How do you get listed? Often, it's automatic. If you have not been listed, tune into your Web server's home page to see if there are instructions, or pick up that antique device called a telephone, and give your provider a call. What if you don't know your provider's URL? Often, it's easy to guess. If your provider is Netcom, for example, a good guess would be something like `http://www.netcom.com`. In other words, just add `http://www/` or `http://` (without the `www`) to the front part of your domain. If your domain name is `server.edu`, try `http://www.server.edu` or `http://www.server.edu`.

Getting Listed in .*announce* Newsgroups

Another way to publicize your Web page is in any appropriate Usenet newsgroup. Usenet is a massive collection of over 11,000 Internet user discussion groups. There are hundreds of newsgroups explicitly for making announcements. If you have a Web page that is of likely interest to readers of that newsgroup, you should post an announcement there. Before doing so, however, read through the newsgroup to make sure that it's really what you think it is.

One user's Web announcement is shown in Figure 12.12. This one was posted in the newsgroup `news:comp.infosystems.announce`. The easiest way to find `.announce` newsgroups is to have your newsreader generate a list of all newsgroups. Then search through it for text matching announce.

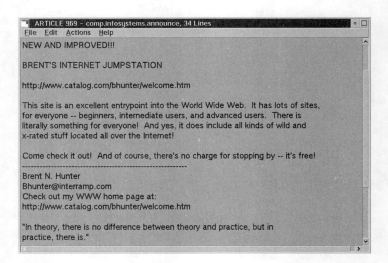

Figure 12.12. *Announcements about new Web pages are welcomed in* `.announce` *newsgroups.*

Note: A newsreader is a program designed to let you read and post articles in newsgroups.

Including Your URL in Your Signature

Many people on the Internet include a lot more than just their signatures—for example, pithy (or not-so-pithy) quotes. Like bumper stickers, signature lines are a way of making a statement without making that statement part of your message. Although some users object to lengthy signature lines that occupy valuable bandwidth, I've never heard anyone object to people including URLs in their signature lines. Signature lines can be used both in e-mail messages and in articles you post to newsgroups. Here's an example:

```
Herb Smith (herb@smith.com)
***Check us out for the best deals on computer memory: http://www.smith.com***
```

Getting Listed in Other Web Documents

Another way to publicize your Web page is to get listed in the Web pages of other individuals and organizations who have similar interests. One way to do that is to cruise the Web looking for likely candidates and then e-mail them indicating how their including a reference to your URL would be useful to others. The best way, of course, is make your Web page the best on the net. That way, others will be sure to include a link to your URL. Some special pages to which you might aspire are The Awesome List (`http://www.clark.net/pub/journalism/awesome.html`), shown in Figure 12.13, Scott Yanoff's Special Internet Connections page (`http://info.cern.ch/hypertext/DataSources/Yanoff.html`), shown in Figure 12.14, and the Webaholics page (`http://www.ohiou.edu/~rbarrett/webaholics/ver2/`), shown in Figure 12.15.

12

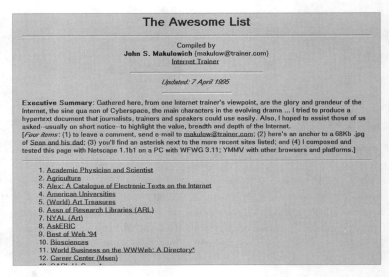

Figure 12.13. *If you can get on The Awesome List, that's awesome!*

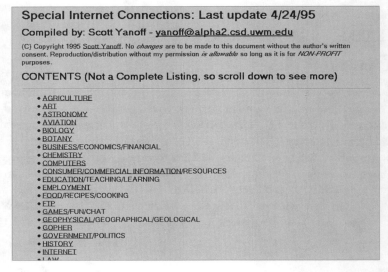

Figure 12.14. *Scott Yanoff's Special Internet Connections page lists hundreds of URLs.*

Figure 12.15. *If you make it to Webaholic's Top 50, you've really made it!*

Summary

Today, you learned about the major resources available on the Internet for publicizing your Web presentation. Undoubtedly, as you will discover, there are more. In particular, there very likely are resources that better fit your particular topic or business. However, if you're new to the Web, you now know where to start.

Q&A

Q **When I ask someone to include my URL on their home page, what's to stop them from saying "No?"**

A Nothing—just as they can't possibly say "Yes" unless you ask them. As you'll soon discover, the Web is a form of computerized exhibitionism. Have you ever met a shy exhibitionist? Don't be afraid to ask. They've been asked before by others.

Q **Should I broadcast a wide e-mail announcement about my Web page to everyone whose e-mail address I can find? After all, e-mail is free for me.**

A No. That's a great way to make enemies. Although e-mail might be free for you, it's not free for a lot of us. People resent getting electronic junk mail, especially if it effectively comes postage due. Train your sights instead at sites that welcome such announcements.

12

271

Q **What about newspapers and magazines?**

A Yes, definitely. If you have a home page of interest to photo hobbyists, for example, letters to your favorite photo mags are in order. You might even consider putting together a press release (electronic and paper) and sending it to the appropriate publicists. Many magazines, newspaper columnists, and newsletters are itching for Web stuff to include, simply because they know how *hot* (don't you *hate* that use of hot?) it is right now.

DAY 7

Advanced Webbery

13

Web Forms
and Image
Maps

Web Forms and Image Maps

So far, you've learned a great deal about how to present information on the Web page to the user. In this chapter, you learn about another option called the image map. You also explore how to *get* information from the user using Web forms. Web forms permit you to receive a variety of different kinds of data from the user. They enable you to conduct surveys, collect potential client information, and even take orders for products and services (with the appropriate precautions, of course). Many users believe that the interactivity provided by the use of forms promises to make the Web *the* communications media of the last part of this decade. Best of all, creating forms using Word is extremely easy. Forms creation is where the Internet Assistant really shines!

First, a caution. Getting Web forms to work correctly requires the use of CGI (common gateway interface) programs, and can be a bit tricky and even downright tedious. What possibilities exist are determined in large part by the operating system of your Web server, what software is available (especially database software), and the policies of your Web provider. Some Web providers don't permit the use of CGI scripts at all, for reasons of security and because of the added burden they can place on mostly passive servers. Heavy use of forms places demands not only on the CPU in a server, but on disk space as well, because an unexpectedly heavy response to a form can easily exceed tightly managed storage areas. Before you invest a lot of time designing forms and writing CGI scripts, make sure that your provider allows forms. Check also with your provider to determine exactly what kinds of CGI programming will be needed to accommodate your forms. What works for one system won't necessarily work for others.

For that reason, today's lesson focuses mostly on designing and writing forms (that is, Web publishing, which is what this book is about) rather than on the programming necessary for using the data that comes back. For in-depth information on CGI programming, you should consult other sources, including your Web server administrator, as well as the excellent tutorial on CGI programming called The Common Gateway Interface (`http://hoohoo.ncsa.uiuc.edu/cgi`).

Web Forms

Web forms enable you to retrieve data in a number of different styles. The Internet Assistant component of Word directly supports forms creation using a modified implementation of Word's own form tools. Using the Internet Assistant tools, you can create the following:

- ☐ Single-line text box fill-in areas
- ☐ Multiline entry areas (similar to the message area in Mailto forms)
- ☐ Radio buttons (choose one item from among several options)
- ☐ Checkboxes
- ☐ Drop-down lists

Today, you learn how to create each type of form element, along with design and layout considerations.

Starting a Form

To begin your HTML document, choose File | New from the menu and specify Html as the document template. Now, from the menu choose Insert | Form. The Internet Assistant displays the notice dialog box shown in Figure 13.1. This tells you that you're not in Kansas anymore, so to speak. This notice appears the first time you enter forms mode for an HTML document, and can be disabled by clicking on the option at the bottom of the dialog box. This notice tells you that you're going into forms mode and that all the stuff you want in your form should be put between the Top of Form and Bottom of Form lines, which are also inserted at this time (see Figure 13.2). The Form Field dialog box appears, along with `html.dot`'s special Forms toolbar. Depending on how the Forms toolbar was last displayed on your system, it might float or it might be attached to one of the window borders. It is floating in Figure 13.2 so that it stands out better.

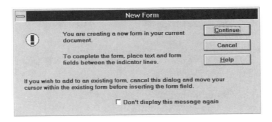

Figure 13.1. *The Internet Assistant alerts you to the fact that all forms elements must be created within the form area.*

Note: If you like doing things manually, or if you need to create multiple forms within an HTML document, you can also insert Top of Form and Bottom of Form lines manually by applying the z-Top of Form and z-Bottom of Form styles, respectively. You can duplicate a form area by copying a Top and Bottom pair to the clipboard and pasting it where you want it to appear. If there are any form elements included, you can delete them, or modify them as needed. This enables you to create multiple form structures within a single HTML document easily, should the need arise. Because you can have multiple forms, it therefore is essential that the Submit and Reset buttons appear only within the designated form area.

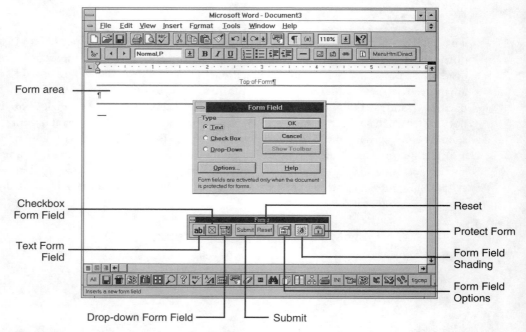

Figure 13.2. *The form area is between the lines; the Forms toolbar is ready.*

The strategy now is to build your form between the Top of Form and Bottom of Form lines. One possible point of confusion is whether just the form fields themselves go into the form area or the forms and the accompanying text (for example, text such as Type Your Name Below). Both the form fields and the instructional text go into the form area.

In HTML language, the top and bottom of the form look as follows:

```
<FORM>
```

```
</FORM>
```

All the forms controls must be placed inside the <FORM> tag area. You can, by the way, have multiple forms in the same HTML document. Just keep them separate.

Forms Toolbar

The Forms toolbar, shown in Figure 13.2, can be used to access form element dialog boxes. From left to right, here are the tools:

> *Text Form Field*—Use this tool to insert a text fill-in area, either single-line or multiline.

> *Checkbox Form Field*—Use this tool to insert a checkbox or a radio button.

Drop-down Form Field—Use this tool to insert a drop-down list.

Submit—Use this tool to insert a Submit button. The Submit button is used to send data to the Web server when the entry is finished.

Reset—Use this tool to insert a Reset button. The Reset button enables users to clear all entries. This is a handy option when users change their minds or realize that colossal entry errors were made.

Form Field Options—Use this tool to edit the selected form element.

Form Field Shading—Use this option to display shading of the form field on-screen. This option affects the display only in Word. It has no effect on the resulting form.

Protect Form—Use this option to protect the Word document from further editing. Given how fragile forms are, it's sometimes useful to lock forms so that you don't accidentally insert stray data anywhere. The protect option serves as an alert to the user that the document isn't an ordinary one.

Single-Line Text Box Fill-In Areas

Now you're going to insert a single-line text box into the form area. Single-line text boxes often are used for collecting names, company names, and addresses. Single-line text boxes are very useful for collecting fixed-length data fields, because the software enables you to limit the data length. Suppose that you are designing a form in which you want to obtain the Web user's name for use in a database. So that you can maintain a tight structure, you want the first, last, and middle names to be distinct. Let's create the form shown in Figure 13.3.

Sample Form

Type your name in the spaces provided below:

Title (MR, MS, MRS, DR, etc., Maximum 10 Characters)

Last Name (Maximum 25 Characters)

First Name (Maximum 25 Characters)

Middle Initial (One Character)

Jr., Sr., III, etc. (Maximum 10 Characters)

Figure 13.3. *A sample form using single-line text box fill-in areas.*

If the Form Field dialog box is still on-screen, press Esc or click on Cancel to dismiss it—you won't need it. You can get it back at any time by choosing Insert | Form Field from the menu. Move the insertion point inside the Top and Bottom form lines, and type some descriptive or instructional text. Keep in mind that the Web is international and not everyone speaks your language, especially not if you use slang or uncommon expressions. Keep it simple, and use examples! If there is a limit on how long the response is, include the limit. To create the form shown in Figure 13.3, type the following:

```
Type your name in the spaces provided below:¶
Title (MR, MS, MRS, DR, etc., Maximum 10 Characters)¶
```

Tip: For some forms, it's useful to have multiple versions—in French, Spanish, and so forth—to accommodate users of different nationalities. You might include links that point to versions of the form in other languages. If you don't want international responses, don't bother with multiple versions. In the latter case, you should also check with your Web administrator. There might be a way to restrict access to your Web page to users in a particular geographical region.

Unless you have some reason to do otherwise, type the descriptive text using the `Normal,P` style. You can use one of the various list styles for the form elements themselves, if desired, to indent the text entry boxes. For the form shown in Figure 13.3, `Normal,P` was used throughout.

Why Have Limits?

Some users use data from forms directly in databases. If, as part of your data definition, you allow a name to be only a certain number of characters, set up your form to allow only that number of characters. If a name has to be abbreviated or shortened in some way, it's a good bet that the user's abbreviation will be more useful than any scheme you or I could create. If you don't believe me, consider an address label on some junk mail I got yesterday, in which I'm referred to as Herbert L. Tyso. Had I known about the 15-character limit, I would have written Herb Tyson.

Some Web browsers, such as Netscape and the OS/2 WebExplorer, recognize the maximum-length parameter and do not accept any data entry in a field beyond that point. Some others, such as InternetWorks Internet Assistant, don't stop the user from entering too much data.

Now insert the text box. Click on the text form field tool on the toolbar. Depending on how your display is set (that is, if nonprinting characters are set to display using Tools | Options | View), the text box appears as a set of tiny shaded circles, as shown in Figure 13.4. If the area isn't shaded, click on the Form Field Shading tool so that it is. This makes it easier to see. Now double-click on the Text box to display the Text Form Field Options dialog box, shown in Figure 13.5.

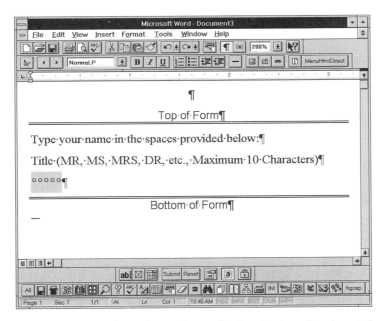

Figure 13.4. *When editing a form, the text box is displayed only as five tiny circles.*

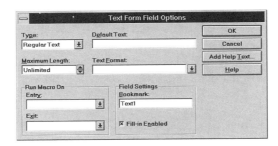

Figure 13.5. *Use the Text Form Field Options dialog box to define the fill-in area.*

Caution: Some of the options in the Text Form Field Options dialog box are not used in HTML documents, so don't waste your time with them. The Type, Text Format, and Macro to Run options are used in Word forms only. Once a document is converted to HTML, these options have no effect.

At this point, you've inserted a generic text box that might not be useful. Use the options in the dialog box to refine the form so that it suits your needs. For the current exercise, leave the Default Text area blank. You can, if you want, pre-enter the expected text. For some text entry items, where the expected entry might be identical 90 percent of the time, it's useful to include the expected text as the default so that the user is spared some entry. In this case, it's not very helpful. Under Maximum length, use the arrows to set an upper limit. The built-in upper limit is 80 characters, but it's often useful to specify something lower. If you need something above 80, see the section "Multiline Entry Areas," later in this chapter.

Even if you're not using a database program, it's a good idea to set an upper limit. Then you won't be faced with being overwhelmed by tons of useless data entered by wiseguys. (You don't want any 80-character middle initials, do you?) In addition to making it harder to deal with data you receive, not having limits also means that your disk space might fill up sooner than you expect.

Now you need to create a name that the browser will use to send the user entry to the server. Click on the Add Help Text box, and then click on the Help Key (F1) tab. Click on Type Your Own and type the name. The name is essential in sending data to the Web server, and in turn, it's essential for getting your CGI script to do something with the data sent. Type the name, and then click on OK to return to the main dialog box.

Note: The temptation is strong to use the Bookmark field in the Text Box Options dialog box for the name of the form field. You can do that; however, the way the Internet Assistant works sometimes prevents the name from showing up in that field if you subsequently edit the text box options. If you use the Help Key (F1), Type Your Own area for the name, it is retained correctly.

When all entry is done, click on OK. In HTML, the form field you just inserted will later appear as follows (assuming you chose 10 as the maximum length and left the default text blank):

```
<INPUT NAME="Title" VALUE="" MAXLENGTH="10" >
```

Congratulations—you've created an HTML form! Of course, it's absolutely useless without a Submit button, so go to the next section immediately before somebody catches you without a Submit button! Before you go, however, note that while editing the Word version of your form, you can go back at any point and make changes (except when it is protected—toggle protection on and off using the Protect Form tool). Now insert a Submit button!

The Submit Button

The Submit button is used to send the completed form to the Web server. Submit buttons typically are placed at the bottom of forms. To insert the Submit button, move the insertion point to where you want the button to appear and click on the Submit tool on the Forms toolbar. The Form Submit Button dialog box appears (see Figure 13.6). Here, you determine the appearance of the Submit button as well as how data gets submitted.

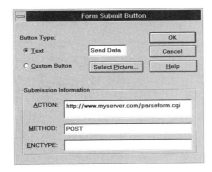

Figure 13.6. *Use the Form Submit Button dialog box to set the appearance of the submit button and how data are submitted.*

Caution: Unlike other forms elements, you cannot edit the definition of a Submit button by double-clicking on it or by choosing the Form Fields Options tool. If you double-click on an existing Submit button, bless its little heart, it tries in vain to submit something. Instead, to change a submit button, you should delete the existing button (select it and press the Delete key) and then create a new Submit button using the Submit tool on the Forms toolbar.

The choices you make in the Form Submit Button dialog box are crucial to getting the form to work correctly. For the Submit button itself, you can make it a text-only button by choosing the Text button type and filling in the adjacent text box with the text you want to appear. Common

choices are Submit, Submit Form, Send Data, Cast Vote, and so on. Alternatively, you can choose a Custom Button by clicking on the Select Picture button. There, you choose an image file (preferably a GIF) to appear in lieu of the standard text button. If you choose the Custom Button option, include some alternative text for folks who don't display graphics. Otherwise, users might go crazy trying to find some way to submit the form.

Under ACTION, type the instruction you want performed when the form is submitted (a URL pointing to a CGI script). The action might be an instruction to start up a database program or perhaps just to cause the data to be appended to the end of an existing text file. Consult with your Web server administrator if necessary to make sure that the Action is entered correctly.

Under METHOD, the two choices are POST and GET. Most HTML gurus (including the people at NCSA and CERN) and guides (including this one) recommend that you choose POST. What's the difference? GET submissions encode the data into the URL. On the server, the data gets assigned to an environment variable called QUERY_STRING. A CGI script can then use the QUERY_STRING variable to access and refer to the data, for parsing or whatever. A problem, however, is that on some UNIX servers, the length of environment variable is limited. This might cause data from some forms to get truncated. Ouch!

The alternative, and better choice, is POST. Using POST, the encoded data is sent directly to the server without using an environment variable. Thus, POST enables you to send any amount of data, preventing possible truncation.

Under ENCTYPE, you include the MIME type for the data being sent. MIME (multipurpose internet mail extensions) is a standard set of data types that tells receiving programs how to interpret data. For HTML forms data, the type should be either Content - type: text/ html or left blank.

When you're done, click on OK to insert the Submit button. When you save the Word document in HTML format, the Submit button appears as follows:

```
<INPUT TYPE="SUBMIT" VALUE="Send Form">
```

Depending on your entry in the other field, another HMTL tag gets created as well, at the top of the form area:

```
<FORM ACTION="http://www.myserver.com/parsehtml.cgi" METHOD="POST" ENCTYPE=
➡"Content - type: Text/HTML">
```

When the Submit button gets "pushed" (usually clicked) by a user who is viewing the form while on the Internet, all the data from the form will be sent, using whatever METHOD and ENCTYPE you specified, to the program specified under ACTION. That program then does something with the data, and (usually) returns some result to the Web browser. It's common practice for many CGI scripts to include some kind of courtesy action, such as saying Thank you Mr. Emily Smith for your submission (alerting you to the fact that you probably clicked on the Mr. button, Emily).

The Reset Button

The Reset button, usually included as a courtesy, enables the user to clear the entire form with a single click. To insert a Reset button, move the insertion point to where you want the Reset button to appear and click on the Reset tool. This causes the following HTML tag to be inserted:

```
<INPUT TYPE="RESET">
```

Multiline Entry Areas

Sometimes 80 characters is not long enough. What if you're having an essay contest, for example? You can use the Text Form Field control, but the instructions are a little tricky. Let's say, for example, that you want folks to tell you why they'd like to be president. First, type some descriptive or instructional text, such as the following:

```
Please use the following space to tell us why you want to be President:
```

Press Enter to go to the next line. Next, use the Text Form Field to insert a text entry field and immediately double-click on the field to evoke the Text Form Field Options dialog box. Click on the Add Help Text button (trust me) to display the Form Field Help Text dialog box. To define the size of the text box area, click on the Status Bar tab at the top. In the Type Your Own box, you would type the dimensions for the text area, where *r* is the number of rows, and *c* is the number of columns:

```
Rows="r" Cols="c"
```

For example, to create a text area that is 10 rows high and 65 columns wide, type the following (see Figure 13.7):

```
Rows="10" Cols="65"
```

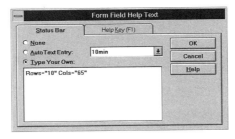

Figure 13.7. *Type the numbers of rows and columns in the Status Bar area.*

To type the name that the fill-in area will be assigned for sending data to the server, click on the Help Key (F1) tab and type this, where *name* is the name of the variable:

```
Name="name"
```

For example, to name the variable Reasons, as shown in Figure 13.8, use the following:

```
Name="Reasons"
```

Figure 13.8. *Type the name in the Help Key (F1) area.*

Then click on OK to return to the main dialog box, where you click on OK again to insert the form field. In HTML, you just created a set of tags that appear as the following:

```
<TEXTAREA NAME="Name="Reasons"" Rows="10" Cols="65">
```

```
</TEXTAREA>
```

When displayed in a Web browser, it appears as shown in Figure 13.9.

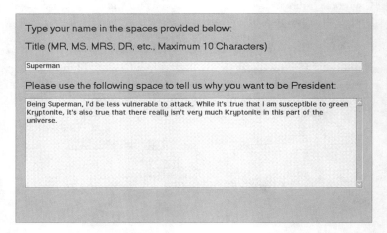

Figure 13.9. *The finished multiline editing box as seen from a Web browser.*

Checkboxes

Another useful option in forms is checkboxes. Checkboxes are useful when you have a list of choices that are not mutually exclusive. For example, you might have one of those "Check all that apply" lists:

```
What features do you require on your new car?
(Check all that apply):
Air conditioning
Steering wheel
Dual air bags
All wheel drive
Ski rack
Sun roof
CD Player
```

To create this kind of checklist, first type the list. When designing checklists, it's often useful and attractive to format the list as an unformatted list (which usually causes the list to be indented on most browsers) and to put the checkboxes at the beginning of each item. If you put the checkboxes at the end, you will not be able to align them. The resulting form isn't as neat and is sometimes more difficult to fill out. On the other hand, scattering the checkboxes throughout the form does decrease the chances that the wrong box will get checked.

Whatever your choice, move the insertion point to where you want the first checkbox to appear. Click on the checkbox tool on the toolbar to insert a checkbox. It will appear at the insertion point. Repeat the procedure for each checkbox you want to create. If you find it easier, copy the first one to the clipboard and then paste it wherever needed.

Tip: If you create a series of checkboxes, one after another, you can insert the first by clicking on the checkbox tool. Until you perform some other editing, inserting the checkbox form field is then assigned to the F4 (repeat) key. You can then use F4 to insert each of the other checkboxes, which might be faster than going back to the toolbar. To add checkboxes to a whole column, use the toolbar to add the first one. Then press the down arrow to go to the next line and press F4. It takes less than five seconds to create 20 checkboxes.

Now, double-click on the first checkbox to display the Check Box Form Field Options dialog box shown in Figure 13.10.

In the dialog box, choose whether the checkbox will be checked by default. You also need to supply a name in which the checkbox state will be stored. For example, you might use AC as the name for the Air Conditioning checkbox. It might be reasonable to assume Air Conditioning is the default, in which case you set the default value to Checked. Similarly,

you might name the Ski Rack checkbox Ski and set the default to Not Checked. Once all the checkboxes are defined, they appear as follows when the document containing the form is saved in HTML format:

```
<INPUT TYPE="CHECKBOX" NAME="AC"   CHECKED>Air conditioning
<INPUT TYPE="CHECKBOX" NAME="Steering"  CHECKED>Steering wheel
<INPUT TYPE="CHECKBOX" NAME="AirBags"  CHECKED>Dual air bags
<INPUT TYPE="CHECKBOX" NAME="AWD" >All wheel drive
<INPUT TYPE="CHECKBOX" NAME="Ski" >Ski rack
<INPUT TYPE="CHECKBOX" NAME="SunRoof" >Sun roof
<INPUT TYPE="CHECKBOX" NAME="CDPlayer" >CD Player
```

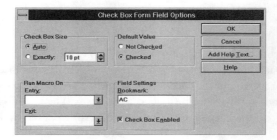

Figure 13.10. *The Check Box Form Field Options dialog box.*

When a form containing checkboxes is submitted to the Web server, the checked checkbox results are sent with the value on. For example, if the URL is http://www.myserver.com/carfacts.cgi, and if the form is sent as shown in Figure 13.11, the values are sent to the server as AC=on&Ski=on. The other variables' names are not sent at all. If all checkboxes are unchecked, no values for the variables (AC, Ski, Steer, and so forth) are sent at all.

Testing a Form

New Car Survey

What features do you require on your new car?

(Check all that apply):
- ☑ Air conditioning
- ☐ Steering wheel
- ☐ Dual air bags
- ☐ All wheel drive
- ☑ Ski rack
- ☐ Sun roof
- ☐ CD Player

Submit Reset

Figure 13.11. *Definitely say "Yes" to a steering wheel!*

Radio Buttons

You also can use the Check Box tool to create radio buttons. Radio buttons are suitable for items that are mutually exclusive, such as gender. With regular checkboxes, each item has a different variable name. To create a radio button, you give all the items the same name. Consider the following list, which you might want to turn into a series of radio buttons to allow the user to select just one:

```
Presidental Straw Poll—Vote Here!
If the Presidential election were held today, for which of the following would
you vote:
Bill Clinton
Bob Dole
Bill Gates
```

First, use the checkbox tool to insert a checkbox in front of each candidate. Next, double-click on the first checkbox to display the Check Box Form Field Options dialog box, as shown in Figure 13.10. In the bookmark field, put the name that you want to be used for the result that gets returned. You can, if you like, just leave the default name (Check1, Check2, and so on). However, a name that actually describes the data you are collecting is better, because it helps document what's being done. For example, you might put vote. Whatever you put, add the text _RD (for radio), so it now appears as vote_RD. To simplify the rest of the procedure, select vote_RD (or whatever you called it) and press Ctrl+Ins to copy it to the clipboard.

Click on the Add Help Text button, and then click on the Help Key (F1) tab. Choose Type Your Own and press Shift+Ins to put the same name you used in the bookmark field (for example, vote_RD), as shown in Figure 13.12. Click on the Status Bar tab and again choose the Type Your Own option. Here, type the following, replacing *name* with the value you want to assign to vote_RD if this particular item is chosen:

VALUE="*name*"

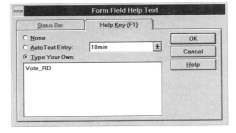

Figure 13.12. *To create radio buttons, all options must have the same name ending in _RD.*

For example, names for each checkbox might be Clinton, Dole, and Gates, respectively. As shown in Figure 13.13, type the following into the Type Your Own text area:

VALUE="Clinton"

Figure 13.13. *Type the value of the option into the Status Bar area.*

Click on OK to return to the Check Box Form Field Options dialog box and then click on OK to accept the choices. Note that in this instance, you do not use the Default Value (Checked or Unchecked) option. If you use that option, it causes that particular item to be the default choice. Sometimes, it's appropriate and helpful to make one of the items the default. For example, if you were giving a choice of Preferred Language, and most respondents were from Mexico, you might make Spanish the default. In the case of a Presidential straw poll, you don't (or shouldn't) want to risk prejudicing the results by suggesting a default.

Repeat the procedure for each checkbox. When the resulting document is saved in HTML format, the tags will look like this:

```
<INPUT TYPE="RADIO" NAME="Vote_RD" Value="Clinton">Bill Clinton
<INPUT TYPE="RADIO" NAME="Vote_RD" Value="Dole">Bob Dole
<INPUT TYPE="RADIO" NAME="Vote_RD" Value="Gates">Bill Gates
```

Next, you should insert a submit button. Move the insertion point (text cursor) where you want the submit button to be, and click on the Submit tool. In the Form Submit Button dialog box, type the necessary information for the submit button, as described under the heading, "The Submit Button." For this particular list, you might customize the text. To do that, set the Type to Text Button and fill in the adjacent text box with the text you want to use, such as Vote. You might also want to include a Reset button. If users change their minds and want to clear their choices so that no radio buttons are selected (or to otherwise return forms to their default status), the Reset button provides that option. The finished straw poll displays in a Web browser, as shown in Figure 13.14.

When the user votes by clicking on the Vote (submit) button, data is sent to the browser in the form *name=choice*. For example, depending on how the user votes, the data sent is vote_RD=Clinton, vote_RD=Dole, or vote_RD=Gates. If the user clicks on the Submit button without making a choice, no value for vote_RD is sent.

Presidental Straw Poll--Vote Here!

If the Presidential election were held today, for which of the following would you vote:
- ○Bill Clinton
- ○Bob Dole
- ○Bill Gates

Vote   Reset

Figure 13.14. *The finished poll.*

Drop-Down Lists

A final type of form field supported by HTML and Word's Internet Assistant is a drop-down, or selection, list. Because they take up less room on the Web page than radio buttons, drop-down lists are a great way to give the user a choice from a number of options. Different Web browsers implement drop-down lists in different ways, as shown in Figure 13.15. Internet Works Internet Assistant and Netscape both use traditional drop-down lists. The OS/2 WebExplorer, however, uses a spinner control.

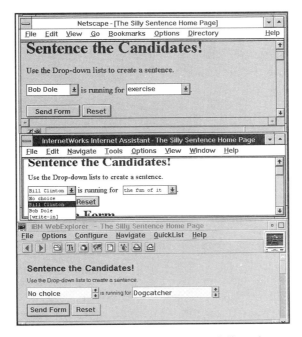

Figure 13.15. *Different browsers display drop-down lists differently.*

To insert a drop-down or selection list in a form, you use the Drop-Down Form Field tool. Actually, however, you can save a step by using the Insert | Form Field command from the menu, because it takes you directly into the Drop-Down Form Field Options dialog box. First, move the cursor to where you want the drop-down list to appear, between the Top of Form and Bottom of Form lines. Next, choose Insert | Form Field from the menu. The dialog box shown in Figure 13.16 appears. Click on the Drop-Down choice and then click on the Options button.

Figure 13.16. *Choose the Drop-Down type and click on the Options button.*

First, the selection result is going to need a name. Let's say you're creating a list similar to the one shown in Figure 13.15, and you're setting up the second drop-down list—that is, the reasons for running. In this case, you might name the result why-run, or perhaps, just reason. Type the name in the bookmark field, as shown in Figure 13.17.

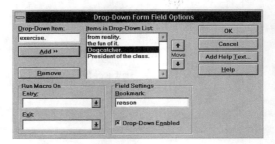

Figure 13.17. *Type the option name in the Bookmark field.*

To create an item for the drop-down list, click the mouse in the Drop-Down Item text box, and type the option. Then click on the Add button. The item is added to the Items in Drop-Down List at the right. In Figure 13.17, for example, you type exercise, and then click on Add. You repeat the procedure for each item you want to add. To remove or edit an item, click on the unwanted item in the Items in Drop-Down List, and then click on the Remove

button. This moves the item from the list back to the Drop-Down List text box. There, you can edit it and click on Add or just proceed to your next choice.

If you want to rearrange the items in the list, you can. Click on the item you want to move in the Items in Drop-Down List and then click on either of the arrows above the word Move. If you click on the Up arrow, the item is moved up one position in the list. If you click on the Down arrow, the reverse happens.

After adding all the choices you want to the list, click on the Add Help Text box and then choose the Status Bar tab. Click on Type Your Own, and type the following, replacing *name* with the same name you wrote in the Bookmark field:

```
NAME="name"
```

Next, click on OK to return to the main dialog box and click on OK to insert the drop-down list. When the document is saved in HTML format, the drop-down coding appears as follows—including the first drop-down list as well, so you can see the transition:

```
<SELECT NAME="Candidate" >
<OPTION SELECTED>John Smith
<OPTION>No choice
<OPTION>Bill Clinton
<OPTION>Bob Dole</SELECT> is running <SELECT NAME="reason" >
<OPTION>from reality.
<OPTION>for the fun of it.
<OPTION SELECTED>for President of the class.
<OPTION>for exercise.
<OPTION>for Dogcatcher.</SELECT>.
```

Notice that, in order to have the two selection sets appear as a sentence, the first one (`Strawpoll`) ends in the same line that the second one (`reason`) begins. Also notice that two items, `John Smith` in the `Strawpoll` set and `for President of the class` in the `reason` set, are also given the `SELECTED` attribute. This means that the two checkboxes will be filled in with those two results when the form first shows on-screen.

In the Internet Assistant for Word, the drop-down list displays as shown in Figure 13.18. Not too flashy, eh? Well, remember, at this moment, you're using Word as an HTML editor, not as a browser.

The finished list displays as shown in Figure 13.19 when using Word as a Web browser. Unlike the other browsers, the Word Internet Assistant doesn't display the drop-down arrow until you click on the item. For a silly sentence game such as the one shown here, this makes the result look more like a sentence (especially if field shading is not turned on). Of course, it also makes it likely that the user won't even realize that there are drop-down selection boxes!

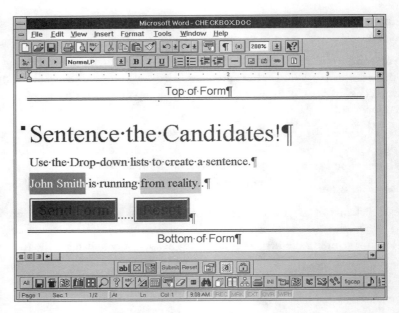

Figure 13.18. *Drop-down lists display rather blandly in Word when you create an HTML document.*

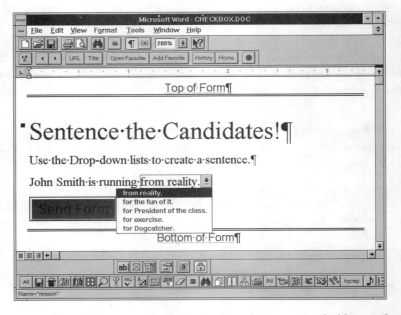

Figure 13.19. *When you browse with Word, the drop-down arrow is hidden until you click on the drop-down field.*

When the form is submitted, this result is sent as the following:

```
candidate=name&reason=why
```

where *name* is replaced by one of the candidate's names, and *why* is replaced with one of the reasons you created. Your CGI script can then parse and use the results as you see fit.

Image Maps

An image map is a picture (usually a GIF) for which you assign different actions to different parts of the picture. Using the image map shown in Figure 13.20, for example, different URLs get loaded based on where you click. One good application for image maps is a geographical map. If you are setting up a weather information server, for example, you might use a map of the U.S. to offer the user a way to select states or regions.

Figure 13.20. *IBM uses a composite of various images for an image map.*

To insert an image map, you need your image, as well as the help of your Web server administrator. Let's go as far as you can with Word; then you'll see what else you need to accomplish. The following are the general steps:

1. Create or choose an image file (GIF or JPEG).
2. Create a map file (MAP).
3. Insert the image file and link into your HTML document.

Creating or Choosing an Image File

The first step is the most important and probably the easiest. In deciding on an image file, you should choose something that's relatively compact (so it doesn't take minutes to download it). You should also choose an image that has well-delineated regions. Very busy pictures, with lots of different things happening and subtle color changes, don't work well. Pictures with definite geometric shapes and distinct areas work very well. Geographical maps can work pretty well, but defining areas to minimize problems of overlap can be pretty difficult.

Another interesting idea that some Web designers use is to create a composite image made from a number of different images. This approach works especially well because the boundaries between the different images often form squares or rectangles. You also can create image maps by taking one definitive object, copying it, and then using different versions of it to represent different choices. Consider the image shown in Figure 13.21, for example.

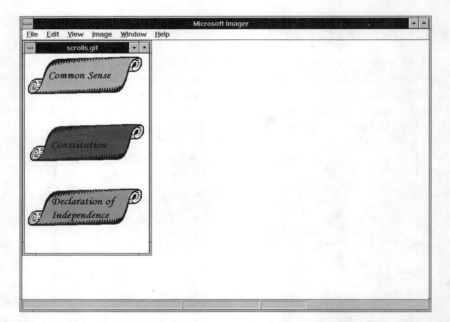

Figure 13.21. *An image created with Windows Paintbrush and converted to a GIF using Microsoft Imager.*

To create this image, you load an image of a scroll into Windows Paintbrush, then copy the scroll to the clipboard and duplicate it twice. Next, you fill in the background of each scroll with a different color. Then use Matura MT Script font to type the names of three documents: Thomas Paine's Common Sense, the U.S. Constitution, and the Declaration of Independence. Then save the image as SCROLLS.PCX. Next, open SCROLLS.PCX using Microsoft Imager (described in Chapter 5, "Tags and Styles") and immediately resave the file in GIF format as SCROLLS.GIF. This image can then be used as an image map to point to URLs for the three different documents.

Creating a Map File

The second step is to create a map file. This step is particularly difficult because the map file format is different for different kinds of Web servers. However, the basic idea is to divide your image into distinct geometric shapes (circles, polygons, and rectangles). Next, use plane

geometry to determine the coordinates of the different regions. For example, you define a circle by specifying the coordinates of the center (in pixels) and the length of the radius. To define a polygon, you specify the coordinates of each of the corners. To define a rectangle, you specify the coordinates of the upper-left and lower-right corners.

In describing image maps, the upper-left corner of the picture is the *origin*, (0,0). Each point on the picture is described as (x,y), where x is the number of pixels to the right of the origin, and y is the number of pixels below the origin.

It's often useful to print out an enlarged version of your image for starters. Then, using Microsoft Imager, choose File | Open and load the image. Use the View menu options to turn on the display of the ruler and the status bar. If the units are displayed in something other than pixels (as indicated by the square where the two rulers intersect), click the right mouse button on the intersection square and choose Pixels. You should have a view like that shown in Figure 13.22. Now it should be clear exactly where the origin is. The rulers give you a clear idea of the coordinates of parts of the picture.

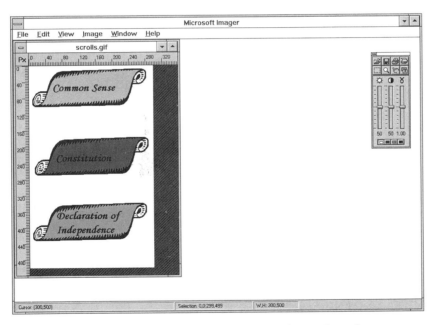

Figure 13.22. *When you turn on the rulers, Imager shows the pixel coordinates.*

Using Imager as you move the mouse on the picture, notice that numbers appear on the status bar at the bottom of the window (see Figure 13.22). If you move the mouse to the upper left, it reads 0,0. If you move the mouse to the lower right, it reads 299,499. To find the coordinates for a polygon, move the mouse pointer to the first corner. Write the coordinates on your print-out. Then move to the next corner, and so on, until you completely describe the polygon.

To find the coordinates for a rectangle, move the mouse pointer to the upper-left corner of the rectangle and write the display from the status bar. Next, move the mouse pointer to the lower-right corner of the rectangle and write those coordinates.

To find the coordinates of a circle, move the mouse pointer to the center of the circle, and write the coordinates. Note that the y value (the second number), is the vertical distance between the top of the picture (where $y=0$) and the center of the circle. Watching the X-coordinate, move the mouse pointer so that it is on the bottom edge of the circle (the X-coordinate is the same as it was when you pointed at the center). Write the y value at that location, and subtract the y value from the center. For example, if the center is at (`90,100`) and the bottom edge of the circle is at (`90,180`), the radius is the difference between the two y values, or $180 - 100$, which is 80. Thus, the coordinate definition of the circle is (`90,100`) `80` (the center and the radius).

Map files are stored on the Web server computer and are different for different systems. The following is the general structure for CERN HTTPD map files, which are the most common:

```
polygon (x₁,y₁) (x₂,y₂)... (xₙ,yₙ) url
rectangle (x₁,y₁) (xᵣ,yᵣ) url
circle (x_c,y_c) r url
default url
```

The parameters are defined as follows:

> x is the horizontal distance from the origin.
>
> y is the vertical distance from the origin.
>
> url is the URL to which control is passed when the noted area gets clicked.
>
> Subscripts of $_1$, $_2$, and $_n$ indicate coordinate points for an n-sided polygon.
>
> Subscripts of $_1$ and $_r$ indicate the upper-left and lower-right coordinates of a rectangle.
>
> Subscript $_c$ indicates the center of a circle.
>
> The variable r is the radius of a circle.

You can define as many different geometric areas as you like. That is, you are not limited just to a single circle, polygon, and rectangle. There might be a practical limit however, based on how patient you are and exactly what you want to accomplish. If you have a very complex shape—a state such as Michigan or Florida, for example—you might need to define a number of points for the shape. If you search the Web, however, you are likely to discover that someone else has already done an image map of the U.S. and has both it and the corresponding map file available for downloading.

An image map works in the following way. When you click on an image map area, your graphical Web browser *knows* where you click. Because the thing you click on is defined as an image map, your Web browser knows that it is to pass the coordinates to the Web server, along with the URL of a CGI program (htimage) to execute. Based on the coordinates passed,

the CGI program determines which, if any, areas you clicked of those defined in your map file. It then passes control to the corresponding URL or to the default URL if you did not click in any defined area.

> **Tip:** Now that you know how it works, you might want to use a less precise strategy if parts of the image are not clearly delineated. For example, the scrolls shown in Figure 13.21 might loosely be described using a polygon (specifically a parallelogram). You might rather use three larger rectangular areas so that clicking near one of the scrolls works as well as clicking on it.

Now that you have your map coordinates, you need to create a map file. A CERN map file for Figure 13.21 might appear as follows:

```
default http://~tyson/web/default.html
rectangle (0,0) (299,110) http://~tyson/web/comsense.html
rectangle (0,120) (299,300,) http://~tyson/web/usconst.html
rectangle (0,310) (299,499) http://~tyson/web/declare.html
```

Once you create this file, calling it docs.map or something similarly descriptive, you need to transfer a copy of it to your Web server. You also need to find the location of the htimage program. You might additionally have to make a copy of it in your own Web files area, depending on what kind of access you have. Your Web server administrator can tell you. For now, assume that htimage is on /cgi-bin and that the map file is on ~tyson/web. Note: remember that ~ refers to your home directory on many UNIX servers.

Inserting the Image File and Linking into Your HTML Document

Now that you've done all of the groundwork, you're ready to install the image map into your main HTML document. First, move the insertion point to where you want the image map to appear in your HTML document. Next, click on the HyperLink tool on the toolbar. If necessary, click on the URL tab at the top of the dialog box.

Click on the Image button to display the Insert Picture dialog box. Use the Drives, Directories, and List Files of Type controls, as needed, to navigate to the location of the file you want to use. Click on the file so that its name appears in the File Name box. In the Alternative text area, type a useful comment that will be displayed if the user doesn't have graphics enabled. Something such as the following works nicely:

```
If graphics are not available, you see this message instead of an image map.
```

Next, click on the Advanced button. In the Advanced Picture Options dialog box, click on the Sensitive Map option. Choose the desired alignment, as well, and then click on OK to return to the Insert Picture dialog box and click on OK again to return to the HyperLink dialog box.

Now you need to type the URL. This varies by the type of server. Because you're describing a CERN site, let's use the CERN format. Check with your Web server administrator to see exactly what's needed for your system. The URL for the htimage program is a little kinky. It's a composite of the location of htimage and the location of your map file. If htimage is on /cgi-bin and the map file is ~tyson/web/docs.map, the URL should be the following:

```
/cgi-bin/htimage/~tyson/web/docs.map
```

This is kinky for several reasons. First, no http:// is used. Second, the location of docs.map is added to the end of the htimage script name. I don't know why it's done this way—it just is!

When you're done, using the parameters described here, the image map appears in your HTML document. If you look at the raw HTML code directly, it should be this (ideally):

```
<A HREF="/cgi-bin/htimage/~tyson/web/docs.map>
<IMG SRC="scrolls.gif ISMAP>
</A>
```

I said *ideally* because, if you have to navigate to the location of your GIF file, there will be some directory information shown before scrolls.gif. If there is, you need to modify the location so that it correctly describes the location of scrolls.gif on your Web server. This harkens back to Chapter 11, "How To Install Your Web Presentation onto a Web Server," where you learned that you have to modify the URLs to match the expected locations on your Web server. Of course, if you set up a subdirectory structure on your own Web workspace on your own computer that matches the subdirectory structure on your Web server, you should be all set.

Summary

In this chapter, you learned how to create interactive forms using the Internet Assistant. You explored how results are sent to the server and learned about image maps, including some ideas about where to get the images, how to create map files, and how to set them up for a CERN server.

Q&A

Q You said that we should always offer text alternatives to image maps. Is that some kind of rule?

A No, but it oughtta be! It's just common sense and common courtesy. There are millions and millions of people on the Web. Many of them—including me, I might add—connect at speeds that make using graphical Web browsers nearly intolerable. In browsing the Web, I've been alarmed recently at the number of Web pages that assume—often incorrectly—that everyone is using a graphical browser, and that they have their graphics turned on. Worse, many of these don't bother using the Alternative text field in the Insert Picture dialog box that might otherwise alert users that something worthwhile is missing.

Q My image is 200 by 300. How come it goes up to 199 by 299 only?

A Because it starts at 0,0 rather than 1,1. If it went up to 200 and 300, your picture would really be 201 by 301. And why, pray tell, does it start at 0,0 rather than at 1,1? It's a carryover from geometry. Do you remember that you drew an X-axis and a Y-axis, dividing the graph into four quadrants? And the 0,0 point was in the middle, rather than at the upper-left corner? The four quadrants—working counterclockwise from upper right—were numbered I, II, III, and IV. All of the points in quadrants II, III, and IV had either all negative coordinates (quadrant III), or a mixture of positive and negative, depending on whether they were to the left of the Y-axis or below the X-axis. (Is any of this coming back to you?) It's stupid to think of pictures as having negative pixels, so we use just quadrant I to describe them. Why do we begin at the upper left rather than the lower left? Who knows?

14

Other Tools for Web Publishing from Word

So far, you've learned how to use the Internet Assistant for Word to create HTML documents. Using the Internet Assistant appears to be an effective, no-cost (except for downloading) way to prepare Web pages for publication on the World Wide Web. Not everyone likes using the Internet Assistant, however, because of the following reasons:

- ☐ It works only with Word 6 for Windows and does not work with Word for Windows 2.0.
- ☐ A number of users find that it increases Word's already high use of resources, making memory-related crashes more likely.
- ☐ It makes Word slower.
- ☐ It turns off the Wrap-to-Window feature each time you change windows within Word.
- ☐ It changes the meaning of the GoBack command (Shift+F5), eliminating a key way to return to your former editing position when opening a Word file.

The first reason alone is enough to cause some users to seek other solutions. Before the Internet Assistant was released, in fact, a number of other solutions had been placed into shareware. Today, you learn about other Word-related approaches to HTML publishing. This comes with a caveat, however. If you are attracted to any of these alternatives, you should bear in mind how they came about. Most were developed at a time when Microsoft had not announced the Internet Assistant. Now that the Internet Assistant—which is free—is here, it would not be unreasonable to assume that some of the third-party add-ons for Word will cease being developed. However, several of the developers have indicated that the existence of the Internet Assistant has actually increased interest in their products and that development is continuing.

Today, you explore two of the other HTML solutions in detail, creating sample HTML documents with CU_HTML.DOT and GT_HTML.DOT. You also get a window-shopper's tour of something called ANT_HTML. Other Word Web authoring tools *not* looked at here are Quarterdeck's Web Author for Word (the demo version of which expired before I even knew it existed), and TagWizard (for which I could find only a 5MB .DOC file but nothing else).

CU_HTML.DOT (Chinese University Template)

CU_HTML is a freeware package for creating HTML files using WinWord versions 2 or 6. It was written by Kenneth Y. P. Wong and Anton S. Y. Lam of the Chinese University of Hong Kong. The CU approach to HTML is similar in some respects to the Internet Assistant

approach. It works using a template called `CU_HTML.DOT`. The template is available in versions for Word for Windows 2 and 6. The fact that it is not just for Word 6 makes it an attractive alternative for some user. CU also uses several DLLs (dynamic link libraries). CU is straightforward and easy to use, but it doesn't offer as full an implementation of HTML as the Internet Assistant does. Here is a summary of the salient points of CU:

- [ ] It works with versions 2 and 6 of Word for Windows.
- [ ] It doesn't slow down Word.
- [ ] It doesn't change Word's normal operation (except in the HTML document).
- [ ] It is free, as is the Internet Assistant.
- [ ] It doesn't provide support for forms.
- [ ] It doesn't provide support for image maps.
- [ ] It automatically can convert `.htm` extensions to `.html` when writing the HTML file.
- [ ] It provides no support for logical formatting tags (as opposed to physical formatting).
- [ ] It supports only the following tags:

`H1-H6`	Headings 1–6
`OL`	Numbered list
`UL`	Unnumbered list
`ADDRESS`	Address
`PRE`	Preformatted text
`TITLE`	Title
`HR`	Horizontal rule
`IMG SRC...`	Inline GIF image
`A HREF...`	HREF
Anchor Names	
`B`, `I`, and `U`	Bold, italic, and underline
`BR`	Line break
`P`	Paragraph break

Installing CU_HTML

Installing CU_HTML is quick and easy, but manual—there's no SETUP program. Before installing, you need to obtain the latest copy of `CU_HTML.ZIP`. You can ensure that you have the latest by downloading it from the source at the Chinese University of Hong Kong: `http://www.cuhk.hk/csc/cu_html.htm`. When you load the latter `.htm`, the installation instructions point you to the download site at `ftp://ftp.cuhk.ck/pub/www/windows/util/cu_html.zip`.

First, unzip `CU_HTML.ZIP`. The zip packet for CU_HTML version 1.53 contains the following files:

BUTTONS.GIF	GIF.DLL
BUTTONS2.GIF	GIF.GIF
COPYRIGH.TXT	LINK.GIF
CU_HTML.DLL	LOCAL.GIF
CU_HTML.DOC	README.TXT
CU_HTML.HTM	SAVE.GIF
CU_HTML.INI	URL.GIF
CU_HTML2.DOT	WORD2.GIF
CU_HTML6.DOT	WORD6.GIF
DELETE.GIF	

To keep the files straight, create a CU subdirectory off your Word directory stem and unzip the files to that subdirectory. Next, depending on which version of Word you are using (version 2 or 6), rename either `CU_HTML2.DOT` or `CU_HTML6.DOT` as `CU_HTML.DOT`. Then move `CU_HTML.DOT` to your Word template directory (often called `WINWORD\TEMPLATE`).

Note: The `.ZIP` extension indicates that the file is a zipped archive file, which is used to store a number of files in compressed format in a single file. If you don't have the Zip utilities, you can find them on just about any local computer bulletin board system. If files are arranged by subject, you'll often find Zip utilities listed under archiving or file utilities. One of the more popular unzip routines to look for is PKUNZIP.

Next, move the following files to your main Windows directory (usually `C:\WINDOWS`):

```
CU_HTML.DLL
CU_HTML.INI
GIF.DLL
```

These files are used by some of CU_HTML's macros for handling HTML files and GIF files. Once those files are in place, installation is complete. The other files are mostly for documentation and image files for `CU_HTML.HTM`. Before using the CU approach, use a Web browser to open `CU_HTML.HTM` and read it through.

Using CU_HTML

Creating an HTML file using CU is as easy as using a Word template. To start, choose File | New and select the Cu_html template from the template list. A new document window is opened. At this point, you are working in a regular Word document that happens to be based on CU_HTML. No special WLLs or DLLs are used to display anything or to modify Word's built-in behavior. When the document first appears, it's possible or even likely that the HTML toolbar is not displayed. If not, choose View | Toolbars, click on the HTML toolbar, and click on OK. The HTML toolbar and menu display is shown in Figure 14.1.

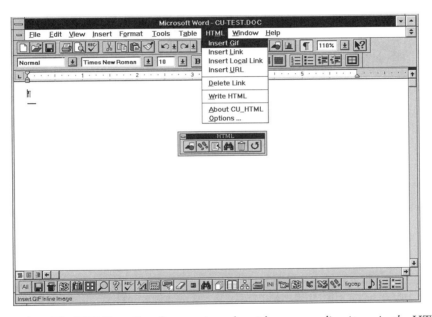

Figure 14.1. *The HTML toolbar features six tools, with corresponding items in the HTML menu.*

All HTML tags are created in one of four ways:

☐ Using the toolbar

☐ Using the HTML menu

☐ Applying character formatting (bold, italic, or underlining)

☐ Applying styles

Let's start by taking a look at the HTML toolbar and menu.

HTML Toolbar and Menu

The HTML toolbar features six tools (see Figure 14.1). The tools are shown in Table 14.1, along with their menu counterparts.

Table 14.1. The HTML toolbar and menu.

Toolbar	HTML Menu	Function
GIF	Insert GIF	Insert an inline image
Link	Insert Link	Link to an external file
Local Link	Insert Local Link	Link to a bookmark in the current HTML document
URL Link	Insert URL	Link to a URL
Delete Link	Delete Link	Delete the link at the insertion point
Write HTML	Write HTML	Create an HTML file from the current file
none	About	Copyright and authorship
none	Options	CU_HTML Options (stored in `CU_HTML.INI`)

All the tools have corresponding items in the HTML menu that is added to the main menu. One aspect of the CU_HTML Link tools that takes a little getting used to is that you must select text in order to use the tool. The selected text is used as the display text for the link. Contrast this with the Internet Assistant, which enables you to use selected text or add the text in the Display Text fill-in area in the HyperLink dialog box. Even so, if you follow the rule about making links work in context, CU_HTML's behavior shouldn't be a problem.

Another curious aspect of CU_HTML is that the Delete Link tool does not require that the cursor be on a link. If the insertion point is not on a link, the next link in the document is selected and you are prompted to confirm the deletion. Look carefully, however. If the cursor is not on a link when you choose the Delete Link tool, the next one in the document is selected—which might not be the nearest one. If the insertion point is beyond the last link in the document, you will get the No link found message, shown in Figure 14.2, which might be a little disconcerting until you understand what it's doing.

Figure 14.2. *If the insertion point is after the last link, the* No link found *error is displayed.*

CU_HTML Options

One other interesting feature is the CU_HTML Options dialog box, shown in Figure 14.3. Four options are stored in CU_HTML.INI, which is kept in the main Windows directory:

Treat MS Word files as HTML files—When a link dialog box displays, files matching *.DOC are displayed as if they already had .HTM extensions. This enables you to program the links to files you have not yet converted to HTML.

Assume HTML files have .html extension—This option causes all HTML file links to be written as .html instead of .htm. This is useful if you are going to move your files to a UNIX server. This option must be enabled before creating the links to work. If you insert a link and later enable the option, only links inserted after the option gets enabled have .html extensions.

Verify path after selecting from dialog—When checked, this option pops up a dialog box to enable you to verify or modify the path and filename used for the link (see Figure 14.4). This feature enables you to link to files and paths that don't actually exist on the current directory.

Language Dependent—CU_HTML defaults to English. If you use a Web browser that requires that tags be written in a different language, this option enables you to specify the translation to be used.

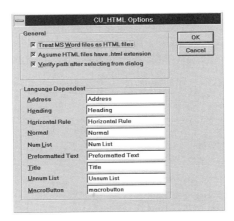

Figure 14.3. *The CU_HTML Options dialog box.*

Figure 14.4. *The Verify path option enables you to write links for files and paths that don't exist on your local PC.*

Creating a Sample HTML File Using CU_HTML

Okay, down to brass tacks. Let's create a sample HTML file using each of the features of CU_HTML. First, create a new document by choosing File | New, selecting the Cu_html template, and clicking on OK. Make sure you choose Cu_html and not Html. The latter is for the Internet Assistant!

First, let's give this baby a title. Using the style tool on the formatting toolbar, choose Title. Now type this title and press Enter:

```
Sample HTML File Created Using CU_HTML¶
```

Note that, unlike when using the Internet Assistant, the title displays in the current document. Later, when you write the HTML file, text with the Title style is given the appropriate HTML tag. Recall that the HTML title displays in the title bar of graphical Web browser, but is not displayed as part of the Web page itself. Notice also that when you press Enter after typing the title, the style of the next paragraph inserted is back to Normal. The Normal style is used for creating ordinary text in an HTML document.

Next, create a top-level heading that will be used as the HTML document's inside title. Using the style tool, apply the Heading 1 style. Then type the following and press Enter:

```
Using CU_HTML¶
```

Excellent! Notice that once again the style returned to Normal. Let's take advantage of that fact and type some ordinary text. Type the following and then press Enter:

```
This is ordinary text. There is nothing special about it, except of course that
I'm typing it only because some book told me to. Hey, why am I typing what a
book tells me to type? Can't I type something original, instead?¶
```

The purpose of making the preceding rather long is so you can see how the text wraps to fit the margins. Now type some preformatted text, using spaces to align the columns. First, apply the style called Preformatted Text. Then, type the following, pressing Enter after each line and typing the indicated number of spaces where shown:

```
Name<15 spaces>City<20 spaces>State¶
Henry<14 spaces>Davidsonville<11 spaces>Texas¶
Deborah<12 spaces>Boulder<17 spaces>Colorado¶
```

Notice that the style does not revert back to Normal after pressing Enter. That's because the Preformatted Text style is set up to repeat itself, and one-line-oriented styles such as headings

and the `Title` style have the following style set as `Normal`. After typing these three lines, text should appear in three columns, neatly aligned in ugly monospaced text.

Caution: Make sure that the line following the `Deborah...Colorado` line is not formatted with the Preformatted Text style. If it is, a bug in CU_HTML might prevent you from being able to write out the finished file later.

Next, create a numbered list. Make sure that the insertion point is in the blank line following the `Preformatted Text` section, and apply the `Num List 1` style. Then type the following, pressing Enter after each line:

```
Put your left foot in.¶
Put your left foot out.¶
Put your left foot in, and shake it all about.¶
```

Hey, you're not just writing HTML, you're doing the hokey pokey! In any event, notice that the `Num List` style remains in force each time you press Enter, and that each item has a number in front of it. Now create a numbered list inside the third item. In the line presently numbered 4, apply the `List Num 2` style. Notice that the line gets indented, but that the number remains at 4. Don't worry about it. The numbers are an artifact of Word, anyway. When the document is written out in HTML and viewed from a Web browser, the numbering will be correct. Just be careful, however, when referring to item numbers! Now type the following, continuing to use `List Num 2` and pressing Enter after each line:

```
You do the hokey pokey¶
And you turn yourself around.¶
That's what it's all about.¶
```

You should now have seven numbered lines. Apply the `Normal` style to the item that is numbered 7, and the 7 disappears. Now type the following with these attributes: boldface the word **bold**, italicize the word *italic*, and underline the word <u>underline</u>. Press Enter at the end of the line.

```
It is bold of me to push the italic key, and it's also fine if I underline.
Now let's see some bullets:¶
```

Now apply the `Unnum List 1` style and type the following, pressing Enter at the end of each line, and applying the bold, italic, and underlining as indicated:

```
Press Ctrl+B for Bold.¶
Press Ctrl+I for Italic.¶
Press Ctrl+U for Underline.¶
```

Do you have a blank line following the last bulleted item? Good, let's turn it into a horizontal rule. Using the style tool, apply the `Horizontal Rule` style and then press Enter. So far, what you've done should appear as shown in Figure 14.5.

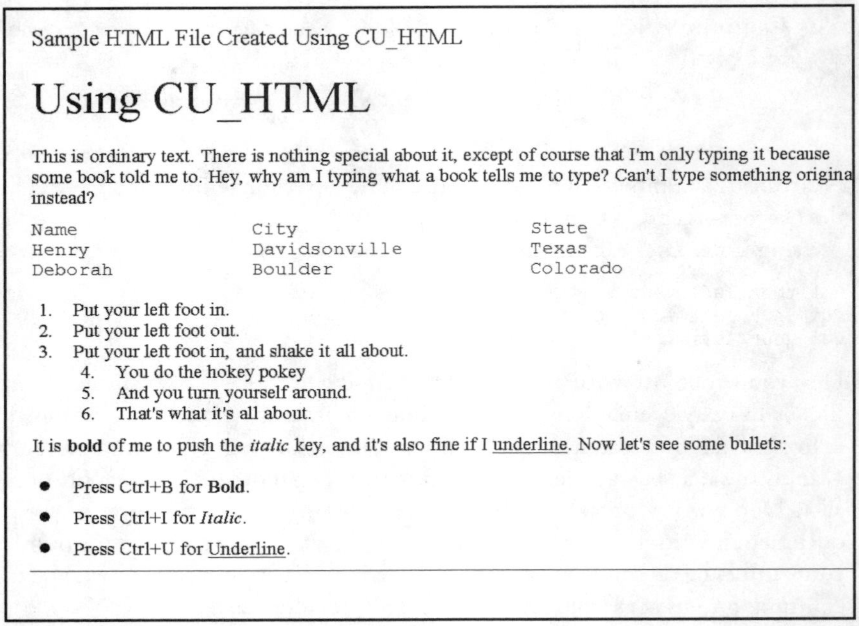

Sample HTML File Created Using CU_HTML

Using CU_HTML

This is ordinary text. There is nothing special about it, except of course that I'm only typing it because some book told me to. Hey, why am I typing what a book tells me to type? Can't I type something original instead?

```
Name            City              State
Henry           Davidsonville     Texas
Deborah         Boulder           Colorado
```

1. Put your left foot in.
2. Put your left foot out.
3. Put your left foot in, and shake it all about.
    4. You do the hokey pokey
    5. And you turn yourself around.
    6. That's what it's all about.

It is **bold** of me to push the *italic* key, and it's also fine if I <u>underline</u>. Now let's see some bullets:

- Press Ctrl+B for **Bold**.
- Press Ctrl+I for *Italic*.
- Press Ctrl+U for <u>Underline</u>.

Figure 14.5. *Your sample HTML document so far.*

Next, create some links below the horizontal rule. Type the following and press Enter:

```
Jump to the top, Read CU_HTML.HTM, or visit Macmillan Computer Publishing¶
```

You're going to create three links. First, however, you need to insert a bookmark at the top of the document, so press Ctrl+Home to go to the top and choose Edit | Bookmark from the menu. The Bookmark dialog box appears as shown in Figure 14.6. Type the word top into the bookmark field and press Enter (or click on Add, but it seems silly to take your hands off the keyboard to reach for the mouse when the Enter key is probably a lot closer). This inserts a named anchor at the top of the document.

Now go back down to the bottom of the document and select the word top. Click on the Local Link tool (it looks like a printed page with an arrow). If you're living right, the Select Destination Bookmark dialog box pops up, with the top bookmark already selected, as shown in Figure 14.7. Note that the linked word (top) and the bookmark name (top) don't have to be the same; however, they can be. If the top bookmark is already selected, click on OK. Now watch the screen. It should look pretty weird; the selected word top is replaced by a quote field that serves as the link marker when the document is written out in HTML format.

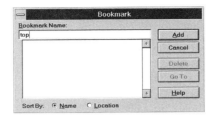

Figure 14.6. *Use Edit | Bookmark to insert anchors for local bookmarks.*

14

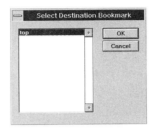

Figure 14.7. *The Select Destination Bookmark dialog box enables you to pick the bookmark for a local link.*

Tip: Word has a feature called ScreenUpdating, which can be turned off in a macro. Apparently, the CU_HTML editors thought that seeing the link being created would give you something to do while you're waiting. If you prefer less on-screen writhing, you can get it. Create a replacement macro for `InsertLocalLink` that turns screen updating off. From the menu, choose Tools | Macro, and type something such as `InsertLocalCalm` as the name. Under Macros Available In, choose `CU_HTML.DOT`. Then click on Create. In the space provided, type the following macro:

```
Sub MAIN¶
ScreenUpdating 0¶
InsertLocalLink¶
CharRight 1¶
CharLeft 1¶
End Sub¶
```

Note that the last two lines are sometimes necessary to correct a minor screen display glitch. When you're done, press Ctrl+F4 to close, and indicate Yes to saving the macro. Next, use Tools | Customize to replace the built-in Local Link tool with the quiet version. If you like the result, do the same thing for the

InsertLink, InsertURL, and DeleteLink macros. If prompted later on, don't forget to save changes to the template. The details are left as an exercise for the student. If you need additional assistance, consult the *Word for Windows 6 Super Book* (ISBN 0-672-30384-1, published by Sams Publishing and written by Herb Tyson).

Next, select CU_HTML.HTM and click on the Link tool—it looks like a pair of feet. When the Select Linkage File dialog box appears, navigate to the location of CU_HTML.HTM, click on it, and then click on OK. This creates a local link to the CU_HTML manual. Note, however, that if you have allowed the Assume HTML files to have the .html extension option, the resulting link probably won't work—unless your file actually has that extension (for example, under Windows NT's NTFS or OS/2's HPFS).

Now insert a link to a URL—the Macmillan Computer Publishing home page. Select the word Macmillan and click on the URL tool. It's the one that looks like a pair of binoculars. Why? I guess because the URL is supposed to be far away. Type the following in the text box:

http://www.mcp.com

Next, insert an address at the bottom. Use the style tool to apply the Address style to the blank line at the bottom. Type the following, substituting your own e-mail address for *e-mailaddress*:

Contact the author via e-mail at *e-mailaddress*.

Convert the e-mail address into a Mailto URL. Click on the URL tool on the HTML toolbar, and type the following into the text box:

mailto:*e-mailaddress*

Substitute your e-mail address for *e-mailaddress*; for example:

mailto:smith@jones.com

Okay, you're down to the wire. The last thing you need to do is bring in an inline graphic. At the top of the document, move the insertion point to the end of the heading Using CU_HTML. Click on the GIF tool—it looks like a triangle, circle, and square. The dialog box shown in Figure 14.8 appears. Navigate, if necessary, to the location of the CU_HTML files, and click on BUTTONS.GIF. Then click on OK. The display should convulse for a moment and then a replica of the HTML button bar should appear. Congratulations! You're done.

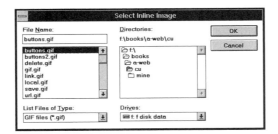

Figure 14.8. *The CU_HTML image tool doesn't provide a way to control the alignment or to include alternative text.*

Note: CU_HTML doesn't provide options for controlling the alignment of the graphic or for including alternative text.

Well, almost done. Save the file, naming it something descriptive, such as CU_TEST.DOC. Then click on the Write HTML button—it looks like most of a circle with an arrow—to write a copy of the file in HTML format. Again, because CU_HTML doesn't use the ScreenUpdating command, you can see the creation of the HTML document before your eyes. Unlike Word, however, which confusingly renames the current document by the save-as name (thus leading you to believe you're viewing the HTML file when you're still viewing the .DOC version), CU_HTML leaves the .DOC version in the window and keeps the .DOC name. The .HTM version is now safely on disk. If you followed all the instructions, the finished HTML document is as follows:

```
<A NAME = top></A><HTML>¶
<TITLE>Sample HTML File Created Using CU_HTML</TITLE>¶
<H1>Using CU_HTML<IMG SRC =¶
"../buttons.gif" ></H1>¶
This is ordinary text. There is nothing special about it, except of course that
I'm typing it only because¶
some book told me to. Hey, why am I typing what a book tells me to type? Can't
I type something original,¶
instead?<P>¶
<PRE>¶
Name            City                  State¶
</PRE>¶
<PRE>¶
Henry           Davidsonville         Texas¶
</PRE>¶
<PRE>¶
```

```
Deborah            Boulder              Colorado¶
</PRE>¶
<P>¶
<OL>¶
<LI>Put your left foot in.¶
<LI>Put your left foot out.¶
<LI>Put your left foot in, and shake it all about.¶
<OL>¶
<LI>You do the hokey pokey¶
<LI>And you turn yourself around.¶
<LI>That's what it's all about.¶
</OL>¶
</OL>¶
It is <B>bold</B> of me to push the <I>italic</I> key, and it's also fine if I
<U>underline</U>. Now¶
let's see some bullets:<P>¶
<UL>¶
<LI>Press Ctrl+B for <B>Bold</B>.¶
<LI>Press Ctrl+I for <I>Italic</I>.¶
<LI>Press Ctrl+U for <U>Underline</U>.¶
</UL>¶
<HR>¶
Jump to the <A HREF = "#top">top</A> , Read <A HREF =¶
"/books/a^~web/cu_html.htm">CU_HTML.HTM</A> , or visit <A HREF =¶
"http://www.mcp.com">Macmillan</A>  Computer Publishing<P>¶
<I><ADDRESS>Contact the author via e-mail at <A HREF =¶
"mailto:smith@jones.com">smith@jones.com</A> .</ADDRESS></I><P><I>¶
</I></HTML>¶
```

Using a Web browser, it appears as shown in Figure 14.9. Although the output is generally okay, it's clear that there are some problems that might need touching up. For example, the preformatted lines are too far apart. Each of the preformatted lines is taken one at a time, and unlike with the Internet Assistant for Word, when you use Shift+Enter rather than just Enter, the desired linebreak <BR> tags are not used. In this HTML file, the problem can be alleviated by removing the extra transitions between each preformatted line. In other words, replace what's shown previously with the following:

```
<PRE>¶
Name          City             State¶
Henry         Davidsonville    Texas¶
Deborah       Boulder          Colorado¶
</PRE>¶
```

Figure 14.9. *A Web page produced using* `CU_HTML.DOT`.

GT_HTML.DOT (Georgia Tech Template)

The Georgia Tech template, written by Jeffrey Grover, John Davis, and Bob Johnston, is a template that helps in the creation of HTML documents. According to the documentation that comes with it, it is not intended as a complete HTML authoring tool. GT_HTML is available in versions for Word for Windows 2 and Word for Windows 6. Both versions are still listed as "alpha" (pre-beta), and it's unlikely that the Word 2 version will undergo any additional development. The Word 6 release is dated August, 1994.

The `GT_HTML.DOT` template has a different approach than either the Internet Assistant or CU_HTML. Rather than creating a normal-looking Word document, GT_HTML inserts the HTML tags as you go along. Because the tags are inserted as hidden text, you can hide them if you want. However, the tags are part of the Word document. The conversion process really is just saving the finished work as a text file. Also unlike either of the other approaches discussed so far, GT_HTML doesn't use any DLL or WLL files. The whole approach is contained in a template file. In comparison with the Internet Assistant, GT_HTML has the following salient points:

☐ It is available for versions 2 and 6 of Word for Windows.

☐ It doesn't slow Word down.

☐ It doesn't change Word's normal operation (except in the HTML document).

☐ It is free, as are the other solutions discussed so far.

☐ It doesn't provide support for forms.

☐ It doesn't provide support for nested lists.

☐ It doesn't provide support for image maps.

☐ It doesn't provide support for logical formatting tags.

☐ It supports the following tags:

> Bold, italic, and underlined text
> Headings
> Ordered and unordered
> Lists
> Anchor Names
> Hypertext links
> In-line graphics
> Preformatted
> Text
> Horizontal rules

The version for Word for Windows 2 was released in alpha form in 1993 and does not appear to have been updated since then. If you are inclined to try it, you should know that it is designed for Word for Windows 2, not version 6. It works with version 6, but it might be a little tricky.

Installing GT_HTML

Installing GT_HTML is merely a matter of copying the appropriate version of GT_HTML.DOT to your Word template directory, which usually is WINWORD\TEMPLATE. First, however, you need to download the latest version. As this book is being written, versions for Word for Windows 2 and 6 are available by using the Download link in the following URLs:

```
http://www.gatech.edu/word_html/ver_2.0/release.htm
```
(for Word for Windows 2)

```
http://www.gatech.edu/word_html/release.htm
```
(for Word for Windows 6)

GT_HTML comes as GT_HTML.ZIP. When you unzip the one for Word for Windows 6, you should see the following files:

```
GT_HTML.DOT
HTMLINST.DOC
README.TXT
```

Note: The versions for Word for Windows 2 and 6 are quite different. However, because this book is about Web publishing using Word 6, that's the version covered. The basic philosophy of the two GT_HTML versions is the same; however, the authors seem to have elected to continue their development for Word 6, leaving the one for version 2 essentially orphaned.

To install, copy GT_HTML.DOT to your Word template directory (usually WINWORD\TEMPLATE). Beyond that, there also is a configuration option that you exercise by clicking on the Setup tool once you start a new document based on GT_HTML.DOT. To perform setup, choose File | New from the menu, and choose GT_HTML.DOT as the template; then click on OK. Word opens a new Document window.

Depending on your settings, the GT_HTML.DOT toolbars probably are not displayed at first. To display them, choose View | Toolbars and click so that an X appears next to Toolbar 1 and Toolbar 2. Then click on OK. The two toolbars should appear as shown in Figure 14.10. Once on-screen, they can be dragged to wherever you want them to be.

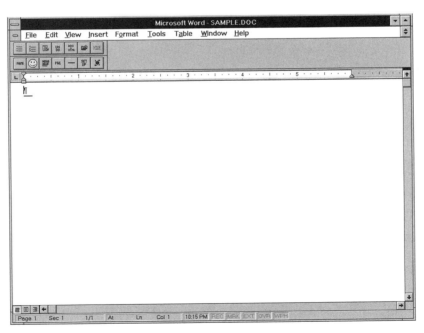

Figure 14.10. *The initial location of GT_HTML's two toolbars varies.*

Begin the setup routine by clicking on the Setup tool. The dialog box shown in Figure 14.11 is displayed. Enter the path you want to use for your HTML files and the location of your default Web browser. Note that the setup dialog box won't take no for an answer. It will not accept anything at all for the Web browser. Moreover, it accepts only a Windows program. After typing your choices, click on OK and you're ready to roll. Your setup choices are stored in GT_HTML.CFG on your main WINWORD subdirectory.

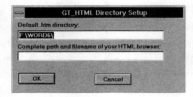

Figure 14.11. *The GT_HTML Directory Setup dialog box won't allow you to leave either choice blank.*

Using GT_HTML

You've already started, just by choosing File | New and specifying GT_HTML as the template. In addition to the toolbars, GT_HTML.DOT adds items to the following menus:

> File
> Edit
> View
> Insert
> Format

Let's take a look at the toolbars and menu items that are added.

GT_HTML Toolbars and Menu

GT_HTML adds two toolbars, each with seven tools. The tools and corresponding menu additions are described in Table 14.2.

Table 14.2. GT_HTML toolbars and menu additions.

Toolbar	Menu	Purpose
bulllist	Format	HTML Bulleted List	Creates unordered list
numlist	Format	HTML Numbered List	Creates ordered list
urllink	Format	HTML HyperText Link	Inserts link to a URL
unhtml	Edit	HTML Undo	Removes HTML tags from selected text

Toolbar	Menu	Purpose
html save	File | HTML Convert and Save	Saves the current file as an HTML text file
opendoc	File | HTML Open Doc	Opens the .DOC version of the selected filename (filename must be selected on-screen)
hide	View | HTML Hide	Toggles hidden text on and off
name	Format | HTML Name Tag	Inserts an anchor name tag
graphic	Insert | HTML Graphic	Insert an inline image
heading	Format | HTML Heading	Formats text as an HTML heading
pre	Format | HTML Preformatted Text	Formats text as HTML Preformatted
horizontal ruler	Insert | HTML Horizontal Rule	Inserts a horizontal rule
setup	File | HTML Setup	Starts HTML setup
browser	File | HTML Browser	Starts the default browser

Note: The tools and menu commands correspond to a number of macros contained in GT_HTML.DOT. Unlike in CU_HTML.DOT, the macros in the Georgia Tech offering are not protected, so you can modify them if you need to. This makes adding the ScreenUpdating command a bit more straightforward, because you can just modify the existing macros rather than having to write new ones.

Creating a Sample HTML File Using GT_HTML

Creating a document is different than creating the other HTML add-ons. Let's create a sample document to see how the features work. First, note that there is no facility for creating an HTML title. (Given how much I've emphasized the need for a title—and a good one, at that—I guess I'll have to call that strike one. However, given that GT_HTML does not purport to be a full-service HTML editor, and given that it's free, can I complain?) However,

given the way GT_HTML works, you can manually insert anything you want and it is saved with the resulting HTML file. So, to create a title, type the following and press Enter:

```
<TITLE>Sample HTML Document Created Using GT_HTML</TITLE>¶
```

Note: Although it isn't necessary, if you really want the whole document to be as WYSIWYG as possible and consistent with the GT_HTML approach, you can format the tags as red and hidden and format the title text as hidden. That way, when you click on the Hide button, the tags and title are toggled on and off. Because the title is not visible in a Web browser, it's appropriate for the title text itself to be hidden as well.

Next, insert a heading to serve as a visible title on the Web page. On the blank line following the title, type the following, but don't press Enter:

```
Sample GT_HTML Document
```

Once it's typed, click on the Headings tool and choose Heading 1. Watch what happens! The text grows in point size in steps of two until it's 18 points. Watch out, however; if you later apply a different heading level to the same text without first using the Unhtml tool to remove the old, the font growth is added to that which you just saw. Incidentally, do you see red <H1> and </H1> tags surrounding the heading? If not, click on the Hide tool to reveal the hidden HTML tags.

Just for practice, remove the <H1> tags from the text you just formatted. Select the same text—including the opening and closing tags—and click on the Unhtml tool. The tags are removed and the text shrinks back to normal.

In any event, thanks to the magic of UnDo, you can now put the H1 formatting back. Press Alt+Backspace enough times (usually four) to bring back the font growth and the <H1> and </H1> tags.

Notice that the philosophy of working with GT_HTML is such that you *must* insert the text before applying the formatting. Unlike Internet Assistant and CU_HTML, GT_HTML works mostly with selected text, rather than with styles. Thus, you need to type the text before applying the formatting.

Now type the following:

```
This is ordinary text. The following is preformatted text:¶
```

Is your text red? If so, you need to watch out. One problem with GT_HTML is the propensity for text that is typed following an HTML tag to adopt the red formatting. Sometimes the hidden aspect gets carried over (inherited) as well. If this happens to you, the easiest solution

usually is to select the text that's not supposed to be hidden and press Ctrl+Spacebar to remove the extraneous formatting. The best prevention is to press Enter an extra time after the last item, *before* you apply the GT_HTML formatting.

Next, type the text you want to be preformatted, pressing Enter after each line. As before, type the number of spaces indicated. Press Enter an extra time after `Colorado` to try to get rid of the red hidden-inheritance problem.

```
Name<15 spaces>City<20 spaces>State¶
Henry<14 spaces>Davidsonville<11 spaces>Texas¶
Deborah<12 spaces>Boulder<17 spaces>Colorado¶
¶
```

Select the three lines (including one paragraph marker after `Colorado`—press Ctrl+Shift+8, if necessary, to turn on the display of nonprinting characters). Now click on the Pre tool on the toolbar. Move the insertion point to the second paragraph marker that follows `Colorado`, and type the following (pressing Enter once after each line, and twice after `about.`):

```
Put your left foot in.¶
Put your left foot out.¶
Put your left foot in, and shake it all about.¶
You do the hokey pokey¶
And you turn yourself around.¶
That's what it's all about.¶
¶
```

Now you have a problem. You were going to format this as items 1, 2, 2.1, 2.2, 2.3, 3, with items 2.1, 2.2, and 2.3 being nested within the main item 2. However, GT_HTML doesn't support nested lists, so just make it all a single numbered list. First, select all six lines (including the paragraph marker that follows `about.`). Then click on the Num List tool on the toolbar. With hidden text displaying, it should appear as the following (`<Tab>` is substituted for the tab character):

```
<OL>1.<Tab>Put your left foot in.
2.<Tab>Put your left foot out.
3.<Tab>Put your left foot in, and shake it all about.
4.<Tab>You do the hokey pokey
5.<Tab>And you turn yourself around.
6.<Tab>That's what it's all about.
</OL>
```

Now put the insertion point two paragraph markers after `about.`. Then type the following and press Enter:

```
It is bold of me to push the italic key, and it's also fine if I underline.
Now let's see some bullets:¶
```

When you type the words **bold**, *italic*, and underline, use normal Word formatting to make those three words bold, italicized, and underlined, respectively. Next, type the following, pressing Enter once after each line, except twice after the final line:

```
Press Ctrl+B for Bold.¶
Press Ctrl+I for Italic.¶
Press Ctrl+U for Underline.¶
¶
```

Again, use normal Word controls to apply the bold, italics, and underlining. Now, select the three lines, up to and including the paragraph marker that follows `Underline.`, and then click on the Bullist tool. Next, move the insertion point to the second paragraph marker following `Underline.` and click on the hr tool to insert a horizontal rule; press Enter. Put the insertion point at the end of the document and type the following:

```
Jump to the top, Read README.TXT, or visit Macmillan Computer Publishing¶
Contact the author via e-mail at jones@smith.com.¶
```

Now insert some links. Create an anchor name at the top of the document. Recall that when using CU_HTML and the Internet Assistant, you were able to use Word's bookmark feature. No such luck with GT_HTML. Instead, move the insertion point to just before `<H1>` near the start of the document. Press Ctrl+Spacebar and type top so that the line now begins with the following:

```
top<H1>
```

Select just the word top and click on the Name tool on the toolbar. It gets changed to this:

```
<A NAME="top">
```

Now go back to the bottom and modify the next-to-last line so that it appears as follows, inserting text after the word top, `README.TXT`, and `Macmillan`:

```
Jump to the top #top, read README.TXT /winword/gt/readme.txt, or visit
Macmillan http://www.mcp.com Computer Publishing.¶
```

Do you see what you did? You added the linkages after the words that will be used for the display. In the case of `/winword/gt/readme.txt`, I'm assuming that you put the GT_HTML files in a subdirectory of the `WINWORD` directory, called `GT`. If not, modify the path so that you can find GT_HTML's `README.TXT` file. Next, select the text top `#top` and click on the URL Link tool. Then, select `README.TXT` `/winword/gt/readme.txt` and again click on the URL Link tool. Finally, select `Macmillan` `http://www.mcp.com` and click on—you guessed it—the URL Link tool. The line should now appear as follows:

```
Jump to the <A HREF="#top">top</A>, read <A HREF="/winword/gt/readme.txt">
README.TXT</A>, or visit <A HREF="http://www.mcp.com">Macmillan</A> Computer
Publishing.¶
```

Add a Mailto URL to the last line. First, add the URL so that it appears as follows:

```
Contact the author via e-mail at jones@smith.com mailto:jones@smith.com.¶
```

Then select `mailto:jones@smith.com` and click on the URL Link tool. Unfortunately, GT_HTML does not provide a command for inserting address tags, which help in making

the address line more distinctive in a busy Web page. However, you can add them manually, if you like, by adding <ADDRESS> at the beginning of the line and </ADDRESS> at the end:

```
<ADDRESS>Contact the author via e-mail at <A HREF="mailto:jones@smith.com">
jones@smith.com</A>.</ADDRESS>¶
```

If you have a spare GIF or other picture file hanging around, you can try to include it as an inline image. First, move the insertion point to where you want the picture to appear. Type the name of the file, including any necessary path and following usual HTML requirements by using / instead of \. For example, using the samplpic.bmp file that comes with the Word for Windows 2 version of GT_HTML (assuming that it's located on the indicated directory), type the following:

```
/winword/gt/samplpic.bmp¶
```

Select the whole file reference, and click on the GIF tool on the toolbar. GT_HTML is supposed to convert the selected text into a reference and also try to display the graphic. Unlike CU_HTML, GT_HTML does not bring any inherent GIF-handling capabilities with it. To display them, you need to make sure that Word's GIF format import feature has been installed. Note that in addition to the fatal error noted, GT_HTML does not appear to have any built-in way to specify ALT (alternate text to display for nongraphical browsers).

> **Note:** I would love to demonstrate what this looks like when processed by GT_HTML, but I can't. Each time I click on the GIF tool, Word abruptly ends with a GPF (general protection fault).

You're almost done! You need to explicitly perform an HTML Save command to complete the conversion of the document into a .HTM file. Recall that some formatting, such as bold, italic, and underlining, is not handled until conversion. First, save the document as a regular Word document (for example, as GTSAMPLE.DOC). Then click on the HTML Save tool on the toolbar. The finished HTML document looks similar to what you got when using CU_HTML:

```
<html><TITLE>Sample HTML Document Created Using GT_HTML</TITLE><P>¶
<A NAME="top"><H1>Sample GT_HTML Document</H1><P>¶
This is ordinary text. The following is preformatted text:<P>¶
<P>¶
<PRE>Name               City                    State<P>¶
Henry              Davidsonville           Texas<P>¶
Deborah            Boulder                 Colorado<P>¶
</PRE><P>¶
<OL><LI>Put your left foot in.<LI>Put your left foot out.<LI>Put your left foot
in, and shake it all¶
about.<LI>You do the hokey pokey<LI>And you turn yourself around.<LI>That's
what it's all¶
about.</OL><P>¶
```

```
It is <B>bold</B> of me to push the <I>italic</I> key, and it's also fine if I
<U>underline</U>. Now¶
let's see some bullets:<P>¶
Press Ctrl+B for <B>Bold</B>.<P>¶
Press Ctrl+I for <I>Italic</I>.<P>¶
Press Ctrl+U for <U>Underline</U>.<P>¶
<HR><P>¶
<P>¶
Jump to the <A HREF="#top">top</A>, read <A HREF="/winword/gt/readme.txt">
README.TXT</A>,¶
or visit <A HREF="http://www.mcp.com">Macmillan</A> Computer Publishing.<P>¶
<P>¶
<ADDRESS>Contact the author via e-mail at <A¶
HREF="mailto:jones@smith.com">jones@smith.com</A>.<P>¶
</ADDRESS><P>¶
</html>¶
```

Using InternetWorks Internet Assistant, the document appears as shown in Figure 14.12. Notice that you again have a problem with the display of the preformatted text area. You can fix this by removing the <P> tags that occur after the first two lines of the preformatted text in the .HTM file. Change that area so it appears as follows:

```
<PRE>Name              City              State¶
Henry             Davidsonville     Texas¶
Deborah           Boulder           Colorado<P>¶
</PRE><P>¶
```

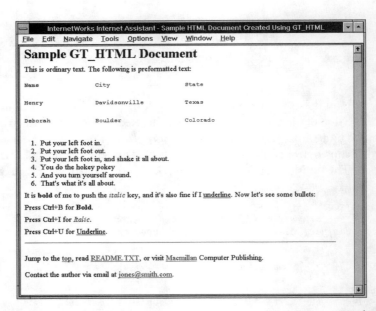

Figure 14.12. *GT_HTML's finished sample document, as seen in InternetWorks Internet Assistant.*

ANT_HTML.DOT (Jill Smith Template)

The ANT_HTML approach, by Jill Smith, is a commercial program. A demonstration version called ANT_DEMO is available using the URL `ftp://ftp.einet.net/einet/pc/ANT_HTML.ZIP`. The operation philosophy appears to be similar to GT_HTML, wherein you write the text and then use the supplied tools to format. Tags are inserted using red and hidden formatting. Jill's template is quite a bit more full-featured than either the Chinese University or the Georgia Tech program. From the demo, it appears that the full-featured ANT_HTML has the following characteristics and features:

- ☐ It supports logical character formatting *(strong* rather than *bold).*
- ☐ It supports forms directives.
- ☐ It doesn't slow down Word.
- ☐ It doesn't change Word's normal operation (except in the HTML document).
- ☐ It doesn't support image maps.
- ☐ It works with Word for Windows version 6 and for Macintosh.
- ☐ It doesn't work for Word for Windows version 2.

Using ANT_HTML

Because I don't have the full version, I can't take you through an exercise the way I did with the CU_ and GT_HTML templates. However, using the demo, I can give you some of the flavor. ANT_HTML works similarly to the CU, GT, and Internet Assistant approaches. You start off by creating a new document based on `ANT_HTML.DOT` (for the demo, it's `ANT_DEMO.DOT`), which you place into the `WINWORD` template directory. The demo version is set up to look for a file called `ANT_HTML.INF` on the root directory of the current drive. If it's not there, many of the features will not work.

When you create a new ANT_HTML document, the ANT toolbar appears, as shown in Figure 14.13. Most of the formatting tools are set up to insert tag pairs. For example, when you click on the tool labeled "1" (for H1), the following is inserted:

```
<H1> </H1>
```

You then can type the heading text between the tags. Alternatively, you can type the text, select it, and then click on the H1 toolbar button to have the tags inserted around the text. One of the tools, the S (style) tool, however, shows you a list of code styles in the resulting dialog box (see Figure 14.14). As you can see, ANT's approach uses several logical styles, which most HTML guides recommend over physical styles. Curiously, however, *emphasis* is absent.

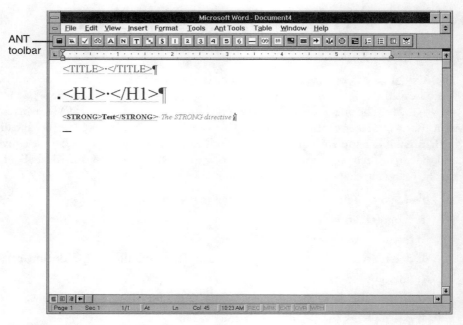

Figure 14.13. *The ANT toolbar.*

Figure 14.14. *ANT's Styles dialog box enables you to choose a variety of tags.*

ANT does not change existing menus; it adds a new menu to the main menu bar, as shown in Figure 14.15. Most of the menu commands offer an alternative to the toolbar.

Figure 14.15. *ANT adds the ANT Tools menu to the menu bar.*

Summary

Today, you had a closeup look at CU_HTML and GT_HTML. If you prefer to use Word for Windows version 2, either of those approaches might be worth investigating because the Internet Assistant is for Word for Windows 6 only. You also had a quick look at ANT_HTML. Although more capable than either CU_HTML or GT_HTML, however, ANT also is only for Word 6—and it isn't free.

Q&A

Q When I'm using `CU_HTML.DOT`, why can't I edit the macros so I can look at them?

A Because they're protected. When you create a macro in Word 6, you have the option of making them execute-only. This enables the author to provide macros that you can run, but cannot view. For developers, this provides a measure of copyright protection. In some network environments, it also promotes security. Some users don't like hidden macros, because you can't see what they might be doing. If you don't like them, CU_HTML probably isn't for you. However, there is no way I know of to unprotect the macros.

Q I'm using `GT_HTML.DOT`. When I selected a filename and clicked on the GIF tool, I received an error message, and the selected text disappeared. Why?

A Because the file was not found, and `SAMPLPIC.BMP` (a placeholder graphic that seems to come with some `GT_HTML.ZIP` packets, but not all) wasn't found. It was also because the underlying macro wasn't written carefully enough to allow for both kinds of errors. The macro copies the text internally and plans to use it later. When it doesn't find the file you specified, and can't find `SAMPLPIC.BMP`, however, all bets are off. Rather than restoring the zapped text, the macro just aborts. You can get the text back, however, by pressing Shift+Ins (paste), because that's where the macro copied it.

Q When trying the ANT_DEMO, I got the brief message `This file can not be found: \ANT_HTML.INF` and then another `Command failed`. Furthermore, when I clicked on the H1 and T tools (along with some others), nothing happened. Why?

A ANT_DEMO wants a file called `ANT_HTML.INF` to be on the root directory of the current drive. It gets necessary information for the Heading and Title tools—along with some others—from that file.

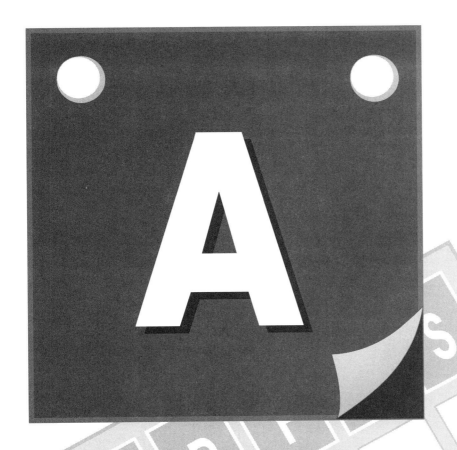

Appendixes

HTML 2.0 Summary and Word Equivalents

HTML 2.0 Summary and Word Equivalents

The following table is a summary of Word procedures for producing HTML level-2 tags. Note that, in some cases, the Internet Assistant won't apply the HTML formatting until the file is saved, although the style is applied immediately.

HTML Command	Word Procedure
`<A HREF=...>`	Insert | HyperLink or HyperLink tool
`<A NAME=...>`	Edit | Bookmark
`<ADDRESS>`	Apply the Address paragraph style
`<B>`	Apply Bold character formatting (Ctrl+B or Bold tool)
`<BLOCKQUOTE>`	Apply Blockquote paragraph style
`<BODY>`	Automatic
` `	Press Shift+Enter
`<CITE>`	Apply the Cite character style
`<CODE>`	Apply the Code character style
`<DFN>`	Definition; automatically applied when you create a definition list with the terms and definitions separated by a tab
`<DIR>`	Apply the Directory,DIR paragraph style to a list of items
`<DL>`	Create a definition list in the form *Term*<tab>*Definition*<enter>, then apply the Definition List,DL paragraph style to the list
`<DL COMPACT>`	Create a definition list in the form *Term*<tab>*Definition*<enter>, then apply the Definition Compact,DL COMPACT paragraph style to the list
`<DT>...<DD>`	Definition Term; automatically applied when you use DL or DL COMPACT
`<EM>`	Apply the Emphasis,EM character style
`<FORM>`	Choose Insert | Form Field or use the Forms tools on the Forms toolbar
`<H1>` through `<H6>`	Apply the paragraph styles Heading 1 through Heading 6
`<HEAD>`	Automatic

HTML Command	Word Procedure
`<HR>`	Choose Insert | Horizontal Rule or click the Horizontal Rule tool
`<HTML>`	Automatic
`<I>`	Apply Italic character formatting (Ctrl+I or Italic tool)
`<IMG>`	Choose Insert | Picture or use the Picture tool
`<IMG...ISMAP>`	Choose Insert | Picture or use the Picture tool, then click the Advanced button and choose the Sensitive Map option
`<KBD>`	Apply the `Keyboard,KBD` character style
`<LI>`	Automatically inserted when you create a list
`<MENU>`	Apply the Menu paragraph style to a list of items
`<META>`	Choose File | HTML Document Information or the Title tool, then click the Advanced... button
`<OL>`	Apply the `List Number,OL` paragraph style to a list
`<P>`	Default, or apply the `Normal,P` paragraph style
`<PRE>`	Apply the `Preformatted` paragraph style
`<PRE WIDTH= ...>`	Apply the `PRE WIDE` paragraph style
`<SAMP>`	Apply the `Sample` character style
`<STRIKE>`	Apply the Strikethrough character style
`<STRONG>`	Apply the Strong character style
`<TITLE>`	Choose File | HTML Document Information or the Title tool
`<TT>`	Apply the Typewriter character style
`<U>`	Apply underlining character formatting (press Ctrl+U or use the Underlining tool)
`<UL>`	Apply the `List Bullet,UL` paragraph style to a list
`<VAR>`	Apply the Variable character style
Special characters	Word automatically adds the & character when writing HTML files; therefore, for example, to cause `<B>` to appear in the output file, you do not need to type `&<B&>`

B

Web and Internet Glossary

<BODY> The <BODY> area of an HTML document is the main part of the document that is displayed on the Web (that is, visible when using a Web browser).

<HEAD> The <HEAD> area of an HTML document contains information about the document. That information is available to Web browsers and to Web search programs. Graphical Web browsers usually use the <TITLE> part of the HTML document to display the window title bar in OS/2, Windows, UNIX X Window System, and when using a Macintosh computer.

anchor An HTML tag used to create links or cross references. You use anchor name tags to mark areas as locations to jump to. You use anchor references to create the jump itself.

bandwidth A term that refers to how much information can be passed over an electronic pathway. In radio signals, bandwidth is the amount of space taken up by a signal (for example, a signal might occupy a full Mhz of space). In data line signals, bandwidth is the amount of data per second that can pass through the line, such as 28.8Kbps, 56Kbps, and so on. It gets the "width" component inasmuch as a 1MB connection might accommodate a number of users, each at 56KB, or a 128KB connection might accommodate a number of lower-speed connections.

character style A Word 6 style that can be applied to part of a paragraph without affecting the entire paragraph.

client A computer that obtains information or services from other computers. Servers and clients are logical complements.

daemon A special kind of server computer program whose function is to wait for requests from clients. The workings of the Web are controlled by HTTPDs (HyperText Transfer Protocol Daemons).

digital audio A computerized recording of sound.

digital video Multiple-frame video images stored in computer files. Frames are played back at a speed that simulates motion, much as old-fashioned movie film takes a series of discrete pictures. When played back at an appropriate speed, the multiple frames give the impression of movement.

external image An image that is linked to a Web page, but which is presented separately, often using an image program external to the Web browser itself.

external media Any file (text, video, audio, or image) that is not an inline part of an HTML document.

fixed font Another name for monospaced.

form An HTML instruction that enables users to input data in a variety of ways.

FTP File Transfer Protocol. On the Internet, FTP is the primary method (protocol) for transferring whole files between computer systems. It is analogous to Zmodem and Xmodem (common data-transfer protocols used in ordinary non-Internet BBS communications).

gateway An electronic link for transferring information between two computers. In Webese, a gateway is used to transfer data input by the user to the Web server, and to transfer data retrieved back to the Web client (user).

GIF CompuServe Graphics Interchange Format, which is an image format optimized for electronic downloading.

Gopher A point-and-click system for accessing Internet resources. In many ways, gopher was a precursor to the Web. Gopher is still very much in use but is being rapidly pushed aside by the World Wide Web.

GUI Graphical user interface.

home page A home page is a starting point on the Web. From the user's standpoint, it's where you begin your Web browsing each time you start your browser. From a server's standpoint, it's the primary point of presence on the Web.

horizontal rule A thick horizontal line through your document. A horizontal rule creates vertical separation of distinct parts of your HTML document. Insert a horizontal rule using Insert | Horizontal rule from the menu.

hot link An image or text that you click that leads to something else.

HTML HyperText Markup Language. HTML is a system for formatting documents for presentation on the World Wide Web.

HTML tag HTML tags are commands from the HyperText Markup Language. They consist of angle brackets, < and >, surrounding a keyword instruction of some kind, along with additional information such as the text of a comment or a URL.

HTTP The Internet protocol used for HTML documents.

hyperlink Text or a picture that is linked to another computer resource. For example, if the words *computer* and *picture* were links, then clicking your mouse on them might lead to information about computers and pictures, respectively. On the Web, hyperlinks are linked to other parts of the same document, other documents, and to other URLs.

image map A picture with different areas or regions that are mapped to different hyperlinks. Clicking on different areas produces different results. An image map needs a graphic image (GIF or JPEG), a map file, and an executable CGI script on the Web server computer. The graphic is displayed, the locations the user clicks with the mouse are interpreted by the map file, and processing is handled by the CGI script.

inline image An image that is presented on the Web page of a graphical Web browser, along with text and other images.

Internet Assistant An add-in for Microsoft Word that lets you use Word as an HTML editor and as a Web browser. The heart and soul of the Internet Assistant consists of `WORDHTML.WLL`, `HTML.DOT`, `WEBVIEW.DOT`, and `HTMLCONV.CNV`.

InternetWorks A stand-alone Web browser included with the Internet Assistant. The stand-alone `IWIA.EXE` is not essential for using the Internet Assistant.

JPEG Joint Photographic Experts Group (JPEG), which is an image format optimized for electronic reproduction of photographs.

Lynx A text-only UNIX Web browser.

Mailto The Internet protocol used for sending e-mail via a Web browser.

Microsoft Imager A free program available from Microsoft for registered Word users, which lets you convert among various graphics formats and resize images, as well as perform other image transformations.

monospaced A font set that has characters which each consume the identical amount of horizontal space. For example, 10 periods, 10 *i*'s, and 10 *M*'s all would be exactly the same width.

Mosaic A graphical Web browser for Windows.

multimedia Any combination of text, graphics, audio, and video.

Netscape A graphical Web browser for Windows.

News The Internet protocol used for reading newsgroups (such as Usenet) via Web browsers.

news server A computer that serves as a repository for the contents of newsgroups.

newsgroups An extensive collection of more than 10,000 discussion areas organized by subject.

origin In computer graphics, the origin is the starting point from which every part of the image is measured. The origin is the upper-left corner of an image and is referred to as 0,0.

paragraph style A Word 6 style that affects all of every paragraph included in the selection.

proportional A font in which different characters consume spacing different amounts of horizontal space. Ten periods, 10 *i*'s, and 10 *M*'s would each be different widths.

protocol A collection of procedures or methods for sending and receiving information between different computers, much as the fax, cellular telephone, and U.S. mail are methods for exchanging information.

server A computer or computer program that provides information or services to other computers or computer programs, called clients. Web pages are installed on servers. Web browsers are clients.

Telnet The Internet protocol used for accessing terminal-based servers.

thumbnail image A small version of a larger image, usually about an inch square (or so) on the screen.

UNIX A computer operating system (much as DOS, OS/2, and Windows NT are operating systems). UNIX is popular in military, scientific, and educational research settings, which form the heart of the Internet.

URL Uniform resource locator. A URL is a way of specifying an Internet address and protocol for Web browsers.

WebExplorer A graphical Web browser for OS/2.

C

Web Resources

Web Resources

This appendix presents the Web resources that were useful in writing this book. If you need additional help, you should find much help in these sources. In particular, see the "Gateway Tools and Information" listing for help in putting together CGI scripts for particular types of UNIX servers. Here's a list of the categories covered:

- ☐ General World Wide Web Resources
- ☐ Windows Web Browsers
- ☐ Gateway Tools and Information
- ☐ Other Word for Windows HTML Resources
- ☐ HTML References and Guides
- ☐ WWW Server Software
- ☐ Web Listings and Indexes
- ☐ Other Resources

General World Wide Web Resources

CERN   The birthplace of the WWW
`http://www.cern.ch/CERN/WorldWideWeb/WWWandCERN.html`

The World Wide Web   The home of the WWW
`http://www.w3.org/`

INRIA—HOME PAGE   The worldwide host for WWW development
`http://www.inria.fr/welcome-eng.html`

The World Wide Web Consortium   A collection of Web authorities
`http://www.w3.org/hypertext/WWW/Consortium/`

Windows Web Browsers

Cello: An Internet Browser
`http://www.law.cornell.edu/cello/cellotop.html`

NCSA Mosaic for Windows
`ftp://ftp.ncsa.uiuc.edu/PC/Windows/Mosaic/`

WinWeb
`http://galaxy.einet.net/EINet/WinWeb/WinWebHome.html`

WebWorks Mosaic (Commercial version of NCSA Mosaic)
`http://www.quadralay.com/products/WebWorks/Mosaic/index.html`

Netscape
http://home.mcom.com/

Quarterdeck Mosaic
http://www.qdeck.com/beta/prodinfo.html

Gateway Tools and Information

CGI Archive   An archive of gateway scripts
ftp://ftp.ncsa.uiuc.edu/Web/httpd/Unix/ncsa_httpd/cgi/

The Common Gateway Interface
Specifications for the Common Gateway Interface
http://hoohoo.ncsa.uiuc.edu/cgi

WWW Gateway Software   Gateway programs
http://www.w3.org/hypertext/WWW/Daemon/Gateways.html

Supporting Forms with CGI   CGI scripts for processing forms data
http://hoohoo.ncsa.uiuc.edu/cgi/forms.html

WWW Common Code Library   Programming code library
http://www.w3.org/hypertext/WWW/Library/Status.html

Other Word for Windows HTML Resources

ANT_HTML   Commercial HTML .DOT template
ftp://ftp.einet.net/einet/pc/ANT_DEMO.ZIP

CU_HTML (Chinese University)   Shareware .DOT template
ftp://ftp.cuhk.hk/pub/www/windows/util/

GA_HTML (Georgia Tech)   Shareware .DOT template
http://www.gatech.edu/word_html/release.htm

SGML TagWizard   Shareware .DOT template
http://infolane.com/infolane/nice/nice.html

HTML for Word 2.0   Shareware .DOT template
ftp://ftp.cica.indiana.edu/pub/pc/win3/uploads/html.zip

HTML References and Guides

A Beginner's Guide to HTML
http://www.ncsa.uiuc.edu/demoweb/html-primer.html

Composing Good HTML
http://www.willamette.edu/html-composition/strict-html.html

Hypertext Markup Language (HTML) Specification
http://www.w3.org/hypertext/WWW/MarkUp/HTML.html

Style Guide for Online Hypertext
http://www.w3.org/hypertext/WWW/Provider/Style/Overview.html

Device Independence Style Guide
http://www.w3.org/hypertext/WWW/Provider/Style/DeviceIndependent.html

How to Write HTML Files
http://www.ucc.ie/info/net/htmldoc.html

Introduction to HTML
http://melmac.harris-atd.com/about_html.html

HTML Quick Reference
http://kuhttp.cc.ukans.edu/lynx_help/HTML_quick.html

Dan Connolly's WWW Research Notebook (One of the originators of the Web)
http://www.w3.org/hypertext/WWW/People/Connolly/drafts/web-research.html

WWW Server Software

CERN   Web server for UNIX, Windows, Windows NT, and NeXTSTep
http://www.w3.org/hypertext/WWW/Daemon/Status.html

NCSA httpd   NCSA Server for UNIX
http://hoohoo.ncsa.uiuc.edu/docs/Overview.html

GoServe: A Web and Gopher Server
IBM's Web and Gopher Server for OS/2
http://www2.hursley.ibm.com/goserve

Windows httpd   Windows Web server for 16-bit Windows
http://www.city.net/win-httpd/

WebSite   Web server for Windows 95 and Windows NT
http://gnn.interpath.net/gnn/bus/ora/news/c.website.html

Quadralay WebWorks   Web server for Windows, UNIX, and Macintosh

`http://www.quadralay.com/products/products.html`

Gn   Free Web server for UNIX

`http://www.ncsa.uiuc.edu/SDG/Software/Mosaic/Notes/gn-1.0-release.txt`

Perl   Web Server for UNIX

`http://www.cs.indiana.edu/perl-server/intro.html`

MacHTTP   Web server for Macintosh

`http://www.w3.org/hypertext/WWW/MacHTTP/Status.html`

HTTPS for Windows NT   Web server for Windows NT

`http://www.w3.org/hypertext/WWW/HTTPS/Status.html`

Netsite   Web server for UNIX

`http://home.mcom.com/MCOM/products_docs/server.html`

Web Listings and Indexes

World Wide Web Virtual Library   Subject-oriented Web catalog

`http://www.w3.org/hypertext/DataSources/bySubject/Overview.html`

Yahoo   Subject-oriented Web listing

`http://www.yahoo.com`

The Awesome List   Collection of special URLs

`http://www.clark.net/pub/journalism/awesome.html`

World Wide Web Yellow Pages   Commercial Web advertising and listing service

`http://www.yellow.com`

Scott Yanoff's Special Connections   Collection of special URLs

`http://www.w3.org/hypertext/DataSources/Yanoff.html`

Webaholics Page   Collection of special URLs

`http://www.ohiou.edu/~rbarrett/webaholics/ver2/`

Other Resources

Cern Clickable Image Support   Help for image map preparation

`http://www.w3.org/hypertext/WWW/Daemon//User/CGI/HTImageDoc.html`

Geographical Map Information Tutorial   Help for geographical image maps

`http://wintermute.ncsa.uiuc.edu:8080/map-tutorial/image-maps.html`

SYMBOLS

video files

Add to Your Sams.net Library Today with the Best Books for Programming, Operating Systems, and New Technologies

The easiest way to order is to pick up the phone and call

1-800-428-5331

between 9:00 a.m. and 5:00 p.m. EST.

For faster service please have your credit card available.

ISBN	Quantity	Description of Item	Unit Cost	Total Cost
0-672-30737-5		World Wide Web Unleashed, Second Edition	$35.00	
0-672-30667-0		Teach Yourself Web Publishing with HTML in a Week	$25.00	
1-57521-005-3		Teach Yourself More Web Publishing with HTML in a Week	$29.99	
0-672-30714-6		The Internet Unleashed, Second Edition	$35.00	
0-672-30520-8		Your Internet Consultant: The FAQs of Online Life	$25.00	
0-672-30459-7		Curious About the Internet?	$14.99	
0-672-30485-6		Navigating the Internet, Deluxe Edition (Book/Disk)	$29.95	
0-672-30595-X		Education on the Internet	$25.00	
0-672-30599-2		Tricks of the Internet Gurus	$35.00	
0-672-30562-3		Teach Yourself Game Programming in 21 Days (Book/CD-ROM)	$39.99	
0-672-30669-7		Plug-n-Play Internet for Windows (Book/Disk)	$35.00	
0-672-30612-3		The Magic of Computer Graphics (Book/CD-ROM)	$45.00	
0-672-30590-9		The Magic of Interactive Entertainment, Second Edition (Book/2 CD-ROMs)	$44.95	

❏ 3 ½" Disk

❏ 5 ¼" Disk

Shipping and Handling: See information below.	
TOTAL	

Shipping and Handling: $4.00 for the first book, and $1.75 for each additional book. Floppy disk: add $1.75 for shipping and handling. If you need to have it NOW, we can ship product to you in 24 hours for an additional charge of approximately $18.00, and you will receive your item overnight or in two days. Overseas shipping and handling adds $2.00 per book and $8.00 for up to three disks. Prices subject to change. Call for availability and pricing information on latest editions.

201 W. 103rd Street, Indianapolis, Indiana 46290

1-800-428-5331 — Orders   1-800-835-3202 — FAX   1-800-858-7674 — Customer Service

Book ISBN 0-672-30764-2

PLUG YOURSELF INTO...

The Macmillan Information SuperLibrary™

Free information and vast computer resources from the world's leading computer book publisher—online!

FIND THE BOOKS THAT ARE RIGHT FOR YOU!

A complete online catalog, plus sample chapters and tables of contents give you an in-depth look at *all* of our books, including hard-to-find titles. It's the best way to find the books you need!

- STAY INFORMED with the latest computer industry news through our online newsletter, press releases, and customized Information SuperLibrary Reports.

- GET FAST ANSWERS to your questions about MCP books and software.

- VISIT our online bookstore for the latest information and editions!

- COMMUNICATE with our expert authors through e-mail and conferences.

- DOWNLOAD SOFTWARE from the immense MCP library:
    - Source code and files from MCP books
    - The best shareware, freeware, and demos

- DISCOVER HOT SPOTS on other parts of the Internet.

- WIN BOOKS in ongoing contests and giveaways!

TO PLUG INTO MCP: ➔   WORLD WIDE WEB: **http://www.mcp.com**

GOPHER: gopher.mcp.com

FTP: ftp.mcp.com

What's on the Disk

The disk contains the Microsoft® Internet Assistant for Word for Windows® as well as icons and templates to help you create your first Web pages.

> To install Microsoft® Internet Assistant for Word for Windows®, you'll need the following:
> - [ ] Personal Computer with 80386 or higher processor
> - [ ] Microsoft Word for Windows 6.0
> - [ ] 4MB memory (6MB recommended)
> - [ ] 2MB free hard disk space
> - [ ] MS-DOS 3.0 or higher
> - [ ] Microsoft Mouse or other compatible pointing device
> - [ ] Microsoft Windows 3.1 or higher, Windows for Workgroups 3.1 or higher, Windows NT, or Windows for Pen Computing
>
> Web-viewing support requires an existing Internet connection, including TCP/IP support and a `WINSOCK.DLL`. You must obtain Internet connectivity separately from an Internet service provider.

Installing the Software

To install the software from the disk accompanying this book, follow these instructions:

1. Insert the disk into your disk drive.
2. From the File Manager or Program Manager, choose Run from the File menu.
3. Type `drive:INSTALL` and press Enter, where `drive` corresponds to the drive letter of your disk drive. For example, if your disk drive is drive A, type `A:INSTALL` and Press enter.
4. Follow the on-screen instructions in the installation program. The installation program will copy the icons and templates to your hard disk and will automatically launch the setup program for Microsoft® Internet Assistant for Word for Windows®.

Obtaining Technical Support

If you experience problems with the disk or the installation, contact Macmillan Computer Publishing at the following numbers and addresses:

Internet E-mail	Send a message to `support@mcp.com` with a detailed description of the problem you're having.
CompuServe	`GO SAMS` to visit the Macmillan Computer Publishing forum, and leave a message in the Operating Systems message area (Section 6).
Phone	(317) 581-3833
Fax	(317) 581-4773
U.S. Mail	Macmillan Computer Publishing Attention: Technical Support 201 West 103rd Street Indianapolis, IN 46290

Software LICENSE

1. GRANT OF LICENSE. COMPANY grants to you a nonexclusive, royalty-free right to make and use an unlimited number of copies of the software provided with this Agreement ("Software"), provided that each copy shall be a true and complete copy, including all copyright and trademark notices.

2. COPYRIGHT. The SOFTWARE is owned by COMPANY or its suppliers and is protected by United States copyright laws and international treaty provisions. Therefore, you must treat the SOFTWARE like any other copyrighted material (e.g., a book or musical recording) except that you may either (a) make one copy of the SOFTWARE solely for backup or archival purposes, or (b) transfer the SOFTWARE to a single hard disk provided you keep the original solely for backup or archival purposes.

3. OTHER RESTRICTIONS. This License is your proof of license to exercise the rights granted herein and must be retained by you. You may not reverse engineer, decompile, or disassemble the SOFTWARE, except to the extent the foregoing restriction is expressly prohibited by applicable law.

LIMITED WARRANTY

NO WARRANTIES. COMPANY expressly disclaims any warranty for the SOFTWARE. The SOFTWARE and any related documentation is provided "as is" without warranty of any kind, either express or implied, including, without limitation, the implied warranties or merchantability, fitness for a particular purpose, or noninfringement. The entire risk arising out of use or performance of the SOFTWARE remains with you.

NO LIABILITY FOR CONSEQUENTIAL DAMAGES. In no event shall COMPANY or its suppliers be liable for any damages whatsoever (including, without limitation, damages for loss of business profits, business interruption, loss of business information, or any other pecuniary loss) arising out of the use of or inability to use this COMPANY product, even if COMPANY has been advised of the possibility of such damages. Because some states/jurisdictions do not allow the exclusion or limitation of liability for consequential or incidental damages, the above limitation may not apply to you.

U.S. GOVERNMENT RESTRICTED RIGHTS

The SOFTWARE and documentation are provided with RESTRICTED RIGHTS. Use, duplication, or disclosure by the Government is subject to restrictions as set forth in subparagraph (c)(1)(ii) of The Rights in Technical Data and Computer Software clause at DFARS 252.227-7013 or subparagraphs (c)(1) and (2) of the Commercial Computer Software-Restricted Rights at 48 CFR 52.227-19, as applicable.